Anti-Racist Pedagogy in the Early Childhood Classroom

Race and Education in the Twenty-First Century

Series Editors: Kenneth J. Fasching-Varner, Louisiana State University; Roland Mitchell, Louisiana State University; and Lori Latrice Martin, Louisiana State University

This series asks authors and editors to consider the role of race and education, addressing questions such as "how do communities and educators alike take on issues of race in meaningful and authentic ways?" and "how can education work to disrupt, resolve, and otherwise transform current racial realities?" The series pays close attention to the intersections of difference, recognizing that isolated conversations about race eclipse the dynamic nature of identity development that play out for race as it intersects with gender, sexuality, socioeconomic class, and ability. It welcomes perspectives from across the entire spectrum of education from Pre-K through advanced graduate studies, and it invites work from a variety of disciplines, including counseling, psychology, higher education, curriculum theory, curriculum and instruction, and special education.

Recent Titles in Series

Anti-Racist Pedagogy in the Early Childhood Classroom by Miriam Tager

Latinx Experiences in U.S. Schools: Voices of Students, Teachers, Teacher Educators and Education Allies in the Age of Trump, edited by Margarita Jimenez-Silva, Janine Bempechat, and Laura Gomez

Implications of Race and Racism in Student Evaluations of Teaching: The Hate U Give, edited by LaVada Taylor

Technology Segregation: Disrupting Racist Frameworks in Early Childhood Education, by Miriam B. Tager

Surviving Becky(s): Pedagogies for Deconstructing Whiteness and Gender, edited by Cheryl E. Matias

Latinx Curriculum Theorizing, edited by Theodorea Regina Berry

Intersectional Care for Black Boys in an Alternative School: They Really Care About Us, by Julia C. Ransom

Culture, Community, and Educational Success: Reimagining the Invisible Knapsack, edited by Toby S. Jenkins, Stephanie Troutman, and Crystal Polite Glover

Whiteness at the Table: Antiracism, Racism, and Identity in Education, edited by Shannon K. McManimon, Zachary A. Casey, and Christina Berchini

The Classroom as Privileged Space: Psychoanalytic Paradigms for Social Justice in Pedagogy, by Tapo Chimbganda

Anti-Racist Pedagogy in the Early Childhood Classroom

Miriam Tager

LEXINGTON BOOKS
Lanham • Boulder • New York • London

Published by Lexington Books
An imprint of The Rowman & Littlefield Publishing Group, Inc.
4501 Forbes Boulevard, Suite 200, Lanham, Maryland 20706
www.rowman.com

86-90 Paul Street, London EC2A 4NE

Copyright © 2022 by The Rowman & Littlefield Publishing Group, Inc.

All rights reserved. No part of this book may be reproduced in any form or by any electronic or mechanical means, including information storage and retrieval systems, without written permission from the publisher, except by a reviewer who may quote passages in a review.

British Library Cataloguing in Publication Information Available

Library of Congress Cataloging-in-Publication Data

Names: Tager, Miriam B., author.
Title: Anti-racist pedagogy in the early childhood classroom / Miriam Tager.
Description: Lanham : Lexington Books, [2022] | Series: Race and education in the twenty-first century | Includes bibliographical references and index.
Identifiers: LCCN 2021053809 (print) | LCCN 2021053810 (ebook) | ISBN 9781793638380 (cloth) | ISBN 9781793638403 (paper) | ISBN 9781793638397 (epub)
Subjects: LCSH: Early childhood education—Curricula—United States. | Racism in education—United States. | Racism—Study and teaching (Early childhood)—United States. | Racism—Study and teaching (Higher education)—United States. | Student teachers—Training of—United States. | Early childhood education—Social aspects—United States.
Classification: LCC LB1139.4 .T36 2022 (print) | LCC LB1139.4 (ebook) | DDC 372.210973—dc23/eng/20211116
LC record available at https://lccn.loc.gov/2021053809
LC ebook record available at https://lccn.loc.gov/2021053810

Contents

List of Figures		vii
Preface		ix
Acknowledgments		xi
1	An Introduction to a Critical Study	1
2	Characteristics of an Anti-Racist Educator	13
3	Just Say No to Black History Month	31
4	Racial Equity	43
5	The ARTS	59
6	Our History Revised	77
7	Racial Literacy	97
8	Teaching Activism	115
9	Critical Reflection on Biases	131
10	Dealing with Administrators and Parents	147
11	Get On Board	163
Appendix A		177
Appendix B		181

Glossary	183
References	187
Index	193
About the Author	195

Figures

Figure 1.1	No More Racism Poster (Ms. Verano's Kindergarten)	4
Figure 5.1	Watercolor Self-Portrait (Ms. Broadbent's First Grade)	62
Figure 5.2	Bulletin Board Watercolor Self-Portraits (Ms. Broadbent's First Grade)	63
Figure 5.3	Light Browny Bark Skin Tone (Ms. Fern's Kindergarten)	64
Figure 6.1	Posters on Wall (Ms. Alice's Second Grade)	90
Figure 7.1	Other Side Illustrations (Ms. Fern's Kindergarten)	99
Figure 8.1	Poster (Ms. Verano's Kindergarten)	118
Figure 8.2	Poster (Ms. Verano's Kindergarten)	118

Preface

I was almost finished with my research phase of this project when COVID-19 hit us hard in the United States. I struggled with the universal trauma that was affecting all of us and I realized once again, as I have in the past, that inequities related to race exist in the present tense. COVID-19 is just another example of how white supremacy operates within our democracy. The truth is that black and brown people are dying at much faster rates. They also cannot get a piece of the federal emergency stimulus funds supposedly ear marked for small businesses. Technology Segregation (Tager, 2019) is dominating the news, as white middle class students have more access to technology and therefore remote schooling in a time of crisis. BIPOC are usually in more risky jobs, in which they must go to work every day without feeling safe (i.e., retail, maintenance, hospitals, fast food chains, transit, sanitation, factories, etc.). BIPOC are also in the majority in prisons, immigration detention centers, and homeless shelters, all with higher rates of infection. The political climate and news coverage have pulled back the curtain to reveal these racist structures and highlight these racial inequalities. Also, it must be noted that the racial unrest of black people being killed by police (recently George Floyd), the movement to defund the police, and the Black Lives Matters protests also occurred during this time frame of the pandemic and made a huge impact on how I framed this book. It seemed that my research was now even more timely and significant than before, but we all know that it has always been an issue that threatens our democracy. It is just now more visible.

How did COVID-19 affect my research on Anti-Racist pedagogy? Well, for starters I could not finish three observations for all of my participants because schools closed in mid-March of 2020. I struggled with how to do interviews with these three participants as we were still in the reopening stages during the summer of 2020. I decided to finish all work remotely—with zoom interviews and electronic findings. It is important to note that it did affect my findings and interfered with my research process, mainly because I was unable to continue my relationships with the students involved and/or see progress in their thinking on the topic by the end of the year. There are always ethical dilemmas within the research process, as research is never neutral, but working on a research project and writing a book during a pandemic crisis is substantially harder. It interferes with the process and makes the researcher have to creatively reimagine how to mitigate any possible validity issues.

I want you to keep these issues in mind as you navigate this book. This is not a disclaimer but rather an important piece of the research project and how it evolved. It did not proceed the way that I had planned (as no one was expecting a global health crisis that would shut down schools), however, the information, including effective strategies and activities that I observed and discussed, were very helpful and insightful. I learned a lot through this research process and I hope you, the reader, do as well.

It is important to note that I am a white middle class researcher who has experience in both early education classrooms and higher education classes. Being white and reflecting the majority of the population of early childhood educators in this country (over 85%) is revealing in itself (Tatum, 2017). This means that I do carry my own biases and perceptions into my research. I am, hopefully, more aware of my biases, and I have critically reflected on my own racial identity. This does not mean that I don't still have a lot more to learn about race and racism in our society and how it effects young children. I am a lifelong learner, something that I encourage in my higher education students. Now, more than ever before, it is essential to be open minded, and, as a white person, be a listener. I constantly reflect on this as I interact with my BIPOC colleagues and BIPOC students in my classes.

This is not a definitive book on how to utilize Anti-Racist practices/pedagogy in the higher education classroom. I think of this research project as the beginning of something, a way to help us all think about how we organize our early childhood courses and reflect on the various possibilities that we have yet to utilize in the classroom.

The research question for this action research project was: *How do Early Childhood educators efficiently and successfully incorporate Anti-Racist activities and strategies into their curriculum?* This book contains the findings for this question and hopefully will help us better prepare white preservice teachers to confront their own biases and be more actively involved and engaged in Anti-Racist pedagogy.

Acknowledgments

It takes a village to write a book. I appreciate all of the help and support from my colleagues, especially the Anti-Racist education committee at my university, Drew, Wilma, Shannon, Juliet, and Terri. I truly appreciate each moment working with you all; you are like family to me. We work so hard, above and beyond the measures of this job, and we are slowly making a difference in our department and our university. I have learned so much from you and I tell all who listen that I am very lucky to have found you and the department. Many thanks to the rest of the faculty who I have only seen on zoom for the past fifteen months. I miss you so much. By the time this book comes out I will have hugged each of you in the hallway.

I can't thank my family enough for all the care and love you gave me during the research and writing process. A huge shout out to my wife and life partner, Robin. She is no longer surprised when I say "I am going to write another book now." Instead she gives me the time and space to create meaningful work, and I truly could not do this without her. I am so lucky to be blessed with two wonderful daughters: Lily, who at 9 is a master video gamer, and Ella, who just turned 16 and is a full-fledged teenager conquering the world. I want to especially thank her for telling me at 10 years old to follow my dreams when I got a job in another state and had to uproot the entire family.

A big warm thank you to Rondi and her mom, Valerie, for hosting me in Cape Cod for two writing retreats. In a pandemic it is much harder to write undisturbed and they came to the rescue by offering their tree house cabin to me for days at a time. I will never forget your hospitality!

And of course, thank you to my friends, who listen to me talk about my research non-stop and give me such wonderful support and love during the whole process. Thanks Mark, Shannon, Juliet, Rondi, and Tracy.

Special thanks to my friends at RECE (Reconceptualizing Early Childhood Education), whom I miss very much, since it has been two years since our annual international conference. I can't wait to travel again and collaborate with you on another wonderful presentation.

Lastly, I would like to express my gratitude to my research participants, Ms. Houston, Ms. Verano, Ms. Broadbent, Ms. Fern, Ms. Maltes, and Ms. Alice. By the way, they all chose their own pseudonyms. You guys were the heart and soul of this project and you gave me access to your classrooms and gave me hours of your time for this important cause. I truly appreciate all of your warmth, humor, and candor during this research process. It was a joy to work with all of you and get to observe your inspirational teaching. Continue to do what you do! We need you in early childhood education!

Chapter 1

An Introduction to a Critical Study

Ms. Broadbent is doing a lesson on classification of books with her first graders. She has the children dump all the book bins in the classroom on the table and asks them to find books that have pictures of all types of people with different skin tones and then she asks them to put the books that do not show all types of skin tones in a separate pile. They write post-its for both piles of books and gather on the rug to share their findings.

Ms. B *(asks WB[1])*: *Do you want to talk about what you discovered?*
WB: *I couldn't find any people with blonde hair and darker skin.*
BIPOC boy: *(shouts) That's racist!*
Ms. B: *Why do you say that?*
BIPOC boy: *They only want to put white people in books—not black people—they are not as important.*
WB2: *Some books do a better job of skin color.*
BIPOC boy 2: *Racist means black people and brown people are not treated right.*
WG: *Like the book we read yesterday (on Wilma Rudolph).*
WG2: *Can we read that again?*
Ms. B: *Yes.*
Class: *(together shouting) Yay!*

This is a first-grade class at the Coltrane School that is actively engaged in Anti-Racist pedagogy. The teacher, a veteran of twenty-plus years, has only recently begun to incorporate more of this pedagogy in her curriculum on an ongoing basis. Clearly, the children (a diverse group) are very excited about this learning as they all want to reread an important biography of a famous African American woman runner (Wilma Rudolf) who was discriminated against during her sports career. In this activity, young children are thinking critically as they sort books, looking for books that are truly representative of the population in their classroom. They are confronted with many books about animals and white people only and are more aware of how the term "racism" affects their daily lives. It is important to note that over 85 percent of all classroom libraries have books that lack diverse representation BIPOC (Tatum, 2017). Most teachers do not engage in these types of critical Anti-Racist activities and therefore a color-blind discourse is represented as the truth, which perpetuates a white supremacist environment in early childhood programs (Derman-Sparks, 1997; DiAngelo, 2018; Husband, 2011; Leonardo, 2009; Sharma, 2005).

This book is geared to the higher education early childhood professor who is dedicated to transforming the pre-service teaching model by focusing on issues of racial identity and racism in the classroom. It can also be beneficial to the in-service, early childhood teacher who wants to learn how to engage in this work within their classroom. This research takes the next step and explores current, early childhood classrooms (in public schools) that are actively teaching Anti-Racist practices. Anti-Racist pedagogy can include helping to identify stereotypes, including books from and about BIPOC populations, utilizing critical thinking related to history, and interrogating power inequities (Husband, 2011). It also includes children having a deeper understanding of their own racial identities (Derman-Sparks, 1997; Derman-Sparks & Phillips, 1997; Sleeter, 2004).

There are many resourceful teachers that are committed to teaching young children about issues of racial equality and equity in general. Classrooms are not neutral spaces, and it is essential that children are taking part in these practices at an early age. It is important to note that researchers (Leonardo, 2009; Tatum, 2017) believe that children notice and talk about race when they are three and four years old. Furthermore, they are able to participate in Anti-Racist activities that will help them to break color-blind practices that are usually perpetuated within the classroom (Bonilla-Silva, 2006; Leonardo, 2009; Phillips, 2016; Randolph, 2013).

Pre-service teachers need to be trained in Anti-Racist practices. Too many early childhood educators say that there "are no real issues of race" in their classrooms. This common declaration is actually more harmful than helpful to this topic, as the majority of teachers, who are white (over 85 percent) and untrained, do not understand how to address issues of race or racism within their classroom (Husband, 2011; Tatum, 2017). Instead, any issue that comes up is brushed aside, and usually the teacher remains unaware of its occurrence. Furthermore, these teachers, who are racially unaware themselves, perpetuate a color-blind discourse, by stating that children are all the same. In my last research project, teachers told me over and over again that race was not an issue in their room, and they did not care if the child was purple, blue, or green as they were all the same. This typical response reveals the expansiveness of this problem. Pre-service teachers who are observing and training within these rooms are then bound to incorporate these color-blind practices, which is damaging to all young children. Children need to be aware of their own racial identity and be understanding and empathetic to other races outside of their own. Their questions must be addressed, discussed within a whole class, and lessons/activities need to embrace racial differences so all children, including white children, are aware of possible biases related to race.

This is what this book is intended to do, give white, early childhood professors and pre-service and in-service teachers an actual map of methods of disruption, by infusing Anti-Racist pedagogy within their classrooms in order to challenge societal racism.

In this book, I observed and interviewed six different white, early childhood educators in the New England area who have been identified by other educators/administrators as Anti-Racist educators. I found that although they all came from different backgrounds, they each exhibited certain characteristics that helped them to succeed as an Anti-Racist teacher, including infusing the work year-round, utilizing an interdisciplinary strategy that focuses on social justice, finding the right books, engaging in hard discussions, working on guiding young children in their discovery of their racial identity, building safe classroom communities, and actively discussing racism as a present-day occurrence and not a thing of the past. I documented many different activities/projects, including follow-up activities that helped them to scaffold the students' learning. Some were more advanced in their work, after many years of focusing on the topic, while others were new to this practice, but all were open and responsive to their children's needs and understandings. Most importantly, they were dedicated to actively increasing their knowledge on this very important topic.

In a follow-up activity in Ms. Broadbent's first grade, all the children voted to write letters to a few publishers advocating for more picture books that represent different skin tones. Like many of the other teachers in this study, they are guiding children into Anti-Racist work themselves as activists. Starting with the notion of fairness, these educators are helping children to discover their own agency as activists and protesters of unfair/racist practices.

Another example of this is in Ms. Verano's kindergarten at Smithfield Elementary, where she read the book *Child of the Civil Rights Movement* and then asked them to brainstorm and create their own Anti-Racist protest signs. Some of the signs included:

We need to make more fair rules!
No more slaves in the whole world

Keep the City Safe No Matter What
No More Racism
Don't be Mean to Other People
I love all people!
Be kind to all people

These signs show that children are not too young to grasp important concepts on racism and unfair practices in our society. This is the main argument of many professionals in education, that children that are four to seven years old are too young to understand the complexities of this topic and that it is developmentally inappropriate for them to be exposed to these types of discussions. This is not true. As a former first-grade teacher myself, I know that children are much smarter than people think. They are aware, for the most part, of what is occurring in our society and they are very concerned with how it affects them in their own lives. Husband states, "Children are constantly constructing meanings and understandings about race as they interact with other children and adults" (Husband, 2011, p. 367). They also have a strong sense of justice and want to be actively engaged in what is right and fair. Teachers usually ignore this, because of their own white discomfort (DiAngelo, 2018). Thus, it is imperative that we break down this discomfort in pre-service teacher education programs so that they are able to positively engage with young children on this topic.

This research study took place in a state located in the northeast region of the United States. Three different school districts are involved and they include five schools overall[2]:

Figure 1.1 **No More Racism Poster (Ms. Verano's Kindergarten).**

Coltrane School (district 1)
Baker Street School (district 1)
Smithfield School (district 1)
Packard Elementary (district 2)
Longwood Elementary (district 3)

It is important to understand the populations of these districts and the schools themselves (see table 1.1). This data reveals that the three different schools in district 1 have very different populations, with only one, Coltrane School, housing more BIPOC[3] students than the others (www. Public school review.com, 2020). The other two schools (within this same town) have higher populations of white students and the highest population of all (at 94

Table 1.1 District Data

District 1

Coltrane School	**Smithfield School**	**Baker Street School**
330 Children	230 children	285 children
57% white	70% white	65% white
21% Latino	21% Latino	18% Latino
10% multi-racial	6% multi-racial	9% multi-racial
6% black	1% black	2% black
6% Asian	3% Asian	6% Asian

District 2

Packard Elementary

135 Children
77% white
11.1% Latino
5.2% multi-racial
4.5% black
9% Asian

District 3

Longwood Elementary

216 Children
94% white
3% Latino
2% multi-racial
N/A black
N/A Asian

percent) is at Longwood Elementary in district 3. This is a rural area with only one pre-k to 5 school. Packard Elementary is in a progressive town with a large state university but still only has 4.5 percent population of black students, with 5.2 percent multiracial. The average school black population in this state is 12 percent, thus, all of the schools are below average in terms of this population. I do think that the data can be confusing when looking at the way they separate the data for African American population and multiracial students. When these two categories are put together it can equal the statewide average. However, it is important to note that the identification of multiracial (more than one race) could be any combination of races including white (i.e., Asian/white, black/white, Hispanic/black, Hispanic/white, etc).

These settings were only selected because of the participants involved in the study, who were referred to me in a variety of ways including through administrators, colleagues, and friends (see chapter 2). I planned to visit each classroom three different times to observe how they were effectively engaging the children in Anti-Racist pedagogy, but because of the pandemic, only ended up with two observations of most of them. I also had three different interviews with each participant, two in person and one virtually during the pandemic.

Critical Race Theory is a visible framework in which to study why Anti-Racist pedagogy is necessary in early childhood pre-service education classes. This specific theoretical framework has been applied to this qualitative research study, and goes hand in hand in the uncovering of ongoing racist practices in early childhood education. With true understanding of this specific topic, the hope is that, we, as critical early childhood educators, can disrupt normative paradigms that marginalize and exclude BIPOC populations and work toward being more inclusive.

According to Ladson-Billings, this theoretical framework purports that race is a social construction that is and will continue to be a significant factor of determining one's value in our society (Ladson-Billings, 2021; Ladson-Billings, 2004). The U.S. economy and history are based on the hierarchy of race and therefore all institutions (i.e., schools) reproduce this deficit paradigm. Both race and socioeconomic class, together, create disempowerment. Blacks, historically denied property rights, the right to vote, and other exclusionary forms of institutional injustice, are always going to be viewed as less than. Critical Race Theory is designed to disrupt these deficit paradigms by bringing awareness to all related subjects, including the need for Anti-Racist pedagogy. Leonardo points out that "Race is no longer only a variable to be plugged into a research study but rather a dynamic that saturates the entire learning process . . . Critical Race Theory argues that race and racism are implicated in every aspect of education" (Leonardo, 2013, p. 3).

Critical Race Theory examines deficit-based paradigms related to young BIPOC students. Since the majority of early childhood educators in the United States are white women, it is more crucial that this research study examines Anti-Racist pedagogy through a Critical Race Theory lens. The whole purpose of this book is to shed light on effective Anti-Racist practices and strategies utilized in the early childhood classroom so as to debunk the myth that this is not possible. This project was designed to critically examine how Anti-Racist pedagogy can be used in order to produce important counternarratives, ones that most white practicing teachers have not yet been exposed to. This goal can only be achieved by infusing Anti-Racist pedagogy into teacher education programs.

It is important to note here that there is currently a political debate surrounding teaching Critical Race Theory in schools, and several states are in the process of passing legislation to ban this ideology in their districts. The critics of this theory (which is not being taught in k-12 schools) believe that this theory is racist against white populations and makes them feel bad for being white (Petit, 2021). They would like to remove all books, such as the classic Ruby Bridges book from the curriculum because there are pictures of white mobs who are angry about desegregating schools. They even go as far as wanting to fire teachers that teach about race or racism and possibly give them body cameras so they can be monitored in the classroom. In Texas, they just decided to remove the term "morally wrong" when referring to the Ku Klux Klan and no longer require the teaching of Martin Luther King's famous "I have a Dream" speech. To be clear, this is not about Critical Race Theory, even though it has been recently politicized as such. Instead, these far-right critics do not want teachers teaching about race and racism, period.

Before we delve into the role of higher education in addressing this matter, we must first work together to agree on what the term "Anti-Racist pedagogy" means. What does it look like? This topic is very complex and may mean more than one thing to different populations, but for this book I think it is important to clearly lay out the terms involved. What is racism? And how is it defined in terms of early childhood schools? What does it mean to identify as Anti-Racist? These are all important questions that in one form or another will be addressed throughout this book.

First, it is important that we define racism, in terms of schooling. Oluo defines it as "a prejudice against someone based on race, when those prejudices are reinforced by systems of power" (Oluo, 2020, p. 27). This means that racism is systemic and is working within all of our institutions, including early childhood programs. "Racism is not abnormal, but inherent in the structures of modern societies" (Cole, 2009, p. 51). Racism, then, is by definition all around us, a part of everyday life. It operates fully in this country under the auspices of the ideology of white supremacy. It is perpetuated and reinforced daily as that is the only way it can continue to live and breathe in a society. A racist is anyone who supports this ideology, unconsciously or consciously. They support it through actions and inactions (Kendi, 2019). This means that being silent on issues related to racism is being complicit. Perpetuating the ideology of color-blindness is an example of an individual being complicit. The message that a lot of early childhood educators try to convey in their classrooms is that "we are all the same." This is harmful to BIPOC children and to white children as well as it perpetuates racism and white supremacy. Clearly, we are not all the same, as we are not treated the same within our society, both in the past and in the present. Kendi believes that you can only identify as Racist or Anti-Racist (Kendi, 2019). There is no option for non-racist. Thus, you are either actively working toward ending racism within our society, including our schools, or you are a part of the problem.

In identifying yourself as Anti-Racist you are committed to being actively involved in trying to disrupt racist practices. This can and should be done within schools, including early childhood programs. "An Anti-Racist approach to education assumes that schools exist as microcosms of the larger United State's society (where racism exists and permeates every institution within)" (Husband, 2011, p. 366). In his 2011 study on Anti-Racist education in a first-grade classroom he concluded that Anti-Racism curriculum/pedagogy should:

- Interrogate power inequities
- Invoke critical thinking within children
- Help identify stereotypes
- Infuse a historical perspective not usually seen
- Help develop positive attitudes toward BIPOC
- Include books by and for BIPOC.

(Husband, 2011)

In my college courses, I show a variety of videos and PowerPoints that explain and unpack the term "Anti-Racist." I feel that the students need to be knocked over the head with the term in order to develop any type of complex understanding of the topic. At first, they are just concerned about being called out as "racist" and so they are initially very uncomfortable with the topic. But it is important to note that discomfort is part of the process and transformation can only truly occur through deep critical reflection of our own biases and assumptions (see chapter 9). Kendi believes that being racist or anti-racist is not fixed in a person's identity (Kendi, 2019). Instead, we, as people, waver between both identities throughout the day. The key is to be aware of all of this and to make choices, good choices at each moment. White people must be actively working toward Anti-Racism on a consistent basis, as that is what makes a person an Anti-Racist (Jewell, 2020). If we do not actively engage in Anti-Racist practices then we are racist. Being silent is not an option and therefore it becomes clearer that pre-service teachers need to try to be actively engaged in Anti-Racist work in their future classrooms, otherwise they are just perpetuating racism and color-blind discourses. "In the absence of anti-racist curriculum, white teachers will continue to participate in the perpetuation of an educational system that reinforces white privilege and domination at the expense of People of Color" (Case & Hemmings, 2005, p. 607).

Sleeter profoundly states that "teaching race does matter" (Sleeter, 2004, p. 163). It matters because the alternative of not teaching about race is detrimental for all young children. What we don't say is just as important as what we do say as teachers. Teachers are role models for young children and therefore everything they say or do has a huge impact on their lives, beliefs, and value systems. Therefore it is key for an early childhood educator to be actively engaged in Anti-Racist pedagogy within their classrooms.

Teacher education programs are the main vehicles of teacher training. These programs are designed to prepare pre-service teachers with the necessary skills needed to become a successful teacher. Teacher education, in general, contains a multitude of courses that help to build these specific readiness skills in pre-service teachers. The following are some of the key courses that presently exist in my own education department:

- Classroom Management
- Literacy and Language Arts
- Math and Science Methods
- Multicultural Education
- Sheltered English Immersion
- Schools in American Culture
- Early Intervention Birth to Five
- Students with Exceptional Learning Needs

It is important to note that there is only one course, on the books right now in my program, that specifically deals with the topic of race and racism in our society (Critical Multicultural Education). I am not suggesting another college-level course that is focused on Anti-Racist pedagogy; instead I am suggesting that we, as teacher educators, infuse this topic into all of our courses so that it lives in all of them simultaneously. This is what my education department is currently trying to do. It is not an overnight process; actually it takes a lot of collaboration and thought, but it is achievable. The point is that Anti-Racist pedagogy is not static and must be developed and nurtured in order to expand into all possible teacher education courses. It must be present and actively utilized throughout, so that pre-service teachers understand the importance of the topic and will be more likely to use it in their future classrooms.

I would like to clarify that just because a teacher says they are an Anti-Racist educator and is actively engaged in the work, does not mean that they have achieved the goal of being an Anti-Racist educator. Anti-Racist teachers are always reviewing, examining, and revising their work. It is always a work in process (see chapter 2). One of the characteristics that was revealed during this study is that Anti-Racist educators are lifelong learners; they are always reading and incorporating new ideas related to the topic. All of my participants, at one point or another, questioned their involvement in this research, as they were not sure if they were good examples of an Anti-Racist educator. In interview two, Ms. Verano addressed this insecurity:

Ms. V: But I almost feel like I have . . . that I signed up (for this Research project) mistakenly because I am saying "Oh, yes I am an Anti-Racist teacher . . ." If you would have asked me last year I would have said, "Yes, I am an Anti-Racist teacher . . ." And when I signed up at the beginning of this year I said, "I am an Anti-Racist teacher . . . and I want to be part of this project . . . this is something that is really important to me . . ." But I am getting . . . I am learning so much more in what I am doing . . . as I am moving forward. . . . That's what teachers should be doing . . . you know . . . that's what we do . . . we have to keep learning . . . that doesn't mean that you are not right to say "I am an Anti-Racist teacher." Do you see what I am saying?

Here, Ms. Verano is questioning her identity as an Anti-Racist educator, as do other participants in the study at one point or another. I think, however, that this is what embodies a true Anti-Racist educator, the ongoing reflection, the hunger for more learning, and the openness to actively engage in the work. Teacher educators and in-service teachers in general can fall into the "imposter" syndrome, where we question our knowledge or competence about our job and yet, within this realm there are no imposters, as long as you are dedicated to the work and trying your best. Also, it is important to remember that "you cannot solve anything that you do not admit exists" (Wilkerson, 2020, p. 385). All of these participants, including Ms. Verano, are aware of the existence of racism and their roles within the system and they want to be actively engaged in disrupting the process.

When reviewing the research data for this book, I realized that certain themes kept coming to the surface over and over again. I decided to turn these themes into different chapters, which are all related to how to teach Anti-Racist pedagogy in both early education classrooms and in higher education classrooms. In the next chapter, I delve into the eleven different characteristics of an Anti-Racist educator that emerged through my interviews and observations. This is also an opportunity to get to know the six teacher participants and the research settings with a clearer lens. In chapter 3, *Just Say No to Black History Month*, I analyze the history surrounding the creation of Black History Month and Black Lives Matter Week, contending that one month or one week is actually more harmful than helpful in the teaching of Anti-Racist pedagogy. Chapter 4 centers on racial inequities and inequalities and how schooling is designed to further engage in white supremacy and the exclusion of BIPOC students. Chapter 5 focuses on the Arts and how this dynamic subject (visual arts, movement/dance, theater, etc.) plays an important role in the active engagement of Anti-Racist pedagogy. The following chapter, chapter 6, delves into the subject of history and social studies and how to actively teach about race and racism by uncovering and unpacking hidden curriculums. Chapter 7 continues this theme by focusing on literacy and read alouds, which are the main venues for these teachers in conveying content on race. Chapter 8, *Teaching Activism*, centers on how to teach activism related to social justice and racial equity, revealing the need to start young and to continue the work in college classrooms. Chapter 9 is a key chapter that focuses on critical reflection, and the importance of this process for teachers in training, as reflecting on their biases and assumptions and racial identity is the only way for them to fully understand this work. In chapter 10, I examine how Anti-Racist educators communicate and build relationships with their administrators and families. And in the last chapter, *Get On Board*, I am signaling all higher education teacher educators to come join us and get on board with this work.

It is important to note that at the end of each chapter there is a section on the higher education classroom, and how to specifically incorporate the theme of the chapter into your daily early childhood courses. This section is designed specifically for the university professor, so that they have variety of ideas/activities that they can utilize right now within their classes. My hope is that this book will have both practical and theoretical application for the Anti-Racist teacher in training and will be a valuable tool in the process of disrupting racism in early childhood education programs. Jewell eloquently states, "Anti-Racism is how we get free" (Jewell, 2020, p. 146). I feel that this is true for all of us, and now is the time to commit to do this work.

NOTES

1. WB is white boy and WG is white girl. BIPOC boy or girl is a student of color. There are numbers used to signify that a new child is speaking, that is, WB2.
2. All names of the schools/districts and participants have been changed.
3. I choose to use BIPOC as a term, rather than POC as it is more inclusive of all marginalized populations that experience racism within America.

Chapter 2

Characteristics of an Anti-Racist Educator

(Ms. Maltes is doing a lesson on skin tone at the rug. She reads a book about similarities and differences in young children and then addresses her kindergarteners.)

Ms. M: *Turn and Talk—Look at your partner's eyes, hair—how are they different? What about skin tone? How is that different or similar?*
   (Students turn and talk loudly.)
BIPOC girl: *My skin is brown—the sun brighter and brighter makes it brown.*
BIPOC boy: *My mom is light skin and dad has dark skin.*
Ms. M: *It is a blend.*
WG1: *I have light skin and it matches that paper (points to construction paper in the middle of the rug each with different shades of brown.)*
WG2: *I found my skin color.*
Ms. M: *Look at your hands . . . what if you turn over your hands what do you notice?*
WB1: *My dad has the same skin as mine.*
Ms. M: *How do you think our skin gets color?*
WG3: *If you go to the beach on a hot day your skin can get brown.*
Ms. M: *Ancestors come from a really warm place if you are brown.*
BIPOC girl2: *Some of my family has the same skin color as me . . .*
Ms. M: *Do you see color that is actually black or white?*
WG4: *No, I see tan and brown.*
Ms. M: *As time goes on it's interesting that people say black and white.*
BIPOC boy2: *My whole family is brown.*
Ms. M: (asks quiet girl) *And what does your family look like?*
   (No response.)
BIPOC boy3: *My mom and dad have different colors . . . she has light skin.*

(Ms. Maltes asks them to find a piece of construction paper closest to their skin tone shade and draw their handprint on it. When they are done, she has them paste it to a large paper, making a mural of handprints with different skin tones.)
Ms. M: *(To class) What are your thoughts or reflections about our mural?*

What makes an early childhood educator an Anti-Racist educator? Well, for one thing they are all committed to do the work. The six early childhood educators in this study had many characteristics in common. In the initial findings, I uncovered eleven common characteristics of these educators:

1) They focus on the building of community all year long—scaffolding this idea.
2) There is continual work on teaching empathy and understanding and appreciating differences.
3) Each teacher gives agency to the children in their room (child centered).
4) They each use key read a louds all year long (see appendix A).
5) Each teacher seems to be very conscious of language they use with children (i.e., enslaved people instead of slavery).
6) They stress that racism is happening now and is not a thing of the past.
7) They Infuse books/activities related to race all year long, not just one month a year.
8) They are lifelong learners and are open to learning about new approaches and ideas.
9) They all teach about intersectionality and combat stereotypes of gender, disability, homophobia, etc. They are committed to teaching social justice.
10) They have good/trusting relationships with families that deal in mutual respect.
11) They are all aware of inequities in education and are actively fighting against it.

In this chapter, I will go into detail on all of the characteristics of an Anti-Racist educator that surfaced during this research project. But first I will talk about these participants and who they are as people and as early childhood educators. What do they have in common besides these eleven character displays? What is different? How does their background affect who they are as teachers? In our interviews, I have in-depth discussions with all six participants and learned a lot about what makes an early childhood educator actively become an Anti-Racist educator.

The six teacher educators who participated in this research study were referred to me in a variety of ways, including word of mouth, principal recommendations, colleague recommendations, and each other. This process, in research, is considered as a snowball effect, as one person would come on board and refer me to another person that they knew about. Some of the participants knew each other, as three worked in the same district, and also two of them are in a long-term relationship. They were all very enthusiastic about the project from the beginning and were very easy to work with. It should be noted that one participant (number seven) dropped out early on after the first interview and observation in round one, so all of her material was discarded. She did not give me a reason, she just stopped responding to any of my emails. I believe that there was some discomfort for her in her participation in the project and therefore she dropped out. I, honestly, had so much data from the other participants that it did not seem to effect the final findings.

These early childhood educators had a lot in common (see table 2.1). Intersectionality, on the whole, was discussed fairly often by these participants as they all identified as either gay or bisexual women. This, to be sure, was not planned on my part. I did not seek out other gay educators, in fact, after all the participants came on board, I was surprised to learn that they were all identifying as queer or queer adjacent. To clarify, there may be a lot of straight teachers in this region who are practicing Anti-Racist pedagogy, but they were not referred to me. Several of the teachers referred other teachers, including Ms. Broadbent who recommended Ms. Fern and Ms. Verano who referred me to her partner, Ms. Houston. It could also be that I am a gay woman myself, which could have affected the referral

Table 2.1 Background of Teacher Participants

Ms. Alice	**Ms. Fern**	**Ms. Maltes**
2nd Grade	K	K
From small town	From region of study	From small town
Fifteen years teaching	Fifteen years	Fifteen years
Majority white school	Diverse school	Diverse school
Diversity experience	Diversity experience	Diversity experience
Bisexual	Gay woman	Gay woman
Grew up hearing racist comments	Grew up hearing racist comments	Did not grow up hearing racist comments
Did not teach preschool	Taught preschool	Taught preschool
Ms. Verano	**Ms. Broadbent**	**Ms. Houston**
K	1st grade	K
From NYC	From Philadelphia	From a nearby city
Over twenty years teaching	Over twenty years teaching	Eight years teaching
Majority white school	Diverse school	Majority white school
Diversity experience	Diversity experience	Diversity experience
Gay woman	Gay woman	Gay woman
Grew up hearing racist comments	Grew up hearing racist comments	Did not grow up hearing racist comments
Taught preschool	Taught preschool	Taught preschool

process. Or it could be that as a part of a marginalized group themselves, they could relate to this topic more. When I asked them about this coincidence of all the participants being queer or queer adjacent, they each had different theories. In my first interview with Ms. Broadbent, she had an interesting take:

Ms. B: It's funny . . . I am thinking of a friend of mine who is a straight white man and he thinks gay people are smarter than any other people in the world. . . . He just has this regard so maybe that's it? I am sure it is not.
R: It is because we are smart?
Ms. B: Well, maybe because we were like a minority group . . . but I know a lot of gay people . . . I know a lot of straight people but I think there is an open-mindedness . . . among the gay people I know . . . or the gay population in general.

Ms. Houston had a similar reaction in her interview:

Ms. H: I think those of us who are in . . . or who identify with one of the marginalized others . . . um . . . tend to think more about it and realize its importance of . . . and I know the focus is on race . . . that's one of the many others . . . because it is part of the social justice umbrella . . . so to speak . . . and race is extremely important and I starting to talk about differences as a starting point.

Others, like Ms. Alice, did not see any possible connection between the majority of participants being gay or gay identified and are also interested in Anti-Racist pedagogy. To be clear, I did not press the issue, but just thought it was worth bringing up to my participants and worth thinking about during the research process.

Another thing they have in common is their love of teaching young children. "Second grade is my happy place," states Ms. Alice. They have all worked with young children for many years, some over twenty. They can't imagine working in any other profession. Many of these teachers grew up in households of educators, including aunts, moms, and grandparents. Like me, they played school when they were young; most of them knew early on that this was the right profession for them. Five out of six participants taught preschool many years before finding their grade of choice. Some worked outside of the region, in other cities, and/or townships, but all settled for the long part of their teaching career in this particular region of the state.

There are other common denominators between the six participants including the fact that many of them grew up in households where they heard racist comments or endured racist discussions from family members. I think this had a profound impact on these participants, including making the issue of the visibility of racism around them. In my second interview with Ms. Fern, she is very frank about the racism within her family:

Ms. F: I don't know that we ever talked about so much about race but there was definitely racist things that were said . . . my grandmother would use racial slurs . . . um referring to people of color . . . There was always a level of "ew . . . this is something weird that grandma says but" . . . as I think back, I don't know what it was that made me go "Ohhh . . . that's icky" . . . I don't remember ever talking about it until I was older.

In Ms. Broadbent's background interview, she also made reference to growing up with racism on display in her household:

Ms. B: I really just . . . I don't even want to say some of the things that were said but I remember thinking . . . well that's not true and that's mean and I wouldn't say anything because there were so many people saying things I didn't want to hear but I internalized it and thought about it and realized it was not true . . . it was wrong and mean and I tried to distance myself from it.
R: Did this shape how you thought about your racial identity?
Ms. B: I guess maybe way back when I thought of myself more as an ally . . . like when my family talked like that . . . I did not feel like I was part of the family . . . I felt like I was part of a different family that was maybe a little more forward in thinking . . . a little bit more open-minded . . . but I really felt distance from them.

Here, Ms. Broadbent opens up about her struggles with coming to terms that she thought differently about race and racism than her family. This may be part of the reason that she is so committed to this work and wants to continue to be a part of it.

It is important to note here that all the participants were at different stages of comfort level in teaching this topic. Some were more comfortable, especially in terms of analyzing the topic and discussing at length in an interview format, and others were still grappling with it, unsure of how to talk about it or needed more prodding. Not all Anti-Racist educators are alike and they can all present differently.

Now that we have taken a closer look at the six participants in this research project, we can focus on the eleven different characteristics that emerged during the data analysis. These findings were presented during interview three (which was conducted virtually) and each participant was asked for their thoughts on these characteristics. Ms. Verano responded,

Ms. V: As I was reading it (the findings) I felt it fit . . . from the people I know that do this work.

R: Was there one characteristic that you thought was ME?
Ms. V: I kinda of felt like that for all of them . . . because it was like . . . yep . . . that's me . . . this is me . . . you know pretty much all of them . . . building community . . . and having empathy . . . having a student centered classroom . . . being conscious of language . . . Teaching through read alouds . . . I mean I felt like all of that was really part of this . . . the heart of my teaching . . . of my pedagogy.

Part of validating my data is going over the findings with my participants. Does this sound right to you? Is this what you said? In terms of all of my research projects, sharing the eleven characteristics that the participants displayed during their interviews and observations, this was the most well-received. They agreed with the data, and were actually all saying, "that's me."

One of the important characteristics that emerged from the data is the need to build community all year long. In general, early childhood teachers tend to really focus on community building during the first several months of the school year. This is a way to train students, at the beginning, to work together in small groups, to feel a part of the larger classroom, and to become interested in doing their part for the greater good of the whole community. What I noticed, though, with these six early childhood educators is that they work on community building all year long. They don't just commit to the first six to eight weeks of community building but instead weave it in throughout the year. I observed them community building in January and March, and probably would have seen more even later in the year if the worldwide pandemic had not interrupted our project. In Ms. Maltes's second interview, she talks briefly about creating an overall climate that is conducive to learning about race and racism:

Ms. M: I think it is more of a general sense . . . again I think it sort of goes back to creating a classroom climate where kids sort of . . . at the same time that they are thinking about race but just learning about what is friendly vs. not friendly . . . I mean so I think they are certainly learning across the year. . . . Learning what is expected by other people.
R: Can you think of an example of this?
Ms. M: Not really. . . . I can see it more in their actions . . . in terms of being inclusive . . . in terms of maintaining friendships with people across the classroom.

Here, Ms. Maltes, along with the other participants, speaks about the importance of creating a climate that is cohesive and friendly, so that all children feel safe and comfortable participating in the work of Anti-Racist pedagogy. In the same interview, she continues her thoughts on building community:

R: Okay, now let's get to strategies . . . are there ways that you use them . . . weave them into your curriculum . . . what's your strategy of how to use it (Anti-Racist pedagogy)?

Ms. M: (Pause) Let's see . . . I think there's the kinda of intentional way from the start . . . the way that it is woven into the curriculum and again it really starts off in the fall in looking at concepts of identity . . . just giving language so that kids can express themselves and share who they are and understand who their friends and peers are . . . it's kinda of . . . and in that way we share topics of conversations in books and that sort of thing . . . and it is a little bit woven into our social emotional curriculum and then kind of on an informal . . . not informal as much . . . but when we are setting up the norms for the classroom and thinking about the rules . . . thinking about the sort of culture that we want to establish in the classroom . . . we will talk a lot about . . . and do a lot of practicing and role playing and problem solving . . . how to express frustration appropriately and how to get your needs met that doesn't involve insulting or belittling or teasing anyone about the way they look or that kinda of thing.

The environment of their classrooms was essential to their teaching strategy of Anti-Racist pedagogy. It had to be a comfortable atmosphere where socio-emotional skills, such as empathy, were taught on a daily basis. Ms. Houston explains why empathy, as a skill, is important in building a safe classroom environment for this work:

Ms. H: As I was reading these books about Martin Luther King and we were talking about them . . . I actually had a couple of kids . . . one in particular who's eyes welled up . . . she started to get really sad . . . And I had another kid who was like "but he was a good guy. . . . He shouldn't have gotten hurt or killed . . . he was the good guy . . . he was trying to be kind to everybody . . . " and I said "I know . . . people were scared just because of what he looked like."

R: So, they were emotional about the assassination?

Ms. H: They were really starting to make that connection . . . I thought that was really touching . . . I wasn't expecting it from my little five and six-year-olds

R: So, you are teaching empathy?

H: I am teaching empathy and I am teaching about the bullshit circumstances based on just what people look like and what I am trying to drive home is that it is not just how you might see yourself . . . it's about how other people might see you because you may have dark skin . . . I think it's about other people's perceptions which is why I think this kindness and empathy is so important to teach.

Ms. Houston, in all of her interviews, emphasizes the need for empathy in a kindergarten classroom. Rather states that "our nation today suffers from a deficit of empathy" (Rather, 2017, p. 101). This is sad but true, as we see in the news and that is why it is essential to teach to young children. It is also one of the socio-emotional standards in this particular state for pre-k and kindergarten children. It builds community in every aspect and is essential to understanding and accepting differences in others.

Ms. Houston uses herself as a model of how people can be misjudged for how they look, so that her children could see that the perception of others can be hurtful and discriminatory. Ms. Houston is larger in stature and has very short hair that presents differently than most female teachers. She is a proud gay woman who shares her family structure with her classroom children and talks about the discrimination that she faces on a daily basis based on her look, which she states is not gender normative. She continually shares stories from her own life, of being marginalized for her look, for her identity, so that the young children in her classroom can understand that we are all different but do not deserve to be discriminated against because of our differences. This, in turn, continually builds empathy in her classroom, as each child is reflecting on their own perceptions and biases based on how a person looks. Some may say that teaching these concepts, including reflection of our own biases and assumptions is not developmentally appropriate for this young age, but the building of empathy must start somewhere. Empathy, as a tool, is very helpful when talking about issues related to race and is essential to building a safe classroom environment.

In Ms. Broadbent's first grade at the Coltrane School, she says she builds community all year round. When discussing how she thinks this and her Anti-Racist work in general affects her children she states,

Ms. B: I am hoping that kids see each other as more than what they see . . . you know what I am saying? That they see each other as people with common experiences . . . common feelings . . . common fears . . . common worries . . . that people are people and what makes them who they are is lots of different things. I like the angle of how we are the same and how we are different . . . that is sort of how I approach this . . . so I am hoping that they are not just tolerant but . . . .that they see each other as full people that have lots of things in their lives that are happening whether good or bad . . . Yeah, I do want kids to respect each other and have compassion for one another and it's a big thing to ask because . . . you know . . . they are six and seven.

Later on, in the same interview, Ms. Broadbent talks about valuing students and making sure that they feel welcomed in her classroom.

Ms. B: You know I keep coming back to this one student who has the mom from Africa and at any moment that it is brought up . . . how good it makes her feel and how I can share that with her . . . and I don't just say "Oh yeah, your mom is from Africa," but we talk about it for a few minutes and she can feel proud and I can continue that feeling in her by showing interest and just . . . paying attention to what is important to her.

R: So, you are valuing.

Ms. B: Yeah . . . that was another word that was just on the tip of my tongue . . . I just think it's important that kids feel good about themselves . . . they feel good about their families. . . . No matter what and that people . . . that kids can start to understand and value and accept and appreciate others.

To her, valuing children and teaching this skill to the class is one way to build community and teach empathy. West states, "Either we learn a new language of empathy and compassion or the fire this time will consume us all" (West, 1993, p. 8).

Each classroom in this study was set up to encourage a degree of agency for these young children. Agency is about a child's capabilities to initiate and design their own projects and pursue their own lines of inquiry (Adair, 2014). It is about freedom, freedom of expression, movement, and thinking. Children who have more agency within a classroom are able to explore different materials, concepts, and actions in their daily work. They are more able to problem solve and think for themselves. Agency also helps with working on their own identities as learners and people within a classroom. Encouraging agency also means noise and sometimes chaos, as children navigate their learning spaces, finding out new things about themselves and others. It can only really occur when empathy and compassion are present, as children move around interacting with one another and learning from one another. It also has to do with giving them options to express themselves as leaders in the community. In Ms. Houston's second interview, she talks about what agency looks like in her kindergarten room at Longwood Elementary:

Ms. H: I make sure that all my kids feel like they are leaders. . . . Like I have a helper a day . . . that rotates and we have share time where they bring something in from home that is meaningful . . . I make sure that everyone does have a voice whether it's my people of color or it's my kiddos who are much lower . . . like everyone has something to give . . . so I really stress community as a whole.

Giving leadership roles to children on a daily basis helps encourage their individualized agency. Here, Ms. Houston is talking about her children that are and have been traditionally excluded from their own agency in their classrooms, special education students, and BIPOC students. She recognizes the need to encourage them in their own agency for learning.

Ms. Alice, who teaches second grade, believes that giving agency in the classroom to her students helps them to further explore topics related to racism and aids them in speaking up when they see something that is unfair or unjust.

R: Have you noticed any changes in your children's thinking and reflections on this work?
Ms. A: I have noticed that they are much quicker to identify incidents as racist. And to use the words racist and racism to describe a comment or event. And they speak up very quickly if they believe something to be racist . . . this past year, the students came in from recess and immediately ran to me to tell me that . . . had said something racist. They told me what had been said and to whom. Their quick identification and refusal to accept the incident allowed us adults to handle it much more quickly and effectively.

In this case, Ms. Alice believes that giving the students voice and agency to be heard helps them to quickly identify problems and issues related to race and racism. To her, they will only speak out and voice their concerns in the world if they feel that they have a right to stand up and say something (see chapter 8).

In Ms. Fern's kindergarten, she sees encouraging agency as an important tool in the fight for racial justice. She believes that it is important to encourage different voices from being heard, especially when it comes to BIPOC children in her room. She discourages the privileging of white students and makes it clear to them that talking over BIPOC students will not be tolerated. In our second interview, she recalls an important event from her classroom.

Ms. F: Last year at the end of the year . . . toward the end of the year the group was talking about . . . um . . . gosh how did it happen? It was a pretty intense conversation about race where a kid who was white started crying about being white skinned and feeling responsible for things that are wrong in the world and um . . . I wish I could remember the whole context but it was an interesting moment where his tears were sort of in response to something a student of color had said . . . um . . . and it was sort of one of those moments where it deflected away from the student of color's comment about their own experience of race in our school.
R: That happens all the time with adults.
Ms. F: All the time . . . so it was this white person cries and then a couple of the kids came over and rubbed the kid's back and I actually interrupted it and I said . . . but so and so was sharing something important and a really big feeling too and I think you are kinda . . . (pause).
R: Co-opting it?

F: I think we used the word "steppin on" . . . . you are stepping on . . . We say that when kids interrupt each other . . . you are stepping on his words right now . . . and you are stepping on his feelings . . . as white people we want to really try hard not to. . . . There was this white guilt moment . . . but they are five so I have to take care of both of those kids.

I have witnessed this before with white adults crying and taking the spotlight from BIPOC who were expressing themselves but I have never seen this with young children. My first thought is that clearly this is a very safe space, because each child, both the white one and the BIPOC student felt safe enough to reveal their feelings to the rest of the class, without fear of judgment. My second thought is that Ms. Fern walks a fine line of encouraging agency and a safe space with balancing the protection of the BIPOC student to feel that same safety. She does not want the BIPOC student to feel "stepped on" for fear that they will not feel safe enough to express themselves freely again and yet she wants to encourage empathy in the white child as well. By stopping the white child from being comforted she is making the explicit point that the BIPOC student, who was talking first, has the right to be heard fully and that other children (especially white children) should give that person the space to freely express themselves without "stepping on" their words. She is also, unwittingly, introducing the term "white guilt," and making sure that they understand that this display of white guilt can take away from the experiences and feelings that a BIPOC student is trying to express.

Another characteristic that kept resurfacing was the fact that they all utilized key read aloud to help teach content related to Anti-Racist pedagogy. Read aloud will be discussed at length in an upcoming chapter but here, it is important to note that it is a key characteristic of these Anti-Racist educators. During our discussions, they make it very clear to me that choosing the right books for a particular lesson or unit is essential in their planning. They are constantly searching for new and relevant books on race and racism that they can purchase and use in their classrooms. It is also a key way that they deliver content related to Anti-Racist pedagogy and fundamental to engaging the young children in the room (see chapter 7).

All of the participants in this study seemed to be very conscious of their word choices when talking to children. They clearly reflect on finding the right way(s) to explain this content so that they are not perpetuating hurtful or dominant language choices (as related to white supremacy).

In Ms. Alice's second-grade classroom, this was very apparent. She actually talked about her language choices with the children so that they could understand why it was so important to reflect on words and the meaning of words in speech. She understands that modeling language choices and being very open about how she chooses words in her lessons is important to their discussions. An example of this is in her second observation where she introduces Sojourner Truth to the class.

Ms. A: When people own other people, they have to work very hard for no money . . . system of slavery . . . people are treated really bad . . . It is awful because they are owned
WG: You can also call them servants
Ms. A: It's different . . . they are actually paid . . . in slavery people are owned . . . It is all over the world . . . the slaves were most often black . . . (She introduces the next vocabulary word on the screen).
Class: (together) Enslaved . . . Enslaved. . . Enslaved.
Ms. A: I learned people had slaves . . . when we call them slaves it is not a nice way to talk about them. They were human beings with hopes and wishes . . . let's not call them slaves . . . if I use that word I will change it . . . they were people that were enslaved.

Here, Ms. Alice makes the distinction between slaves and being enslaved to make sure students understand that these people were human beings and were not inferior to whites. She wants them to understand the difference between these words and why she wants them to use "enslaved" instead of slaves. To her, slavery is a system and people were not slaves but were enslaved by this horrible system of racial injustice. The distinction is clear, saying someone was a slave is demeaning and dehumanizing so she wants them to consider this when they decide to speak on the topic. Later on, when she asks them to do a go-around on what they learned about Sojourner Truth, one white girl states, "She was enslaved" and Ms. Alice smiles as she is happy that her students are thinking about word choice before they speak up.

Another common thread of all six early childhood educators in this study is that they emphasize that racism is happening right now in our society, and that it is not just a problem located in the past. This concept is very important when utilizing Anti-Racist pedagogy in an early childhood classroom, as students can easily be persuaded that the problem of racism no longer exists, that in fact we solved this problem in the 1960s with the Civil Rights Movement. This is dangerous as it leads them to believe that it is no longer an issue and therefore, they do not need to do much about it. It actually perpetuates colorblind discourse and makes it harder for young children to grow up and become actively Anti-Racist themselves. Bonilla-Silva states, "This storyline, then, is used to deny the enduring effects of historic discrimination as well as to deny the significance of contemporary discrimination" (Bonilla-Silva, 2006, p. 79).

When Ms. Houston spoke about Martin Luther King Jr. in her classroom, she made sure to emphasize the fact that racism and discrimination based on the color of a person's skin still exist today.

Ms. H: Again I didn't sugarcoat it . . . I said they hurt him. . . . They killed him unfortunately . . . yes it has gotten better but it is still a problem . . . people are still unfair . . . just because of how people look and their color.

R: So, what you are saying is this is not a thing in the past?

Ms. H: Correct . . . this is still going on . . . I make it about This happens . . . this is happening . . . this is happening with . . . Because I feel that even if they can't really relate to . . . you know the color of people's skin . . . because there is not too much diversity.

Here, Ms. Houston makes it clear to her young children that racism is happening now. She is counting on their sense of fairness and justice to help them to understand that it is a present problem, one that still needs to be addressed.

The six participants also make it clear to me that Anti-Racist work has to be infused into the curriculum all year long. They do not believe in presenting this as a once a year topic, like for Black History Month (see chapter 3) or just for Martin Luther King day in January. Unlike most teachers, they believe it is essential to build the foundation of Anti-Racist pedagogy at the very beginning of the year as they are building community and then to weave it in and out of the various curriculum units throughout the year. This way, they feel that the children are scaffolding their knowledge and constantly engaged in the topic.

When discussing different possible effective strategies in teaching Anti-Racist pedagogy in the kindergarten classroom, Ms. Fern has a plan:

Ms. F: I think the strategy for most things in kindergarten is they need a thread . . . to follow along . . . it connects . . . so everything builds off of this and it starts with who you are . . . it starts with self and we build off from there . . . it is part of our community building in the classroom . . . making an inclusive space in our classroom . . . and how does that translate to inclusion spaces in the world? So, I think in terms of strategy in the classroom. . . . I don't know if I ever thought of them as strategies per say . . . but I think it's sort of this idea of knowing who . . . that you have a place in the community and that your actions effect members of the community and your community is part of a larger community.

Ms. Fern and the others utilize the work all year long by building upon their knowledge, starting with the self, then family, the local community, and the worldwide community. The strategy in this case is to infuse Anti-Racist pedagogy throughout the curriculum while encouraging the students to scaffold their knowledge on the topic. Ms. Fern does this by starting with the child's own exploration of their racial identity at the beginning of the year.

Ms. F: We spend a good . . . September and October sort of building their understanding about noticing differences and noticing similarities and being able to talk about racial identity . . . You know when you live in a town that is mostly white . . . an idea about racial identity is (laughs) . . . most kids do not have a racial identity and kids are such little . . . big hearted beings that they just want everything fair and cool and it's good . . . and it doesn't matter and . . . initially when we talk about race and their own racial identities . . . so we move from the focus of the self . . . we look at family . . . and then we look at different kinds of family makeups in our classroom . . . then we start with who we are and then we branch out to who is in our community and eventually we branch out to who is in our world.

Now the difference here between an Anti-Racist educator and a mainstream educator is that when talking about the self, the focus is on racial identity and not just our favorite hobbies. They then move into the family, also discussing differences in family makeups, outside the norms, and then discuss the community at large. By the time they discuss the world, they have already been exposed to racial differences and racism as a whole and now they can apply it to their world community.

When talking to Ms. Maltes about different strategies utilized, she also focuses on the fact that she discusses it throughout the year at Baker Street School and that this is intentional on her part.

Ms. M: I think there's the kinda of intentional way from the start . . . the way it is woven into the curriculum and again it really starts off in the fall in looking at concepts of identity. Just giving language so that kids can express themselves and share who they are and understand who their friends and peers are . . . how to express frustration appropriately and how to get your needs met that doesn't involve insulting or belittling or teasing anyone about who they are . . . we also talk to the kids about . . . to help them navigate new social experiences and so sometimes . . . usually I will be explicit in saying that these are some of the ways that people talk about skin color but then we don't use skin color ever to make someone feel bad or exclude them.

In this case, Ms. Maltes is connecting her Anti-Racist pedagogy to her teaching of socio-emotional skills. She is building a safe space, a community that is open to discussing race, in a way that is valued and accepted.

Another important characteristic that emerged from this research project is that all the early childhood educators believe in continuing their own education as they move forward. Lifelong learning is an essential component to becoming a committed Anti-Racist educator. Saad states, "Make life-long learning about Anti-Racism one of your values" (Saad, 2020, p. 208). This means that it is important that we encourage young teachers in training to embrace their lack of knowledge on the topic and then want to learn more about it. This is a commitment, lifelong, that starts in teacher education programs. If we teach about lifelong learning, and being open to do more research and read more about certain key topics, such as Anti-Racism, then students will willingly practice this skill.

When discussing her Anti-Racist teaching practices, Ms. Verano questions her own position as an Anti-Racist educator and reflects on how much more she needs to learn.

Ms. V: And when I volunteered for your project, I thought I had an understanding and I felt that in my pedagogy that I did . . . I was teaching Anti-Racist things to my students and I feel like I am . . . but in the work I have been doing in the last year I am learning so much more and I am teaching it so much differently so this year was the first time that in talking about Dr. King and the things he wanted to do . . . I said to the students "We still have a lot of work to do" that we are not done. . . . Like I said before, this is ever changing because I am probably going to do it differently next year or possibly the same things but added on.

Ms. Verano is constantly reflecting on her Anti-Racist teaching practices and this is what makes her a good example of a lifelong learner. It is the constant reflection before, during and after a curriculum unit is presented to a classroom. As educators, we do not know or understand all parts of what we teach on a daily basis and therefore we must continue to open ourselves up, to critically reflect and to reach out for new information.

Ms. Alice, in her second interview, talks about how she will change her teaching of a book I observed in her classroom, "Racism and Intolerance" by Louise Spilsbury.

Ms. A: I teach it in October or November so that the students have some vocabulary on hand, as well as a concept of what racism is, before I teach units about specific historical events. Going forward I am going to teach this book over the course of an entire week so that I can read it slowly and we can delve deeper into discussion.

Here, it is clear that Ms. Alice is constantly reflecting on her teaching of this work and thinking about ways she can improve on it. This is a part of the process of lifelong learning. There has to be a need to search and reflect upon our practices and then find ways to improve them. Some teachers just do the same units, the same lessons, year after year without revising and revitalizing the content and this is not conducive to lifelong learning.

As already noted, each of the six teacher participants focuses on social justice issues other than race and racism. They are intersectionality educators as well as Anti-Racist educators. They are utilizing their own intersectionality, as marginalized individuals from other groups (gay or bi identified) to shed light on injustice and combat stereotypes. Ms. Fern believes that it is not coincidental that all of the participants experience some form of marginality.

Ms. F: And I think the fact that most of your participants have some experience of marginality is not coincidental . . . I mean I think having an experience of being part of a marginalized community brings more of these issues to the forefront to your life in a way that if you don't have that experience you can sort of coast . . . look the other way or whatever . . . read one book.

To her, it is not surprising that intersectionality plays a role in being an Anti-Racist educator. Experiencing marginalization helps these participants to be more open to teaching about race and racism. They have some knowledge of what it feels like to be oppressed and/or discriminated against within the larger society and therefore have more understanding of what needs to be taught in the classroom to counter this normative discourse. Later on, in the same interview, she connects this idea to children and how they think about intersectionality:

Ms. F: I think that is another cool part about early childhood . . . that is how their little brains are. . . . Everything is interconnected already . . . so it's just naturally . . . you can go there with kids . . . they make connections because their brains are patterning in the world still . . . like fitting everything into those pieces . . . I think that five year olds are naturally intersectional because everything is . . . they are just laying it all out for them . . . figuring out where all of these threads go together.

Intersectionality is about our many different perspectives. People have multiple identities, including a racial identity and need to be aware of these identities at all times, especially while teaching young children. I think it is essential for teachers to be aware of all of these identities and perspectives and be able to critically reflect on them on an ongoing basis (see chapter 9). All of these identities intersect and give us insight into how we perceive the world.

What does this look like in the higher education classroom? How can we teach pre-service teachers the various characteristics of an Anti-Racist educator? More importantly, how can we encourage them to obtain these traits and characteristics, to incorporate them in their teaching practice?

First, it is essential that we prioritize and encourage college students to embrace these characteristics and to commit to actively engaging in this work. Inaction is not an avenue or an option. White apathy, as Saad refers to in her latest book, is essentially the problem (Saad, 2020). The practicing of white silence is the opposite of what teachers should be doing in their classrooms. Saad relates this to the process of being open to lifelong learning, evaluating, and reading about Anti-Racist practices (Saad, 2020). Saad states, "The intentional nonaction of white apathy is just as dangerous as these intentional actions of racism" (Saad, 2020, p. 127). Therefore, it follows that higher education teachers must clearly define and encourage critical reflection with their white pre-service teachers. Challenging their biases and assumptions is key to this understanding (see chapter 9). We, as professors, must challenge them to think and rethink about racism and how they can actively work against it in their classrooms.

Language choices, as stated earlier by the participants in this study, is the key to teaching Anti-Racist pedagogy in the higher education classroom as well. It is very important that we use the right language and terms when discussing the issues of race and racism in education. It is essential that professors themselves critically reflect on their spoken and written language (in the syllabi) and revising and correcting themselves when needed. An example of this is the use of any deficit terminology, which is usually not even considered or reflected upon before a lecture. Deficit terms that relate to BIPOC may include the following:

- Culturally deprived
- At-risk youth/children
- Lower class youth
- Disadvantaged

It is also important that higher education professors stop and comment on inappropriate or offensive language being used by the students themselves. Usually, this occurs in writing more than speaking, but sometimes students are not aware enough to see that the language they are using is actually full of bias and assumptions and is detrimental to the cause of Anti-Racism. For example, in my courses, over the years I have had many white students who refer to BIPOC in their writing as "colored," which can be seen as a divisive and inappropriate term. I have also come across students who have used the term "oriental" when referring to Asians. It is our job to reeducate them on their terminology, so that they are more aware of these terms that they are repeating over and over again that actually undermines this work. A good way to do this in your classroom is to provide them with different terms/ words/phrases and have them sort them by piles of words that are helpful and/

or hurtful to the practice of Anti-Racist pedagogy. This may help them to be more conscious of their word choices in their own future classrooms.

Another important way to encourage these powerful characteristics of an Anti-Racist educator is to help them understand the importance of involving social justice practices within all of their teaching methods. Social justice is related to Anti-Racist pedagogy and as noted, teachers that are committed to social justice practices are usually involved in some form or another of Anti-Racist pedagogy within their classrooms. Teaching about racial inequities and disparities is essential to the pre-service teacher's understandings. This should not be taught within one required course in your department, such as multicultural education, but instead should be woven together throughout all of the required coursework. This could mean that a transformation is needed in your education department, and that each course within your program of study be examined diligently. Infusing Anti-Racist pedagogy throughout each course is essential to helping the pre-service teacher really come to terms with the overall concepts. Thus, if you have courses that do not deal at all with Anti-Racist frameworks, such as literacy or special education courses, then it is time to work with your department on incorporating Anti-Racist pedagogy into all courses (see chapter 11). This method helps to create an inclusive environment which then aids pre-service teachers to feel more and more comfortable with working in this area.

Characteristics of an Anti-Racist educator can be taught throughout higher education courses by utilizing a set of character dispositions for your students. In my college we have, as a department, overhauled all of our pre-service dispositions, so that they are inclusive of these basic characteristics needed for becoming an Anti-Racist educator. Students are briefed on these dispositions in each course and are held accountable to them within the field (see Appendix B). This helps them within their courses and within field placements to adhere to the characteristics they are expected to uphold and encourages them to reflect on them for their future teaching career.

As you can see, there are certain characteristics that do define an Anti-Racist early childhood educator; however, there are more that are not listed here. These eleven characteristics are just some of the ones that help to define a teacher as being committed to Anti-Racist pedagogy. We, as professors, have an obligation to encourage the development of these characteristics so that we can ultimately produce early childhood educators that are dedicated to this work.

Chapter 3

Just Say No to Black History Month

> *Ms. F: You know we talk about that there is this thing Black History Month and we talk about whether . . . what we think about that . . . they sort of get that it is a little weird . . . um it comes up with other topics too . . . when gay pride happens and we talk about gay pride and that there is a parade for queer people . . . or Women's History month . . . we talk about how this is . . . you know they get the idea that this is sort of ludicrous . . . that why isn't this all the time? We are talking about these people's stories . . . so I hope by the time we get to Black History Month they have had enough exposure in the classroom and the curriculum with black history that it is not new stuff all of a sudden because it is February . . . I mean that is one of my goals is that when we get to February it is not the first time we are talking about Martin Luther King Jr and who he is . . . or Rosa Parks or people of color and I think it is usually the first time where POC are intentionally included in book selection.*

In my second year of teaching in the 1990s, I worked in a segregated BIPOC school with a majority of the population being West Indian/Caribbean. I was teaching first grade and was very excited about Black History Month. I spent hours designing a special bulletin board display outside my classroom and was very proud of it until my principal, a black woman, approached me. She told me to take down my bulletin board immediately. I was honestly surprised by her response. I expected her to react positively to my bulletin board because I was trying to be culturally responsive to the majority of students in my classroom. Instead, she was not happy. She told me that Black History Month was every day of the school year and that I should be infusing it into my daily practice. It was a hard lesson to learn as a young white teacher trying to do good in the world, but she was right. Why was I falling for this concept that I should only highlight great black leaders and heroes one month a year?

DiAngelo believes that there is no designated white history month because every month of the school is white history month (DiAngelo, 2018).

In this chapter, I will critically examine the background and history of Black History Month and Black Lives Matter Week. I will focus on the various inherent problems/issues within these concepts and how to address this in the higher education classroom.

First, we need to examine the history and the context of how Black History Month came to be a part of the school calendar. Carter Woodson, the founder of Black History Month, believed in the "emancipatory" power of history (Van De Mieroop, 2016). He first introduced it as Black History Week (Negro History Week) in 1926. Woodson strongly advocated for black history to be a part of the school curriculum. At first, the intended audience was African American students, who he felt did not know enough about their own history and culture. He wanted to encourage black students to positively view their own history so that they would see themselves as worthy in our society (King & Brown, 2014). He also clearly thought that it should be a relevant and important part of the curriculum and not used as an additive (King & Brown, 2014). This is important to note, as in many schools today, it is seen as an additive and not as an essential part of the curriculum as a whole. Woodson believed it should be taught all year round in segregated black schools but initially rallied for one intense week as a starting point. It was designed to help African American students to be prideful in their culture as well as give them more self-confidence later on as they entered the workforce (King & Brown, 2014).

In the 1960s, Black History Week officially turned into Black History Month. It was expanded in many schools at the time and started to be taught in newly integrated schools. Thus, more children, including some white children, were exposed to black history for the first time. In 1975, Gerald Ford became the first president to publicly recognize the significance of Black History Month and encouraged its appearance in all k-12 schools nationwide (Van De Mieroop, 2016). At this point, it is fair to note that it was not universally utilized in all classrooms.

Today it is still being highlighted during the month of February and is a key fixture in most k-5 schools. Black History Month is a time when educators teach about key figures in black history, mostly focusing on Dr. Martin Luther King, Rosa Parks, and Harriet Tubman. It is set up as a stand-alone month where all of black history is revealed and discussed. Yet, in most cases, it is a very limited view of black history in this country. This, of course, is a very stereotypical view of how Black History Month is being utilized in general, but it is not far from the actual truth. In reality, early childhood educators are not critically delving into black history, mainly because they have limited understanding or knowledge on the topic themselves. For example, in my class last semester, the majority of students in my literacy course had never heard of Sojourner Truth, a famous abolitionist. Actually, I notice, year after year that they have had very limited exposure to black history and know very little about it in general. In most cases, they receive a whitewashed education about Dr. King and the "I have a Dream Speech" and Rosa Parks not wanting to give up her seat on the bus. Their understandings are minimal and simplistic. For example, most of my students believed that Rosa Parks was just too tired that day to get up and give up her seat to a white person. They do not know her back story as an activist, and/or how she planned this demonstration, nor do they know about other important civil rights leaders and how they impacted the movement. They also have no understanding of important time periods, such as Reconstruction, Jim Crow era, migration patterns up north, segregation in schools, and the Civil Rights era. They have no knowledge of great black artists, dancers, singers, inventors, and more (see chapter 6). So, if they have little to no knowledge of black history how can they, in turn, teach it properly in their classrooms?

There are negative aspects to this particular setup of only teaching black history during one month of the school year. One issue, as stated earlier, is the amount of historical knowledge a child can actually be introduced to during this limited window of time. This leads to a "Tourist Approach" to black history, which can be "patronizing and superficial" (Cole, 2009, p. 72). This may include activities such as children dressing up in Kente cloths from Africa, hosting food festivals on Soul Food, wearing safari costumes, creating parades and assemblies that are white-washing real events in black history (King & Brown, 2014). This "Tourist Approach" is similar to how a lot of K-12 schools deal with multicultural events, including wearing sombreros for Cinco De Mayo, eating rice for Chinese New Year, and so on. These cultural festivals can end up perpetuating stereotypes, and thus, reproducing racist discourses. DiAngelo states, "I am not against Black History Month. But it should be celebrated in a way that doesn't reinforce whiteness" (DiAngelo, 2018, p. 26).

Most teachers focus on just a few key black leaders during Black History Month, which is another problem, as it implies that there are only a few to begin with. They may throw in random images of black people in history here and there but it lacks true depth. This whole enterprise then becomes additive and not a key part of the social studies curriculum (King & Brown, 2014). It also serves as an afterthought, a way to pretend to be interested in black history without really teaching it. "This approach to Black History Month is harmful as it reinforces the hidden curriculum that perpetuates otherness while replicating systems of power and whiteness is presented as normal" (King & Brown, 2014, p. 27). King and Brown believe that this approach to Black History Month can cause more harm than good and essentially defeats its own purpose. There are, of course, teachers who complain about not having a designated "white history month," which is very troublesome as each month in 99 percent of the schools in America is all about white history. Actually, the only history taught is from a white perspective and does not usually include voices of non-white figures. To me, this is not unlike the recent protest by a group of straight people marching for equality for straight people as a counter-protest to gay pride events. It just doesn't make sense.

Another important issue within this controversy of teaching about black history for only one month of a ten-month school year is the way that it reinforces a color-blind discourse within schools (King and Brown, 2014). Early childhood educators (over 85 percent white) constantly talk about how we are all the same, that we are all humans and thus deserve to be treated the same (Tatum, 2017). Some actually actively do lessons that feed into this color-blind discourse. For example, they present a bowl of lemons and have the children peel them to see that the lemons are all the same on the inside. Then they discuss that we are all human beings on the inside, no matter how we look on the outside. I have actually witnessed these same lessons with apples and oranges as well. If this is what teachers are discussing all year long then it makes sense that they are behind the ideology of a month only dedicated to black history events. They don't need to or want to highlight any issues related to race or racism in the world because "we are essentially all the same." This is very worrisome and problematic for several reasons, but the main one being that it just continues to marginalize BIPOC and downplays any issues of race or racism within our society.

Probably, the biggest reason why this existing approach to the teaching of black history exclusively within one month is so problematic is the idea that we live in a post-racial society and therefore this is a problem from the past and is no longer a valid concern (Van de Mieroop, 2016). "Post racial periodization is not a denial of the racist past, it is a denial of the connection between the past and the present" (Van De Mieroop, 2016, p. 23). The post-racial argument, which is still alive and well, is that slavery and segregation are a thing of the past and are no longer a part of our society so there is no reason to dwell on it. Some teachers actually take this a step further and don't even think it warrants a whole month of lessons/activities as it is not a problem anymore. These are the same people who think that by electing a black president, it shows that we live in a post-racial society, one that no longer has a racial divide or issues related to past racist discourse. Some researchers believe that the way most schools currently enact Black History Month is problematic because it continues this discourse of racism as a thing of the past (Van de Mieroop, 2016). "Black History Month celebrations always feature a narrative of racial progress" (Van De Mieroop, 2016, p. 19). Look how far we have come. This is what is presented in early childhood classrooms nationwide, and then children both white and brown/black believe that this inequality is a past occurrence and does not exist today. Many white teachers are happy to just present Dr. Martin Luther King, and his "I have a dream" speech, to show how much better we have it in today's society. It then becomes a very narrow view of black history and as such just perpetuates this post-racial myth.

I think the whole current debate on whether to teach Critical Race Theory in schools is an example of this post-racial myth. Many white families that are contesting this practice in K-12 schools (where it ironically is not taught) believe that we should just drop this whole race/racism issue as it is no longer a problem in our society. They believe that by discussing race/racism, white children are being discriminated against and being made to feel bad about their heritage for no real reason (Petit, 2021).

Some people argue that teaching black history will improve racial relations in our society (Van De Mieroop, 2016). This notion is also problematic. Yes, it is important to teach black history so that all populations can honor and understand the significance of hidden history. However, if we just dedicate one month of the school year teaching about this hidden history that has never really been told or honored in any way, then how will we improve racial relations in our society? This strategy just reinforces the hierarchy of the races because there are nine months of the school year where we focus on white history (mainstream history) and just one month that we focus on 400 years of black history. This just furthers the argument of the "other" and continues to marginalize BIPOC populations in our society. Black history needs to be a part of everyday lessons in the classroom, infused throughout the year, in order for it to be an authentic part of how we define and talk about the history of the United States.

One of the common characteristics of the participants in this study is that they all believe that black history should be infused throughout the school year. They do not believe in the ideology of Black History Month and the idea of teaching about race and black historical figures during this one particular month. As noted earlier, Ms. Fern refers to this as "ludicrous" and "weird" and realizes that the children in her kindergarten class feel the same way about this idea. These teacher participants actually push against this notion. They actively go against the grain. Ms. Broadbent, in her second interview, makes this point when talking about her first-grade social studies curriculum that focuses on great heroes and changers in society:

Ms. B: . . . this is the kinda of work with great changers is all year long.
R: So, if I can ask you then . . . do you do Black History Month?
Ms. B: During Black History Month? Not necessarily . . . I don't know . . . it is all year for us.

Ms. Broadbent, like the other participants in the study, was actually taken aback by my asking about whether or not they celebrated or actually practiced Black History Month in their classrooms. To them, this was not an option, as they make it clear that it is infused into the curriculum on an ongoing basis. When asked about certain strategies and how they incorporated Anti-Racist pedagogy during the year, Ms. Verano made it a point to combat this notion of Black History Month.

Ms. V: Yeah, I definitely do it more throughout the year because it is something that I think needs to be woven throughout everything . . . throughout the timeline of the year because it is too important to push into one short month.

Ms. Verano believes that Anti-Racist work cannot be crammed into one short month, as it is too important and there is too much to cover. King and Brown state that Black History Month "represents a time to cram everything 'black into the curriculum'" (King & Brown, 2014, p. 25). And this is not what an Anti-Racist educator wants to do. It is also important to note that February is the shortest month of the school year, which is interesting in itself, as to why it was selected. From start to finish it is twenty-eight days and eight of those days fall on the weekend. That means that there is less than three weeks of actual instructional days devoted to this topic. Imagine trying to teach so-called white history in this small amount of time.

In our second interview, Ms. Maltes responds in a similar way as the other participants when asked about Black History Month:

R: So, that gets to my next question . . . do you do Black History Month? How do you deal with that?
Ms. M: I personally don't . . . just because it would be something I try to integrate throughout the year but that being said . . . it's just my own teaching and upbringing I tend not to do like this month is devoted to this . . . this month is devoted to that . . . kinda thing.
R: So, you infuse it throughout the year in your curriculum?
Ms. M: Theoretically . . . whether I . . . except it might just not look as explicit as it would . . . if I were to try and dedicate a month to it .

Interestingly, Ms. Maltes challenges the notion of teaching any topic for just one month. This means that she doesn't highlight Women's History Month either. She is questioning the idea of doing any one topic for one month, separating it out from the year as a whole. When I taught first grade, seven years ago, I witnessed many other early childhood educators embracing this idea of teaching one topic per month. Some teachers even had boxes for each month of the school year so that they could categorize their activities during a specific month, like March (Women's History Month), December (Christmas and other winter holidays), and so on. Each year they pulled out the box for the month in question and only used resources/activities from this specific box. This, to me, always seemed like a very limited approach to teaching, as you can only use what is in one box each month.

Black Lives Matter Week is also in February and is a very recent event taking place in schools nationwide. It is designed to be a week of action within the public schools. It asks educators to look at their own Anti-Racist pedagogy to reflect and challenge themselves to center Anti-Racist pedagogy within their classrooms. It started a few years ago and happens during the first week of February annually. Only one of the participants in this study had heard of this new Black Lives Matter Week for k-12 schools. In an interview, two Ms. Fern delves into the topic:

R: Do you do Black Lives Matter Week?
Ms. F: We did . . . a few years ago when it first . . . we did . . . we got some of the resources you can get online . . . There was some coloring pages and things like that and we put them out and we definitely talked about what they were . . . And then, you know, we live where the Black Lives Matter signs are sort of everywhere . . . so we sort of talk about how it doesn't just have to be a week . . . Black Lives Matter all of the time . . . so I think we try to . . . I think I try to keep the presenting . . . especially when I am presenting visual information to kids through stories . . . through videos we watch . . . or whatever . . . that they are seeing diverse ranges of people in the stories because otherwise it's . . . yeah, that's not relatable.

Ms. Fern understands the importance of teaching about the Black Lives Matter movement. Since it is newly on the scene, all the participants were not sure how to teach this specific week in the classroom, but they are up for the challenge. Clearly, this is an area where the school districts they work in could provide professional development, and hopefully they will in the future. Yet still, it is only designated as one week per year which continues to be a problematic setup.

Black Lives Matter Week is designed to showcase the national demands of the organization and it focuses on improving the school experiences of BIPOC. It is also trying to promote awareness to the fact that all Black Lives Matter and therefore shootings of black/brown bodies by police are not justifiable for any reason. The following are guiding principles to this weeklong celebration:

- Restorative Justice
- Empathy

- Loving Engagement
- Diversity
- Globalism
- Collective Value
- Transgender and Queer Affirming
- Intergenerational
- Black Families
- Black Villages
- Black Women
- Unapologetically Black

These principles need to be examined closely in both the k-12 classroom and higher education classrooms as they are important key characteristics that reveal that black lives do indeed matter. Going over each principle in the classroom will encourage students to want to learn more about black history in general. Furthermore, these principles guide students in their quest for honoring and valuing people from other racial backgrounds.

I think that the study of Black Lives Matter Week, which should be infused throughout the school year, is essential especially in these aggressively violent times where BIPOC are being murdered by agents of the government. Just in the past month of this writing there have been over four incidents nationwide of innocent young BIPOC men and women being shot and killed by police, even at the same time as there is a trial going on to convict the officer who murdered George Floyd by stepping on his neck for over eight minutes. This movement is about civil rights and should be critically examined in all classrooms so that everyone understands the true nature of racism in our current society. These are public lynchings and are not acceptable, not now and not ever and they must be discussed.

On many occasions, I have had to explain in my higher education classrooms what the term "Black Lives Matters" really means. I have had students respond with "All lives Matter" or "Blue Lives Matter" and that is when I know they need more education on this point. I utilize several scenarios that they can understand to highlight how Black Lives Matter is different than these other two sayings. For example, I tell them to close their eyes and imagine a street of single family houses. One is on fire, so the firefighters go to that house first to put out the fire. The other houses are not on fire and therefore do not need immediate attention. The house that is burning down is Black Lives Matter. This is an emergency situation, and the fire needs to be put out in this one house. The emergency situation is that BIPOC are being shot and killed for no apparent reason (no weapons etc.).

When teaching about or critically reflecting on how to handle Black History Month in our higher education classroom is important that we frame this discussion in deficit versus inclusive terms. Questioning the design of this concept of a month devoted to black history is an important part of the discussion. Pre-service teachers do not even question the ideology behind this premise of one month. They need help in reflecting on how this can be seen as deficit based, like referring to young BIPOC as "lower class," "culturally deprived," and or "at-risk." It is important to talk about deficit-based language and how this relates to the concept of Black History Month. If we only talk about black history during one month of the school year, are we really honoring it or making it a priority in our classrooms? Is this strategy inclusive? No, it can't be. If we are trying to frame this Anti-Racist work as important to their teaching, then we must question the lack of inclusion of black history into the overall curriculum.

There will be push back of course, but professors need to be clear, inclusivity and infusing it into the curriculum all year long is the only option that promotes equity. Some students will counter with the idea that there is no extra space in the curriculum for black history. They will question why they can't just focus on it during February, as they have witnessed in most of their pre-practicum classrooms. And this is where you must be firm. If you are committed to teaching pre-service teachers to be open to Anti-Racist work and you actively utilize these principals in your classrooms then you have to be very clear. There are only two options, to try and infuse Anti-Racist pedagogy within the early childhood classroom or continue to perpetuate a color-blind discourse that is dismissive and non-inclusive. This ideology is clear in Kendi's book where he states that there is no such thing as being non-racist. You are either defined as an racist or an Anti-Racist (Kendi, 2019). Taking this idea one step further you are either promoting racist teachers or Anti-Racist teachers. There is no middle ground, especially not now in our current society of extreme racial injustice.

Another important reason to infuse black history all year long in the early childhood classroom is that representation matters. Young BIPOC need to see their history on display because it is inspiring and motivating for their learning. In the higher education classroom, it is important that we make this point over and over again. It needs to become second nature to the pre-service teacher. They must be aware of the books and materials they pick and how they present different content. Is it inclusive? Does it incorporate important BIPOC? Representation builds self-esteem and self-respect, which is crucial for a young BIPOC (Randolph, 2013). It is the teacher's job to build self-esteem and to help children appreciate their own culture and expertise. This can't be accomplished without ongoing representation during the school year. BIPOC young children need lots of encouragement to succeed and to feel as though their voice is being heard within the classroom. Also, it is important to note that the nation is becoming more of a nation of BIPOC and within the next ten years will become even more so (Phillips, 2016). "Because of the cultural and racial diversity of the United States student population, educators must realize the differences among their students and integrate diversity education into the entire curriculum" (Alismail, 2016, p. 139).

Many of these white pre-service teachers do not even give the time to examine how they will be culturally and racially responsive to their young children. Some believe that if they are placed in a mostly white school then they do not need to ever reflect on this topic. They do not think about the one or two token BIPOC in their rooms and therefore they buy into this myth of only teaching black history one month a year. However, research has shown us that majority white classrooms still need ongoing exposure to black history and Anti-Racist pedagogy (Derman-Sparks & Ramsey, 2005).

> We now understand that it is not enough for white people to "accept" and "respect" POC. Rather white people need to undergo a profound shift, from viewing the world through a lens of dominance to a commitment to equitably shared power and resources. (Derman-Sparks & Ramsey, 2005, p. 1)

Derman-Sparks and Ramsey believe that racism also profoundly affects young white children as they grow into their privilege and their sense of superiority (Derman-Sparks & Ramsey, 2005). If the curriculum is more representative of them and their historical view than this reinforces these children's views on racial hierarchy and privilege. Thus, it is important to represent and expose all young children to the counternarrative of black history, so that they accept and honor it as a major part of our overall American history (see chapter 6).

How can we actively promote these ideas in our classrooms? The first thing we need to do is be a good role model. Our course structure/readings should reflect this practice of infusing black history throughout the entire semester. This means that you must scrap the idea of one or two classes solely dedicated to the topic of Anti-Racist pedagogy or black history. This is tantamount to saying that you think only one or two classes should be devoted to this topic. In turn, this sends a message to the students that it is just a tiny matter, one that is not central to the course as a whole. I used to do this without reflection and then one day while examining my syllabus I realized that I had only three weeks devoted to the topic of race and racism and that I had another twelve weeks that did not include much on the topic. This is problematic. We need to reflect and rework our syllabi in order to infuse this ideology throughout the semester. This takes time and thought but is well worth it in the end. You have to look at your topics from week to week and look carefully at your resources/materials, such as videos, PowerPoints, books, and make sure that they all are related to some form of Anti-Racist pedagogy. For example, I teach a class on early intervention and I cover the topic of IEP's (Individual Education Plans) and IFSP's (Individual Family Service Plans). Instead of just reviewing an IEP and discussing the referral process, I include a powerpoint and a video related to how there are more BIPOC referred to special education programs. I also include data sheets so they can see hard data that proves this is happening nationwide. This leads to an important discussion about critically reflecting on the inequities in the IEP process and helps them to understand the bigger picture of institutional racism in terms of schooling.

Recently, I taught children's literature to early childhood and elementary education students for the first time. I created my own syllabus that centered on books by BIPOC authors. Every week, I exposed them to a different genre of children's literature and each week they read books and watched videos about important BIPOC authors. I intentionally searched for BIPOC authors for each genre so that they would be infused into the course and the white pre-service teachers could visualize how they could do this in their own classroom. At the end of the course, they had to present an author study of a BIPOC author who promoted social justice issues. Overall, I think that by infusing this concept of honoring BIPOC authors all semester long, they not only learned more about people they had never been exposed to but they also developed a real respect and understanding of BIPOC authors in general. Thus, I recommend taking the opposite approach of exposure to a canon of classic white authors and instead make it ordinary to showcase BIPOC authors. Most of the students, in their reflections, were very happy to be exposed to literature that they had never heard of and were critical of their past teacher's choices of books in their own upbringing. Yes, they were familiar with *Charlotte's Web* and Dr. Seuss books, but they never had a chance to read *Bud, Not Buddy* and *Roll of Thunder, Hear My Cry*. If we are truly committed to Anti-Racist pedagogy then we must center BIPOC voices throughout the term.

The teaching of black history is more essential than ever before. It needs to be integrated into our social studies curriculum throughout the year in order for it to be seen as important. Representation matters. The problems of hundreds of years of ongoing systemic racism have not been solved. Yet, this takes more than a month to teach, so just say no to Black History Month.

Chapter 4

Racial Equity

Ms. Fern: Yeah, clearly, I am a white woman and I present to the world . . . you know as white . . . I receive white privilege . . . I live in a town where lots of people have that privilege . . . lots of people have that 'woke' awareness . . . so, I live in a great place where there is lots of great dialogue and discussion . . . but then . . . and this has come up in my class . . . from the kids . . . that even though we live in this great town where we talk about these things . . . where are the families of color? I mean I think five-year-olds recognize that . . . last year, a student in my class . . . got upset . . . like physically upset . . . was crying . . . and you know when I talked to him about what was going on for him he said, "It's just really hard because . . . " I think he recognized that . . . nobody looking like me and my family is hard . . . I don't think I understood the concepts of power and privilege and oppression until much later . . . until I was older and kind of did reading and got this idea . . . but I think when you are young and in school . . . and you are in a community where there is not a lot of kids of color . . . and the kids of color that there are often the kids who are having behavior problems or are targeted as such . . . having behavior problems . . . I remember those experiences very clearly about certain kids who I went to school with . . . that were kids of color and were always the ones in trouble . . . they were always getting yelled at . . . They were always . . . you know the ones going to the special classroom or going to the principal . . . it made me uncomfortable . . . I remember feeling uncomfortable . . . I don't know.

Racial equity or the lack of real equity is a theme that kept resurfacing during this research process. The teacher participants consistently made comments within their interviews related to inequities and true inequalities within their school districts. These racial inequities affect how they teach Anti-Racist pedagogy with young children as it continually motivates them to do more. In this chapter, I will closely examine these issues of racial inequity and inequality within the sphere of these teacher's everyday worlds. I will examine issues of power dynamics, privilege, individualism, meritocracy, and how to teach this important topic within a higher education classroom. It is imperative that pre-service white teachers understand these complex topics before entering the classroom, especially since most schools in the United States are still segregated (de facto) and therefore inherently unequal.

According to Delpit, there is a clear culture of power which is a hierarchal structure, with white doctrines/discourses on the top (Delpit, 2006). There are underlying codes and rules that are enforced by institutional racism and they are true reflections of how our society and our schools function. "Whiteness operates as an unspoken norm" (ST. Denis & Schick, 2003). This culture of power continues to operate through a white, middle-class lens primarily because it benefits white people and serves the interests of those in power (DiAngelo, 2010). Schools and, therefore, early childhood programs are representative of this culture of power as they maintain the status quo, white supremacy (Delpit, 2006). This leads to a severe discrepancy in equity issues in differing districts. Ladson-Billings states, "In a racialized society where whiteness is positioned as normative, everyone is ranked and categorized in relation to these points of opposition" (Ladson-Billings, 2004, p. 51).

It is the job of the teacher, who is usually white, to visibly oppose this power dynamic and intentionally teach about racial equality and equity in their classrooms. This does not really happen on a large scale, because most white educators, even those dedicated to social justice issues, have not reflected about this regime of truth at all. And if they do, they are unsure and afraid of challenging the status quo. What ends up happening is that the teacher just avoids the topic of racial inequity or power dynamics in the classroom. Delpit states that "admitting participation in the culture of power is distinctly uncomfortable" (Delpit, 2006, p. 26). This then turns into bias, whether intentional or not, on the part of the white teacher. "Teachers rate black students as exhibiting more externalizing problem behaviors then they do white students" (Downey & Pribesh, 2004, p. 275). This is an ongoing practice in early childhood programs, as mentioned by Ms. Fern in her aforementioned interview. Part of the issue in question is the teacher's views and perceptions of BIPOC students and their lack of knowledge and understanding of cultural and racial differences. In their research, Downey and Pribesh found that "while teachers fail to appreciate black students' unique cultural style or possibly use class-management styles that fail to motivate black students" (Downey & Pribesh, 2004, p. 277). The culture of school is based on white, middle-class discourse and therefore white teachers lack the knowledge and understanding to adjust their classroom practices to different cultures and races. What is worse, in most cases, white teachers actively utilize a deficit discourse when evaluating young BIPOC children. "To deny students their own expert knowledge is to disempower them" (Delpit, 2006, p. 33). Instead of focusing on the strengths of BIPOC students and what they can bring into the classroom, including their own expert knowledge, these white teachers are trying to assimilate them into the culture of the school.

Children, on the other hand, are very aware of unfairness. They will constantly point to the issue of fairness in the classroom, encouraging the teacher to take stock in its concept and asking them to make it paramount. "That's not fair" is a sentence that is common in pre-kindergarten and kindergarten classrooms. They are always searching for fairness and they know that there is a chance of it being made of as an example in the classroom. In my first interview with Ms. Fern, she states,

> Small people are so naturally wanting the world to be good and wonderful and they come to you with their big big open hearts . . . they are ready to make things good. . . . They want things to be fair and for people to feel good and they understand these very vital concepts of justice and love and equity in a way that grown-ups get stuck.

Like parents, most teachers dismiss this notion of fairness, precisely because they want to believe that society, in general, plays fair. Yet, how can it be if there are inherent power dynamics that favor one race over others. And this is how white supremacy as an ideology operates within institutional systems.

A good example of this comes from Ms. Fern's third interview where she is talking about issues of equity and equality, and how it relates to the current global pandemic.

> I have a friend who calls this pandemic a "Time of Reckoning" and I think it really is . . . a Time of Reckoning for people . . . I hope it compels us to make change . . . this reckoning. . . . And say . . . like wait, why is that when I am thinking about my pod I am only thinking about these white families that I know . . . because I have only ever had playdates with those kids . . . I am in the same neighborhood as those kids and I have never reached out to others in other neighborhoods . . . now that we have this pandemic . . . we got virtual teaching and it is just . . . the divide is more evident . . . so when you are thinking about schools re-opening or not re-opening . . . or who gets to go back and who doesn't get to go back . . . who has access . . . who doesn't have access . . . yeah, to technology . . . to support . . . at the early childhood level. . . . And let's face it remote learning requires adult support . . . and not everybody has support and a lot of that support is based around race and class.

Here, Ms. Fern is talking about how the pandemic has dramatically revealed the inequities and inequalities in our schools. She speaks of it as the "Time of Great Reckoning" but it has always been in place, and is just an example of the power dynamics that control our institutions. Just the whole notion of pods, which are groups of people who can play and learn together without worrying about being infected by Covid-19 from others is an elitist concept. White families can build pods with other white families, hire tutors, have one or two educated parents help with remote learning, and not invite families of color to join because they don't know any. They also have all of the technology infrastructure needed: more devices, software, and connectivity (Tager, 2019). Ms. Fern is right when she mentions the inherent inequities related to a global pandemic, yet it was all there operating and fully functioning beforehand. It is just now even more noticeable.

There is a history of deficit thinking in terms of BIPOC students in the United States. Pennington states, "The social construction of race attested to the fact that we automatically made certain assumptions about children based on what we thought of them as a member of an essentialized group of people" (Pennington, 2007, p. 102). One of the main problems in public schools today is that teachers (85 percent white) have lower expectations of BIPOC students than white students (Tatum, 2017). Anti-Racist pedagogy directly combats this idea and as such is helpful in this counternarrative of culturally deficit thinking. Marx states, "Culturally deficit thinking remains firmly entrenched in the American mindset" (Marx, 2006, p. 15). Thus, this type of thinking promotes and maintains white supremacy within its institutions. It benefits white populations of children and victimizes and oppresses populations of BIPOC children (Marx, 2006).

Culturally deficit thinking is an active force in early childhood programs and is a part of a white teacher's mindset. When teachers, for example, use the terms "school ready" or "nonschool ready," they are classifying children into groups that are not equitable. The majority of identified nonschool ready children are BIPOC (Tager, 2017). In my previous book, I challenge these constructions and label them as racist in practice (Tager, 2017). Identification of being nonschool ready is a way for white teachers to exclude BIPOC students from their own learning. They are regulated to academic interventions, behavioral interventions, and to large numbers of referrals to the special education team (Harry & Klingner, 2006). This all relates to the mindset of deficit-based thinking of marginalized populations.

Another issue that majorly affects how teachers view children in terms of racial inequities is the ideology surrounding the term "individualism." The notion of individualism in our country is actually a downfall in terms of racist practices. If one believes in the power of the individual and their strength to overcome all the odds, then it is up to the specific individual as to whether or not they succeed in American society. This ideology, related to meritocracy, is problematic because it is based on the notion that we live in a color-blind society and that all people have equal access to succeed if they work hard. According to this ideology, race is not an issue and there are no intrinsic barriers holding certain populations back (DiAngelo, 2010). This perpetuates the myth that we all have an equal opportunity to do well and that if we don't personally do well it is our own fault. This is the so-called American Dream that all who come to our land of freedom have equal opportunities to succeed. This notion perpetuates racism within our culture because it blames BIPOC for not being able to pick themselves up by their bootstraps and be successful in our economy. "A further problem with the assumption of meritocracy is that it ignores how dominant group identifications facilitate access to social and institutional power . . . meritocracy assumes that power is equally available and distributed" (ST Denis & Shick, 2003, p. 64). We do not start on a level playing field, thus certain populations are actually penalized for not being a part of the dominant class. Therefore, we are essentially lying to the people of this nation by saying that we all have equal opportunities to succeed and rise above the crowd. BIPOC have many more obstacles to overcome in order to do this, which includes issues in housing, job searches, bank loans, mortgages, dealing with the police, health insurance, schooling, and other institutional endeavors.

Individualism and the pride of the individual is really the pride of white supremacy and how it functions in all of our institutions. Teachers, like everybody else in this society, can buy into this notion of equal opportunity and therefore will be a part of the blame game with their student populations that are marginalized. Education is not the great equalizer, as there is nothing equal about institutional racism in our schools. Therefore, it is important that in order to dismantle institutional racism, we must deconstruct and get rid of this long-lasting notion of the individual and meritocracy. First, we, as higher educators, must try not to perpetuate this ideology in our classrooms. We must be clear that race and socioeconomic status matters. "This strategy of denying that race matters supports differences of power reflected in historic, social, political and economic practices" (ST Denis & Shick, 2003, p. 62). We need to challenge the status quo by breaking down this ideology and critically reflecting on how it is more harmful than helpful to reforming our schools/programs.

True racial equity and equality cannot exist until we confront this issue head-on in our schools and early childhood centers. It is important to note that the Office of Civil Rights has filed and will continue to file thousands of lawsuits against school districts in the United States for violating the Civil Rights Act of 1964. An example of this is a lawsuit that was filed in my previous school district in 2014. The ACLU and the Office of Civil Rights looked at the data within this so-called "liberal" district and realized that there were too many BIPOC children being suspended and being referred to special education testing. This happens all the time across the country, as districts have to publish their student data and can suffer lawsuits if there are high proportions of BIPOC students that are affected. In 2013–14 (the year this particular district was sued), 1.1 million of the 2.8 million suspensions were black children (US Dept of Ed, 2013-14).

Another example of this racial divide occurred in my junior high school and still occurs in many junior high/middle schools and high schools today. Tracking students into certain pathways for learning is common and in my junior high school, it was clearly along racial lines. All of the white kids, with some exceptions, were tracked in higher level courses/cohorts where the academic classes were harder and geared to future college entry. The BIPOC students in my school were on lower tracks, such as 5, 6, 7, 8, and were tracked for vocational school with less focus on academics. I was in 7-3, 8-2, and 9-3, always in the upper tracks with higher expectations, better teachers, and more academic rigor. The student populations really never mixed except at lunchtime. This tracking experience took place in New York City, in liberal areas of the city, and as a student, I was surprised by the normalcy of this system. Today, with gifted and talented classes and college-level high school courses, this tracking system is still in place and is perpetuating inequalities in many state school systems.

Greene, a prominent critical educator, states, "There is no question but that some students face fearful obstacles due to inequities in this country" (Greene, 1995, p. 18). Schools are inherently unequal. This is due to a variety of reasons including inequities in school funding, segregated practices, institutional racism, teacher retention issues, and more. Materials, including technology, are inequitably distributed district to district and PTO's in wealthier white communities can raise more school funds than low-income schools with large populations of BIPOC students (Tager, 2019). Even commonplace school practices, like homework, reveal essential inequities within schools. In my second interview with Ms. Broadbent, she brings up this disparity:

Ms. B: Even now we have this homework discussion going on and it's really pissing me off because we are not talking about equity and that's not necessarily around racial lines but there's something

R: (interrupts) Because some people can do homework and some people can't?

Ms. B: Right, because the resources are different in homes and people are dismissing that instead of really talking about how that is an issue . . . . I was at a meeting on Monday . . . "My kids love homework," said a white parent. Really, that's not what we are talking about . . . We are talking about the effectiveness and the value of educational homework and the equity around

it . . . and I was adamant at this meeting . . . we have read the research . . . and so maybe I will be very specific about the articles I pull, because we did this already in our school and we don't do homework because of those issues and now the district wants to just do homework without really looking at the whole picture.
R: Well, it's pushing white middle-class norms on everybody.
Ms. B: Yeah.

Ms. Broadbent is referring to her district's new push to make homework mandatory. She knows that this is unfair because some of her students, low-income BIPOC students, will have a hard time completing homework, as their parents work three jobs and do not have time to supervise. White parents are the ones who are saying, "My kids love homework," which is not completely believable, but it is clear that homework is important to them. They also have more resources at home, including more technology, and have more time to support and supervise their children in this endeavor. Interestingly, this only became a nonissue when the pandemic hit and all homework was banned as schools went completely remote. This issue will probably return to the district after the pandemic is over and is a part of many school district discussions.

Ms. Houston, who works in a majority white school district, was very clear in her interviews that her school has more resources than other schools in high-poverty districts. She is probably more attuned to it as she was herself a student in an inner-city environment with large populations of BIPOC students. In the following excerpt, she makes her opinions on equity and equality known:

R: What are your thoughts now that you are in a school that is predominantly . . . it has a high percentage of whites . . . it is 94% . . . I looked up the data.
Ms. H: That makes sense.
R: What are your thoughts of working in that type of environment which is very restricted?
Ms. H: It's an environment of privilege . . . because we are two thirds school choice . . . um so we get kids from . . . (another town) but school choice is also a place of privilege because you have to . . . be able to get . . . transportation . . . which means you have to have somebody who can bring you to school for eight O'clock and pick you up at three O'clock . . . that alone is privilege . . . um having a job where you can pick up your kid . . . or the means to pay for an afterschool program and pick them up at five.
R: But do you feel like you fit into this school? District? Like if you had an ideal job would it be at this school?
Ms. H: It would be this school with more diversity to be honest.
R: But I don't think that can happen.

Ms. H: Unfortunately, the places that I would want to be in are so over-regulated that . . . even . . . (town 1) and . . . (town 2) are incredibly regulated and so you have to do certain programs . . . you know "same day same page" . . . you are expected to do a lot of these things or you are expected to be able to create an environment where you are still able to meet all of these expectations but also providing what you know is developmentally appropriate.

Clearly, Ms. Houston does not like working in her "environment of privilege" but also can't fathom working in more "diverse" (segregated with majority BIPOC students) schools because they are too regulated and compromise her academic freedom. She doesn't think it is fair for low-income BIPOC students to be overregulated but she does not want to be a teacher there either for the same reasons.

Ms. Alice, who used to work in a segregated urban school district, also observed and experienced differences in equity and is now happier teaching in a predominately white school with more resources and less restrictions.

Ms. A: I liked working in [nearby city] a lot and I actually miss it but I worked in a charter school and I did not like that. . . . Charters are not really good for teachers in terms of us having many rights and we are not unionized and we are very much taken advantaged of . . . but it was more of the system I didn't like not the people I was teaching.
R: What was the population of your charter school?
Ms. A: I would say it was approximately 97% African American.
R: So, it was a segregated school?
Ms. A: Of course . . . yeah . . . but it what was interesting is people from colleges around the area . . . you know teachers in training would bring students to our school because they wanted them to be in a quote unquote diverse school . . . and it would really bother me . . . so one time I said to one these professors this isn't a diverse school . . . it pained me that even these teachers in training were getting a false definition of diversity . . . that if people are brown it is diverse . . . but it wasn't diverse . . . it was the opposite of diverse . . . where I work now it is pretty white. . . . Almost all white.
R: And how was that going from a segregated school of one type to another segregated school?
Ms. A: Well . . . you know what makes you realize that . . . how the churches and schools are the two most segregated places in this country . . . it's crazy . . . I mean it really brings it home . . . so it was definitely my first . . . my first month in . . . (district) was a culture shock which was very interesting because culturally the students and the families are more similar to me culturally but I had just . . . never taught in a setting like . . . never seen things like . . . and I felt like I had to be very careful and everyone was so precious.

Ms. Alice reveals very different experiences in majority white schools and majority black schools. De facto segregated, non-diverse schools are the landmarks of this region and they offer very different things (Tager, 2019). She also talks about the pay and how she can't move again because she is paid so much better in her majority white district. This is another form of inequity, teacher pay, and is the reason why good teachers like Ms. Alice and Ms. Houston do not stay in high-poverty, school districts with large populations of BIPOC.

Ms. Broadbent takes this a step further through advocacy work. She believes it is the teacher's job to advocate for the children in her class, especially populations that lack power within the system. When talking about the current political climate in interview, one Ms. Broadbent brings up advocacy.

Ms. B: Well yes . . . because I feel like I am a voice for some people who can't have a voice . . . that's one thing for sure that people are scared might not want to speak out so I feel like as a teacher it's kind of your responsibility to give voice to people that don't have voices.
R: And to your children.
Ms. B: Yeah . . . because what's happening is wrong on so many levels . . . it's like you can't even pick it apart. . . . It's too big.

To Ms. Broadbent, her job is to be there and advocate for her young first graders, especially in the current political climate where there is a common thread of bias and discrimination from the government.[1] She is worried about her BIPOC families and wants to protect them from the world and from the institution she works in. In her second interview, she digs a bit deeper into this concept:

Ms. B: I get notes a lot from kids and I get lots of hugs lots of kids come to visit . . . and I have to say when I look at who comes back it's really a lot of kids of color . . . which is interesting.
R: So, that means you have impacted them?
Ms. B: I also feel like I am an advocate for these kids . . . When their families can't . . . and it feels like . . . . there is. . . . Disproportionate when I think about kids that are in need in this school and the kids that have parents that have more trouble in that realm . . . for whatever reason . . . whether they had bad experiences as kids themselves or they have jobs that keep them away from the school because they are working a lot . . . but I feel this . . . I feel compelled to advocate for those students and those are usually the ones who come back . . . I get angry sometimes because I feel like the administration knows that they will . . . . they will let it happen . . . that they know that certain parents won't make a stink so they take advantage of that . . . I see it and I feel it and it stinks so that's why.

R: Are you talking about inequities?

Ms. B: Yes . . . kids that need evaluations that the school can't provide . . . there's an example.

R: Special education testing?

Ms. B: Yeah . . . we advocated and got a kid to . . . (city) last year who really needed some serious work up and got the testing back . . . she moved onto another grade but I read the results and then nothing happened because the parent didn't follow through.

R: If it was a middle-class white person it would have been done.

Ms. B: Well, most of the emails I get from parents who want to talk or want to meet with the principal are really the white parents and its' the parents of color that don't reach out to me as much.

Ms. Broadbent is touching upon the power dynamics of her school and of schools in general, where white parents hold more power in terms of their children within the school system. To her, she has no choice but to advocate for BIPOC families who are marginalized within the structures of the school system. "Racism, prejudice and discrimination are shamefully sabotaging our nation's efforts to provide a high-quality education for all children" (Pine & Hilliard, 1990, p. 1).

Another example of inequities and inequalities that circulate within school systems are microaggressions. Oluo defines microaggressions as "small daily insults and indignities perpetuated against marginalized or oppressed people because of their affiliation with that marginalized or oppressed group" (Oluo, 2019, p. 169). They can be and are often cumulative in nature and can cause psychological damage to the victim (Oluo, 2019). If you can imagine this as being very harmful to an adult, imagine a young child who receives this daily from his/her peers and from the teacher or adults around them.

A good example of this came up in my second interview with Ms. Verano at Smithfield Elementary:

Ms. V: So, for example . . . this was last year . . . that I am thinking of one time that there were a couple of girls in the class and like what you said . . . they don't necessarily know that it is hurtful . . . because usually at this age they're not really thinking along those lines . . . so I had a little girl who would always . . . you know she came in with her hair in braids . . . but she would fidget with them . . . she would end up taking them out and when she took them out her hair was . . . you know . . . black hair and that would get kinda of puffy . . . sticking out all over the place and so . . . somebody said to her . . . one of the other girls said, "your hair is sticking out all over the place" and they.

R: Was this a white girl?

Ms. V: Yes . . . so they just matter of factly said . . . she was taking out her braids and so it was kinda of unruly and I said "yeah, isn't that wonderful" and I kinda of rubbed her hair and you know I said, "I wish I had more curls in my hair . . . I don't like that it is flat."

R: But you know that culturally black people . . . hair is very important.

Ms. V: Yes.

R: And you don't want to tell people they have messy hair.

V: Right.

R: She could be offended by it.

V: Correct . . . and I knew that it was going down that path so I.

R: you stepped in.

V: But then I also addressed to the child and I said "Do you like your hair like that? Or would you like me to help you put your braid back in?" and she said "No, I like it" because I had just said "Isn't it beautiful" and then I said to the white student "Everybody's hair is different and we all have different hair and that is what makes it so wonderful."

Here, Ms. Verano is making a conscious effort to address a microaggression by reaffirming the actual beauty of the child's hair by complementing her different hair texture. She feels that by turning the insult around and truly appreciating the diversity of hair texture and style she is modeling how to treat others fairly. Later, I mentioned that this was in fact a microaggression, which she had not considered at the time.

White teachers need to be aware of microaggressions as acts that occur in classrooms on a daily basis. In the above instance, Ms. Verano believed that by turning it around and making it a positive comment then there was no wrongdoing, but it is still a microaggression for that child, one that she will endure many more times in her lifetime as people negatively talk about and ask to touch her hair.

Microaggressions are common in our society as they are ways that people intentionally or unintentionally confirm and maintain the power dynamics of our society. BIPOC experience them on an ongoing basis and they are commonplace in schools and educational programs nationwide. They are used as a way to keep the power structure of our society which is based on white supremacy and 400 years of a slavery system, reconstruction, Jim Crow laws, in place. Later, Ms. Verano shared another example from her kindergarten classroom:

Ms. V: I have an example form last year that I really experienced . . . I had two students that were from Africa that came to this country and started in my classroom last year . . . both boys had pretty dark skin . . . I had a student in my classroom that had some learning disabilities . . . was a white student and he would call them by the other's name so, he would mix up their names . . . I felt like it was important that everyone else in the class knew that it was not okay . . . so we talked about it a lot in the classroom . . . part of responsive classroom is when you greet each other you use each other's names and that is a big part of our community building . . . so we model and we practice if you can't remember somebody's name ask them what is your name again? And that's okay and the kids get used to it . . . but this one particular student had this glitch and just kept doing it . . . and we had done a lot of Anti-Racist work all year long and it was probably the spring time that he said it again . . . and two other students turned to him and said it is not okay that you are mixing up their names because they both have brown skin . . . and I think one of the boys got annoyed at one point and the other boy would kinda of laugh about it . . . but it was uncomfortable and it was the kinda of thing that other kids addressed.

In this example, Ms. Verano was impressed that the other children took issue with this one white boy mixing up the names of the two BIPOC boys from Africa. She felt that the other children really understood that it was not okay to do this on the basis of their skin tone. It is important to note that in another classroom, this kind of microaggression can go unnoticed and is not addressed in the same way. In actuality, at times, many white teachers do this too, mixing up names or mispronouncing the names of BIPOC students. Utilizing Anti-Racist pedagogy all year long helps to expose these issues early on and teaches children how to handle these acts of microaggressions within the early childhood classroom.

Teaching about racial inequity is critical in the early childhood higher education classroom. Without understanding how inequities and inequalities manifest themselves within schools and districts, new teachers will ignore the issue. It is important to note that although issues of social justice are sometimes incorporated into the higher education classroom, issues of racial inequity and the unpacking of these issues within the school system are less likely to be a part of everyday college lectures. In early childhood, it is clear that this varies from institution to institution; however, it needs to be more infused within the structures of teacher education programs. There needs to be a common thread of commitment to teaching issues of equity in order to properly prepare pre-service teachers to enter the real world of de facto segregated schooling in the United States.

How do we teach issues of racial equity and equality in our classrooms? First, it is important to note that professors must understand that language matters and that utilizing the word "diverse" when speaking about de facto segregated schools is more harmful than helpful. Teachers in training need to understand the difference between diversity and de facto segregation within school systems, otherwise, like Ms. Alice witnessed, they think segregated schools are diverse spaces. This is a false narrative and one that can affect how a teacher feels or works on issues of diversity in their classrooms.

There are many ways to infuse the concept of racial equity into our higher education classroom, including through dramatic role play, writing exercises on reflection, discussing segregation and redlining, watching videos on equality or lack of in schools, utilizing specific texts, and making it a part of every assignment. We need to highlight it as an important topic so that we can inspire young teachers to critically examine and engage in it in their classrooms.

The following observation is an example of how this is used in a second-grade classroom at Packard Elementary:

(Ms. Alice is reading a book on racism and intolerance).
Ms. A: Sometimes you have to talk about difficult things (Repeats term Prejudice and gives definition from book).
Ms. A: There is gonna be some people you like . . . you can't dislike people if you don't know them.

(Reads another section of book on refugees experience inequality).

Ms. A: Why is that not fair?
WB1: Because if you talk to them, you might like them.
WG1: It is kinda of like when my mom says you are throwing away foods I haven't tasted and it is a waste of money.
Ms. A: When you do that to people you are causing more harm . . . humans are deeply hurt by it. You are not born prejudiced . . . you come into this world as beautiful human beings . . . naturally loving . . . people are prejudiced because they are taught that . . . we are going to turn and talk . . . if you are at a school and see someone who is left out because they look different . . . what would you do? We all have the power to do things.

(Students turn and talk with their partners.)
(Ms. A claps)

WB1: Ask him to play with me.

(Ms. A teaches them the word Intolerant—and then talks about refugees coming into their community).

Ms. A: A lot of people don't want to talk about things that make you upset . . . (projects a new slide titled 'What can we do') What can we do? We can realize

we are all different and that is a great thing . . . we can accept and be tolerant of other people . . . we can stand up for people who are treated unfairly . . . We can talk about racism and intolerance . . . and we can be willing to listen.
Ms. A: Think of what you learned today about racism and intolerance that is new for you.

(Students turn and talk again).
(Students share out in a circle).
BIPOC boy: Be kind and helpful.

WB: People treat other people badly because of their skin color.
WB2: People are different and that's good.
WB3: Stand up for people.
BIPOC girl1: Treat people fairly.
WB4: People leave their homes to go to safe places.
WG2: I learned what racism is and how to stop it.
WG3: Racism is pronounced differently than I thought.

Ms. Alice was reading the book *Racism and Intolerance*. She uses this book in order to get children to think about issues of racial equity. Young children are being introduced to heavy concepts that are powerful and important in our society. They are not too young to understand the central issue, unfairness, and racial inequality. They are interested in knowing how to address this unfairness and Ms. Alice is providing resources for them to use. At one point in this lesson, she tells the students to go home that night and discuss this book with their parents. She is advocating for a true dialogue, for her children to continue to talk and listen about these issues.

This type of lesson needs to be taught in the higher education classroom. Ms. Alice takes it upon herself to choose this particular book and to have these particular conversations. She also has slides projected on the screen defining hard words, such as prejudice, racism, and intolerance and then in her last slide provides them with action, including being open to listening and discussing these topics. College students, for the most part, do not know how to design this type of lesson. They are uncomfortable in general with discussing challenging topics, especially racism and intolerance and need guidance on how to approach it with young children. I find that after I provide them with tools through a PowerPoint presentation they are more able to brainstorm ideas of how to tackle issues of racial inequality/inequities in the classroom. Practice and more practice helps too. That is why it is important to give them multiple opportunities to brainstorm ideas of how they will utilize all of this information in the classroom. If it is only covered, once then they will not be comfortable taking the risk when they have their own classroom.

Thus, multiple exposures are critical. Professors must provide many different types of opportunities, including modeling of lessons, in order for students to really feel like they will and can incorporate Anti-Racist teachings in their class effectively.

It is important to note here that Ms. Alice's lesson on racism and intolerance was implemented in October, in order to set up her calendar year. She wanted to build their knowledge of these important topics so that she could offer them units on the Civil Rights movement, Women's Rights movement, and more, later on in the year. This lesson is laying a foundation, a background of important terms that will be crucial to their later understandings. In our higher education classrooms, we should be practicing the same thing. We need to present and discuss issues of equity early on, scaffolding each lecture or discussion so that by the end of the semester the students leave with a deeper understanding of these topics and will be more likely to use them in their own classroom design.

Issues of racial equity and equality are of high importance to the higher education classroom. Reviewing deficit-based thinking, such as nonschool ready labels, interrupting microaggressions, comparing and contrasting "diverse" schools with segregated schools, and fully discussing issues of equality within school districts is essential for pre-service teachers in their continued growth of how to effectively utilize Anti-Racist pedagogy in early childhood classrooms.

NOTE

1. This project started during the Trump presidency which included a lot of legislation supporting hate bills.

Chapter 5

The ARTS

(Ms. Houston is on the rug talking to her kindergartners).
Ms. H: We are all different and we are all similar in some ways.
    (Reads The Skin You Live In.)
Ms. H: Can you point to your skin?
WG1: We all have different colors.
Ms. H: We have different shades.
    (Shows picture of different circles of colors.)
Ms. H: What do you think these are?
WG2: That's all people color.
WB1: Those are all skin colors.
Ms. H: Look down at your skin. People may say you are white or black (shows a big white paper to the class) Are any of you white like this?
Class: No.
    (Ms. H shows them a black paper.)
Ms. H: Are people's skin this color?
Class: No.
    (She shows them a box full of crayons.)
Ms. H: I want you to make the color of your skin. Why do we have different shades to choose from? Because we are all different . . . what happens when you mix colors?
    (Ms. Houston draws on experience chart paper. She models mixing colors).
Ms. H: You need to experiment . . . try different colors to try and match your skin.
    (She mixes colors on board.)
Ms. H: How can I make it more like my skin?
WG3: You could use a lighter brown.
Ms. H: Maybe I should use my white crayon to lighten it up . . . think like scientists and artists when mixing colors I think I need it a little dark *(adds more dark*

colors. Puts her arm near the board to compare shade of skin) See if you can replicate it . . . repeat it . . . do it again when done.

(Children go to their tables and mix different crayon colors to find their own shade. Many students ask me if it matches.)

(Ms. Houston calls them to the rug after a while to share their findings.)
Ms. H: *Use your eyes to scan around . . . take a peek at some of the shades you see. (Children look around at other papers.)*
Ms. H: *What did you notice when you were doing this activity?*
WB2: *I tried it again and it didn't work.*
WB3: *I did too much red so I couldn't get close enough.*
WG4: *I noticed that . . . (boy in room)'s color looked like my skin.*
Ms. H: *In the future when making pictures of people I hope you start thinking about skin color and the shade when you draw.*

(She ends the lesson by having them sing We are all the colors of the earth.)

Children learn visually, which is why the study of art is so important in the early childhood classroom. It is also a creative way to teach important topics. "The visual arts can be an important and rich domain of learning for young children" (Eckhoff, 2007, p. 463). In this chapter, I will go beyond the usual tactics of utilizing art to teach Anti-Racist pedagogy. I will examine the overdone handprints and mural ideas and look into the issue of colorism and skin tone in artwork. It is important to look at art in terms of communication and how it effectively expresses ideas on race and racism. I will also examine the expressive arts, such as music, dance, and theater. Later on, we will look at the use of open-ended art projects and how to successfully utilize art in the higher education classroom in order to shed light on topics related to Anti-Racist pedagogy.

When walking around a school, any given school, you are likely to notice murals of handprints, sometimes in various shades of color. This is a fairly typical display that shows the school is involved in teaching multicultural education. Actually, it is the main way teachers share their classroom diversity in the hallway. These artistic bulletin boards show the passerby that these young children are aware that they are different from one another and respect all races and skin tones. It is an oversimplification of a very important topic and yet it is used all the time. In this section, I want to go beyond this superficial approach to skin tone and instead think of more complex ways to share art and the expressive arts in relation to Anti-Racist pedagogy. Greene states that we can "begin to seek out ways in which the arts, in particular, can release imagination to open new perspectives, to identify alternatives" (Greene, 1995, p. 142). She is talking about utilizing art as a way to explore different perspectives and different ways of being in the world. She believes art is a freeing process without limitations, only the limitations of a child's imagination (Greene, 1995). In this case, handprints of every child in this class posted to a bulletin board are not very imaginative or creative. It is a simple out, a tourist approach to very complex issues of teaching about race and skin tone.

In Ms. Broadbent's first-grade class, they have been discussing skin tone and different shades of people since the beginning of the year. Today she is doing a follow-up lesson utilizing watercolors.

Ms. B: Yesterday we went into the hallway and looked at the hall mural of our neighbor. Today we are doing people colors we found that there was only five shades of paper the other day—Not enough choices for us

(She places her hand against the five shades of paper taped to her experience chart paper.)

Ms. B: (moves her hand from paper to paper) It doesn't really match my color . . . we will challenge ourselves and finish our portraits . . . remember we are painting skin . . . which includes what?

WB1: Forehead.

Ms. B: Not lips, hair or mouth.

(She refers to a book she read weeks ago *Two eyes, a nose and a mouth.*)

Ms. B: This is the part that is different (holds up a book she read the day before called *Shades of People*). We are using watercolors.

(She uses the overhead projector and a mixing cup.)

Ms. B: I have a mixing cup. Test your brush first . . . How do I use watercolors? (discussion on how to use them with class) I am trying to make my mixing cup match my own skin color (mixes paints on overhead screen) Is that my color? (yellowish) I am going to dab more colors. I am going to take orange and test it out . . . too dark?

WB2: Too light.

Ms. B: I will put a little brown in . . . now guess what? It is too dark. . . . Here I go . . . got to mix.

WG1: I think yellow.

WB3: Red.

Ms. B: Okay, red . . . I will test it out.

WB4: It's perfect (it is not even close).

WG2: Too yellow.

Ms. B: I am not giving up here . . . what can I do if the color I am mixing is really off?

WB5: Do blue.

WB6: Do green.

WB7: Just put water in it.

WG3: That might work.

Ms. B: I am going to rinse my cup and start again . . . mix, mix until you get as close to your skin shade as you can find . . . once you have

it you can start painting your portrait . . . it's a challenge but first graders have done this before.

In this observation, I noticed that Ms. Broadbent wanted the children to really start from scratch. The process of finding the right color was more important than finding the right color. Children were concerned about finding the color to match their skin tone, but they liked exploring and trying colors to lighten or darken their skin tone. Some were frustrated by the process and lacked patience but they did it anyway. They mixed and mixed and started again and many had trouble replicating the same skin tone on the second go around, but they were committed to the process. Thus, this activity, which was done in some form or another in all of the classrooms I observed, is done throughout the year and is not a one-time event. Young children need to have time, through many lessons, to learn and explore different skin tones. This is key to their understandings of race and their own racial identities. Rather profoundly states that "art is about engaging in candid dialogue with yourself" (Rather, 2017, p. 159). Therefore, it is the process of expressing oneself through the arts that is important in understanding ourselves.

An issue that should be addressed in schools is colorism. In our society, there is a notion of white beauty (Jewell, 2020). The lighter the skin tone you are the more beautiful, or so we are told by the media around us. A major part of Anti-Racist work is to combat this ideology and eliminate it from our mindset. We, as educators, need to challenge this beauty standard, and colorism in general and set up new expectations and standards that highlight the

Figure 5.1 Watercolor Self-Portrait (Ms. Broadbent's First Grade).

Figure 5.2 Bulletin Board Watercolor Self-Portraits (Ms. Broadbent's First Grade).

beauty of darker hues (Kendi, 2019). The darker the skin, the harder it is on the child. Colorism is about racist policies and white supremacy as children are made aware that to be lighter skinned is to be seen as a better person (Kendi, 2019).

Changing this narrative can only be accomplished if the new teacher is open to looking at colorism and in her daily practice tries to eliminate negative discussions related to color.

In interview two, Ms. Fern speaks about her practice on this topic:

Ms. F: We focus on building their identity and self-esteem about who they are . . . who everybody is . . . I think the big idea for five- year olds is that there are ways that we are alike and there are ways that we are different . . . and we can value and appreciate those things. . . . They draw their family similar to how we were using paints to make our skin shades to draw ourselves and then we extend that to our family and thinking about what people in your family look like . . . we get to talk about whether it is the same or different . . . and I looked at whether they were positive about their own racial identity or positive about other's racial identity . . . and so I think some of these kids had some negative comments about their own racial identity . . . those are the kids that stick with me in my mind and I would like to see how the conversation evolves.

Ms. Fern is aware of colorism and how it may affect BIPOC students in her classroom. She is committed to helping them form positive racial identities and knows that she must challenge this practice through her own activities/lessons. Art plays a major role in shaping and transforming these fixed ideas in young children. An example of this occurs after a lesson on mixing paints to match their skin tones where she has each individual child brainstorm a positive title for their found skin tone. Some of these titles included brownish white like a pancake, pinkish red like a peach, brownish tan like cookies, brownish yellow like butter, yellowish white like light olives, brownish tan like peanut butter, and more.

Sometimes teachers have to combat many years of a child feeling bad about their skin tone and they have to work to erase these negative images. The following example highlights a biracial child and her feelings about her own skin tone:

Figure 5.3 Light Browny Bark Skin Tone (Ms. Fern's Kindergarten)..

Ms. F: One of the kids in the class who is mixed race . . . she is brown skinned . . . she said something really positive . . . you know she called herself like chocolate ice cream . . . and talked about her mom who was more vanilla ice cream and her grandparents were coconut ice cream . . . she was adopted and her parents were white . . . and it seemed benign and then she said "But sometimes there is these tiny green spiders that crawl all over me because of my skin shade and they are really itchy" and I don't know exactly what she meant by that . . . when I asked her if she could tell me more . . . she just acted like she was getting all itchy . . . like green spiders were crawling on her . . . so I don't know if that was a funny five year old thing to say or if it was connected to uncomfortability . . . in your skin.

Here, Ms. Fern notices how uncomfortable this young biracial girl is when discussing the color of her skin. She starts off with positive words, related to ice cream colors but then goes on to talk about spiders crawling on her skin and being very itchy. This shows that she has mixed emotions about her skin tone and is unsure of how she fits in the world. It is important to note here that our skin tone has a lot to do with how we see ourselves within the larger society. This young girl is searching for her identity in the world and is unsure of how her skin tone plays a part in the process.

Kendi believes that "Anti-dark colorism follows the logic of behavioral racism, linking behavior to color, studies show" (Kendi, 2019, p.110). In order to maintain the structures of white supremacy, colorism must be perpetuated on a daily basis in all avenues of society. In one of my classes, I show videos on the classic doll experiment, where young black children are asked which doll is the prettiest and which doll is the smartest, and they continually pick the white doll. Students are astounded by this every time I show it, because they can't believe that young black children can actually feel bad about the color of their own skin. The original doll experiment, which took place in the 1940s and 1950s by two black psychologists Kenneth and Mamie Clarke, was conducted to show the negative psychological effects of segregation on black children. This research was introduced to the Supreme Court case of *Brown vs. the Board of Education* as evidence of the need for desegregation of public schools. Logically, it just makes sense that a country that practices white supremacy will psychologically damage children of color throughout their lifetime.

In Ms. Broadbent's first-grade classroom at the Coltrane School, she is always aware of the impact on BIPOC students when discussing skin tone or doing art projects on this topic. In the following excerpt from one of her interviews, Ms. Broadbent discusses how she handles negative comments in her room.

R: Did you ever have people say derogatory things?
Ms. B: Yeah . . . yeah.

R: And how did you handle that?

Ms. B: We usually have a sit down conversation and I try to guide the conversation but let the kids really do the talking but interject when I need to . . . do a lot of validating . . . understanding and . . . I try to listen more than anything but also make sure that everybody comes out of the conversation feeling pretty good . . . um . . . I never had to talk to any parents.

Ms. Broadbent makes an effort not to dismiss anything said in her classroom that can be seen as deficit based. Part of appreciating one's own skin tone is feeling accepted by our peers. This is especially crucial in younger grades as children are discovering who they are in the world and are unsure of their personal identity. Thus, a teacher has to be on top of all negative remarks in the classroom and address them as soon as possible. In this classroom, Ms. Broadbent makes sure that children's voices are heard and validated on an ongoing basis and is ready to interrupt any negative remarks related to skin tone and racial identity.

Art is also an important form of communication. Children express themselves through the visual arts, dance, music, and drama in a variety of ways. They need artistic outlets to help them create meaning. It should be incorporated in all parts of the early childhood curriculum and used as an outlet for creative space and thoughtfulness. Art gives "the ability to see things in new ways" (Fox & Schirrmacher, 2015, p. 5). It should be woven and infused throughout the day and not just at weekly art specials. It is a viable way for children to express their thoughts, ideas on reflections of identity and meaning within the world. The Arts serve a purpose in their young lives and most of the time, since they are just learning to write, it is the key way that they can express themselves. Gunn states that this is a way to "manipulate tools to convey meaning" (Gunn, 2000, p. 155).

In Ms. Verano's kindergarten, she uses art activities all day long. Art is a way that she can assess her students' understandings of content. They are expressing their knowledge through their drawings, paintings, music, dance, and theater. On Ms. Verano's walls, there are self-portraits of the children that are replaced monthly, as she has them do new ones each month. She does this on purpose so she can see their growth in their own self-identity. She can look at drawings/paintings from the beginning of the year and see how an individual child has grown in their own knowledge of self. Kindergarten and first grade are times when children learn about themselves and who they are in the world and they need creative outlets to try and express who they are. This is the first time I have heard of a teacher utilizing self-portraits in this manner. Ms. Verano says that it helps to build self-esteem and makes them more comfortable in their own skin. If you look at the development of these self-portraits, you can see that there is a true growth in how the child views themselves racially as well. As they learn more about skin tone and different tools that help them convey differences in skin tone, their self-portraits become more detailed and more realistic.

In my conversations with Ms. Houston, another kindergarten teacher, she talks about how she encourages children to explore different colors and forms of media to represent their own skin tone and how it helps children to better understand about race and skin tone.

Ms. H: So, if we are doing coloring . . . we are representing since we talked about color . . . I make it a point to talk about skin tone and trying to have that be accurate . . . cause there is a time when kids get to color whatever and do whatever . . . Blue people are fine and what not . . . afterwards I just keep on bringing it back . . . keep the skin tone crayons and pencils out separate from the regular ones and any time we are doing any activity that involves coloring . . . involves people . . . drawing or whatever I try to bring that in and try to remind them . . . You can be accurate . . . we have all the colors . . . all of the skin tones . . . you can draw with people and use that.

Ms. Houston, much like Ms. Verano, is expecting growth in their self-portraits and drawings of people, because she is constantly talking about skin tone and the need to be accurate. There is a time, in the beginning of the year, before discussions on skin tone and race that she sees children using unrealistic skin tones (like blue) but later on, she expects them to be mindful and utilize their new knowledge to more accurately represent people in drawings. Part of this is having the available materials handy, as I noticed all of the participants had multicultural crayons, markers, and paints available in the room for children to use.

In Ms. Maltes' kindergarten, she has noticed the difference in drawings by children who are unfamiliar with exploring skin tone colors and children who actively try to use it in their artwork. And this can be a result of how and if teachers actively engage in discussions and activities related to skin tone. We reflected on her first observation where she noticed the limitations in her own art materials:

Ms. M: I think in this case I had been using a pack of skin color paper . . . I don't know if we just worked our way through the other things but maybe using more variety or starting with paints . . . that can truly be mixed together to really represent a child's skin color vs. them trying to match it . . . . often when they draw themselves . . . part of it is their fine motor skills are still developing . . . I often find that it's not all that common for kids to represent their skin color in their drawings . . . and I don't know if it is because they are relying more on a stick figure kind of sketch or that their drawings aren't all that detailed to begin with but . . . .

R: Have you ever had a student of color draw themselves with no color?

Ms. M: Yeah, or to be sort of resistant to like putting something . . . often I think they sort of want to match their peers or they want to have things in common . . . and I do have one child and it is sort of noticeable that . . . she will go out of her way to find colored pencils that match her skin color . . . and that to me just seems like really healthy.

In her reflection of her lesson, which only provided five shades of skin tone on paper for kids to choose from, she realizes that she should have provided more flexible materials, and that because she did not, some children found it harder to express themselves and their racial identity. She also brings up an important point, that without access to a variety of art materials, children are limited in their creative expression. I have had many BIPOC students in my first-grade classrooms over the years and there were always a few that avoided color and/or drew themselves as white identified. This shows that I did not provide the correct materials or the proper lessons over a period of time on skin tone and thus, they were not comfortable expressing themselves through their art.

Music is another form of The Arts that should be incorporated throughout the day in pre-k to second grade. Children should be singing, listening to different genres of music, writing their own songs, and generally appreciating the creative expression music has to offer. "Music adds beauty to our lives and can be a source of joy and comfort to children" (Jacobs & Crowley, 2010, p. 96).

It is not hard to utilize music in a way that centers Anti-Racist pedagogy. Most teachers do not consider this idea and instead only utilize mainstream songs, such as *The Wheels on the Bus*, instead of incorporating songs by and about BIPOC people. Music is a formative tool that can really help children critically reflect on how to honor our differences both culturally and racially. In Ms. Houston's kindergarten, she uses a song at the end of her lessons, usually related to the content studied. During an observation on skin tone and their exploration of mixing colors, I noticed she had prepared a song on chart paper to sing with the children at the end of the lesson:

We are Made from the colors of the earth
Each color is different
Each color is true
We are made from the colors of earth
And I love the colors that made you!
When I look in the eyes of my friends
I can see topaz. I can see sky
The green and the gray of the sea rolling by

And a dazzling brown river in the morning
When I look at the hands of my friends
I can see chestnut. I can see corn
The color of wheat fields and a dappled brown fawn
And the rain-kissed black trees in the morning.

Ms. Houston used her pointer and sang a line first and then asked the children to sing the line again, making it a shared reading experience. This song helped them to solidify the lesson on how our skin is different shades and also the children really enjoyed ending the lesson by singing a song.

Teaching about race and racism through music helps children gain real insight into inequities and inequalities between populations. An example of this is the book on the history of the song *We Shall Overcome*. Reading this book to young children gives them an understanding of the historical importance of songs and how they are used as protests and voices of the oppressed.

In my first-grade classroom, music was very important in our scaffolding of knowledge in this area of content. We wrote songs about the Civil Rights movement, slavery, Jim Crow laws, and other historical events related to race and racism. We actually wrote an album each year, recorded them with instruments, and had a CD to distribute to the families. The children loved the creative process as well as the finished product. One of the songs we wrote together was called *The Firsts*:

She was a queen on the rap scene
Latifa lives in New Jersey and
Is not mean
They were all the first
But not the worst
They were first
Obama, the president, shoots the hoop
He scores a second term
He is strong and firm
They were all the first
But not the worst
They were first
Rosa Parks boycotted the bus
To save us
Ella Fitzgerald sings Jazz
With a little pizazz
They were all the first
But not the worst
They were first.

They proudly created this song, because it was meaningful to them. They worked on the chorus first and then added different stanzas of some of the important African Americans we studied. Different songs can be provided (see appendix A) as well, so that children can see and hear the important voices of our times.

Part of exploring music and catering to children's musical intelligence is to introduce a variety of musical genres to them. They need to hear jazz, rap, rhythm and blues, Reggae, Hip Hop, Latin music, and so on. They need to be able to understand and identify these genres while appreciating them. I used to introduce a different genre of music bi-monthly in my first-grade class so that they had a true liberal arts exposure to different musical styles. This is a multicultural activity that is also culturally responsive. Children want to be represented in all ways, including in music and they also want to learn about music from different cultures and countries. This opens up their world of musical expression and helps them to appreciate all types of music, especially ones they have not been exposed to.

Dance and Movement are another essential form of creative expression for any early childhood classroom because fundamentally children at this age need to move. We can't expect very young children to stay seated on the rug or at tables/desks all day. Part of the way that they process information is through movement. In the theory of Multiple Intelligences, Gardner makes it clear that teachers must cater to children who show strengths in bodily kinesthetic behaviors (Lazear, 2000). This means teachers need to modify lessons and accommodate the learning needs of children in this domain. A major part of this is creating active lessons, one that involves physical movement inside the classroom. An example of this is when I was teaching first grade, I brought different sports into the classroom and had the children actively engage in these sports so that they could understand how they operated. We played golf, tennis, volleyball, football, and other sports by pretending to recreate all of the moves of these sports. They loved being able to get up and move around in the classroom and at the same time, they were learning about the sport themselves.

Dance is a great way for young children to express themselves artistically. In my first grade, we read about Alvin Ailey (a premier African American dancer) and practiced many of his dance steps in our room. This helped them to connect books on great African American artists and develop a true appreciation for the forms/choreography of these artists. "All artistic experiences are dynamic: each experience leads to more experiences, discovery generates further exploration" (Eckhoff, 2007, p. 464). Dance is about exploration of various moves and is powerful in the feelings it evokes. Children, especially young ones, are not as self-conscious about dancing in front of other people. They love to perform. They also love to evoke a powerful reaction in others. Of course, there are children that are shy and quiet, that do not excel in bodily kinesthetic activities, and it is important that we do not put them on the spot. However, I did find, throughout my teaching career with young children, that if you provide a safe environment where children are validated and heard they are more apt to go outside of their comfort zones and try new things, like dance and movement activities.

It is also important to note that dance and movement activities, while essential to learning new content, are also key in the development of gross motor skills (Gunn, 2000). Children need to practice being active, so that they can continue to grow in this area. Teachers must give them opportunities to move and explore how their bodies can move in order to aid them in their own overall development.

Dramatic play is also essential to the early childhood classroom. Many classrooms have dramatic centers/areas (which usually do not exist after first grade) where children rotate or choose to play in. They love to dress up utilizing costumes and other materials, pretending to be someone else. This is a creative outlet, a way for them to express themselves and it is also a way for them to work through what they are learning about related to race and racism. They will reenact important historical events and other books that teachers share in the classroom. It is a way for them to explore their feelings about the content they are absorbing, a way to work it through to make it more meaningful in their own personal world. It goes without saying that there should be a space and time in the daily schedule for young children to produce their own dramatic play. They must be given the agency to explore materials and subjects through their own creative pretend sessions. The dramatic arts can be transformative for children and it is a way for them to "visit other worlds" by expressing themselves (Rather, 2017).

In Ms. Houston's kindergarten, she sees a direct connection to her dramatic play area and her infusion of Anti-Racist pedagogy through read alouds.

H: I think they are more aware of things (28:20) . . . I think they are . . . when we were . . . in dramatic play I had one of the kids say . . . he was real excited to get into dramatic play . . . he picked up the doll with brown skin and said . . . I want the . . . baby (name of BIPOC child in class) the one student of color (laughs) . . . I just think they are noticing and I think that's . . . but I think it's important to just to get them to notice first and then it would be great if we had this continue because then they could build upon it . . . once you notice then you can start to acknowledge things.

Here, Ms. Houston makes the point that the dramatic play area can be a place where young children process content related to race and racism. She feels that they need time and space to really delve into the topic and incorporate it into their artistic world. This serves many functions, but mainly helps young children to be more aware of racial identity in general. This young white boy is processing what it means to possibly be the only BIPOC child in a classroom and he wants to explore this through playing with dolls.

The way to make the most of your dramatic play centers is to utilize prop boxes. These boxes should have different materials, costumes, props to help children explore a variety of storylines. You can have a post office box, with a mail carrier bag for playing postal worker, a restaurant box that includes menus and other dining props, and/or a veterinarian box with various medical supplies for animals. It is important to encourage children to think creatively and engage in problem-solving through play. They can use different props in different areas without question. For example, a child may want to use a menu in the block area and this is more than acceptable. It is important that we teach our pre-service teachers that children need agency when they play dramatically and we should not restrict their play in any way. This gives them the ability to explore issues of race freely through dramatic play, as we have set up a creative space with lots of personal agency. The more freedom they have to explore different play materials, the more creative their play will become and this helps them to process important topics covered in class.

What does this all look like in the higher education classroom? How can we effectively teach about art and the expression of art within Anti-Racist pedagogy? I think it is important to start with accessing the proper materials, that is, skin tone crayons, markers, paints, and more. It is also necessary to continually, as Ms. Houston does, bring it back to discussions of skin tone and different hues and colors that are a part of our racial identities. As will be noted in the Critical Reflection chapter, it is essential that we foster a safe classroom environment that encourages transformations and reflections on student's racial identities. The only way to do this is to keep broaching the subject and having students explore various visual mediums to discover and learn more about their own racial identity. This will also help build community in the classroom and individual self-esteem, especially for BIPOC students, as their self-portraits are hung on the wall for the world to praise.

It is also important to teach college-age students about their role as art educators in the classroom. How can they help and support their children in the exploration of The Arts? They need to be grounded in the idea that they are there to guide them, to support them in all of their explorations. Positive feedback is essential to this point. I remember, when I was in graduate school and I took a course on art education and early childhood; one of my main takeaways from this course was that there is a certain way to give positive feedback when it comes to children's art. We were taught that teachers must be specific when giving feedback in art. It is not acceptable to say things like "that is a beautiful drawing" or "nice work." These comments are too vague and not at all encouraging. Children need specific feedback and guidance to feel like they are on the right track—although art is an individual expression and should never be viewed as being done one way. Therefore, college professors must take the time to model and practice how teachers respond to children's artwork. Comments should be tailored to the individual child like, "I like the way you are mixing colors" or "Your use of lines and circles is incredibly creative." Children will feel more confident in their artistic endeavors which will in turn lead them to feel more comfortable exploring new materials or creating imaginative and original art pieces.

Be creative with the materials you provide. For example, I used paint swatches that go from lighter shades of brown to deeper shades. I put them in the middle of the table for reference points so that they could mix their paints close to these shades. Another good idea is to use a variety of nuts, which come in many shades of brown as well. (It should be noted that if using nuts in the classroom teachers should be aware of the various allergies in the room beforehand.) You can also use dry tempera paint mix in a bowl so students can add water and find different hues of brown/pink (Kissinger, 2017).

Be sure to encourage pre-service teachers to be creative when teaching The Arts. They should not be utilizing adult ready-made art projects. These projects stifle children's creativity and do not let them think outside the box. Prescribed art projects are not going to foster open-mindedness and critical thinking in a young child. Instead, teachers should provide open-ended art projects that do not end up with all the same products (Jacob & Crowley, 2010). So, it is important that we, as the higher education teacher, model open-ended art projects instead of modeling a set way to express oneself. "By offering experiences in the arts we can help children value and respect their own work, as well as that of others" (Jacobs & Crowley, 2010, p. 91). Therefore, it is essential that we provide these pre-service teachers with open-ended art materials for their own exploration and construction of art projects. Providing a variety of materials for the pre-service teacher gives them agency and also models giving agency to young children. We must highlight the importance of seeing value in the art-making process and not in the final product. This is also culturally responsive and respectful of all the different cultures in the room and gives them a chance to express themselves artistically in a manner that suits their needs and values their culture.

The following are projects related to The Arts and Anti-Racist pedagogy that may be helpful to include in the higher education classroom:

- Mixing paint colors to find a match to the student's skin tone.
- Creating murals (or parts of murals in small groups) that portray famous BIPOC in history.

- Sharing and modeling artwork from famous BIPOC artists.
- Using dramatic role play to act out a scene from a biography of BIPOC.
- Have the students create a dance or movement activity for young children related to the exploration of racial identity.
- Using multicultural crayons/markers to draw a portrait of another peer.
- In small groups give out roles (architect, visualizer, sculptor, drawer) for the production of an open-ended art project.
- Connection to Literacy—Have them illustrate a page from a chapter book (biography or story of BIPOC).
- Create comic books that are related to social justice issues.
- Write a song that relates to the Civil Rights Movement.
- Study and replicate a fine art drawing of a great BIPOC artist (Hokusai, Frieda Kahla, Diego Rivera, Jacob Lawrence, and more).
- Prepare innovative choreography that tells a story related to Jim Crow through dance/movement.

The Arts and the creative expression of art in many forms plays a huge part in the construction of racial identity and knowledge of BIPOC within the early childhood classroom. It is important that we, as higher education professors, utilize this form of expression in our own classrooms. It is another way to have students process their understandings of Anti-Racist pedagogy. It is also a way to encourage understandings related to racial identity and therefore is key for pre-service teachers to use thoughtful and intentionally. "Our art is our story. It grows with the inclusion of different peoples and cultures, and we are stronger for it" (Rather, 2017, p. 171).

In my last interview with Ms. Broadbent, during the summer of the pandemic, she wanted to share with me the important news from Crayola:

Ms. B: The other thing I wanted to pass on to you because this is one of the things we did a lot and you observed . . . what colors Crayola is putting out for their art work . . . Crayola has a whole new line of skin tone crayons . . . thirty-two different shades.

R: Wow!

Ms. B: Yeah . . . so I bought them . . . they are newly released . . . it is kinda hard to get . . . I had to order it online and be on a waiting list and all that kind of stuff but on the box, there is a beautiful display of all the colors and I think this is another way we can enrich the curriculum . . . like we don't have to have eight crayons . . . We have thirty-two . . . how does that fit us? Is that going to work? Well, someone listened I guess, right? We have more colors now.

R: Did this come out during the racial unrest right now?

Ms. B: It was over the summer . . . they are skinny ones but I don't care because people's eyes are open now, I think . . . perhaps and mine are more open as well and maybe the resources will improve.

Needless to say, we were both so thrilled about this new possibility of more shades of skin tone crayons to utilize in the early childhood classroom. Crayola has come a long way but we all still have a long way to go.

Chapter 6

Our History Revised

(Ms. Houston is talking to her kindergartners at the rug.)
Ms. H: Before today we talked about an important person in history . . .
WG1: Ruby Bridges.
Ms. H: What is she known for?
WG1: Smiling at other people.
Ms. H: She was very kind . . . What else?
WG2: First kid with dark skin to go to school with white skins.
Ms. H: What is that word . . . for whites only? It begins with an S.
WB1: (calls out) Segregation.
Ms. H: It sounds like separation—put things away from each other . . . segregation is like separation. . . . We see those signs a lot when looking at these books.
  (She holds up a biography of Ruby Bridges.)
Ms. H: White People could go everywhere they wanted . . . it was people with dark skin that couldn't go places . . . separate parks . . . entrances . . . theaters . . . whites only. If you had a chance to go to a beautiful school . . . a nice restaurant . . . or sit away from everyone else . . . in a place falling apart that was for people with dark skin What would you choose?
WB2: (Screams) The one that is not falling apart!
Ms. H: How many people agree with . . . (boy's name)?
  (Lots of hands are raised.)
Ms. H: Does that sound fair?
Class: (Yells) NO!
  (Ms. Houston then puts on a projector that shows two images on the screen. It is a picture of two different schools—one is a huge white school that has a pretty playground and two white children laughing and the other image is a run-down school building with no playground and two brown skin children looking sad.)

Ms. H: What do you notice?
WB3: That the white people were in a school that is really good and the black one doesn't have a good school or a playground.
WB4: I see two cracks on two windows.
BIPOC girl: This one looks like a church.
WG3: I noticed that the little girl with dark skin is crying.
Ms. H: Why?
WG4: Their school doesn't look pretty . . . no playground . . . they want to go to the other school.
Ms. H: What if you had a choice?
WG5: I would go to the school that is good.
Ms. H: Even though it is illegal to say you have to go there because you have dark skin there are places like this . . . which one looks like our school?
WG5: The white one.
Ms. H: (to BIPOC girl) You came from a school in another city.
BIPOC girl: Looks like that one (points to run down school) but no cracked windows.
Ms. H: Friends in your class had white or dark skin?
BIPOC girl: A lot had dark skin.
Ms. H: There are still a lot of places that look like that . . . in places with kids with dark skin. . . . Nice noticing my friends.

Ms. Houston is teaching her Civil Rights unit to her kindergarten class at Longwood Elementary. She says that she does this unit every year but recently she has added the contemporary model of segregation so that the children understand that the system continues to this day. She is excited that she just recently got a new BIPOC student from a nearby urban center (one that she grew up in herself). There is only one other BIPOC child in this class, a boy who is biracial and has been a part of the school since pre-kindergarten. In our debriefing, Ms. Houston talks about her struggle with asking the BIPOC girl about her old school because she doesn't want to put her on the spot. However, she wanted the majority white class to know that de facto school segregation still exists even in their local region. Since this is a school with a population of over 90 percent white children, Ms. Houston feels that it is even more important to teach about race and racism in America. Unfortunately, most teachers actually do the opposite and think that since they are teaching to a majority white population it is less important to teach about other races and or histories of other races.

Every year when I get a new crop of pre-service teachers in my Early Childhood Curriculum class, I am immediately challenged by their lack of knowledge about the history of the United States. Their history teachers in K-12 schools have all failed them. Since most of my students come from majority white schools in majority white neighborhoods, they lack exposure to historical perspectives of marginalized populations. Sadly, they also have limited knowledge on traditional history (white male normative perspective) and no nothing at all about the missing history (the history of BIPOC), with the exception of Martin Luther King Jr. and Rosa Parks.

Gregory, a Civil Rights activist/author states, "We've all been told the same lie" (Gregory, 2018, p. 27). He is referring to history and how it is taught in schools from a dominant white perspective (Asim, 2018). DiAngelo refers to this as a "discourse of universalism" (DiAngelo, 2010, p. 4). This dominant discourse on history and social studies is perpetuated in early childhood classrooms, through state standards. The standards of this particular state in which the study took place will be deconstructed and critically reflected upon in this chapter. "They (students) are subliminally socialized, enculturated and oriented to believe that the western experience and world view are superior and dominant" (Pine & Hilliard, 1990, p. 4). The "western experience" is the white experience. Other perspectives or counternarratives of our history are not incorporated into our class curriculums. Scholars and historians believe that history, and the teaching of history, is objective, but that is clearly untrue (Gregory, 2018; Pine & Hilliard, 1990). History, as it is currently taught, through social studies curriculum standards actually reinforces racism and white supremacy. It is narrow and non-inclusive of important historical events from outside the white person's lens. In order to be more inclusive and truly practice Anti-Racism in this field, we must critically examine what we are doing as we teach social studies to young children.

In this chapter, I will unpack and examine the following topics related to how pre-service teachers need to actively teach about history in a more inclusive way: culturally responsive history, educating white children, great heroes and changers that are BIPOC, dealing with the social studies standards k-2, all topics that must be studied (slavery, Civil Rights movement, etc.) and the issue of historical solidarity. At the end of the chapter, I will provide connections to how this affects teaching pre-service teachers in a university setting.

Being culturally responsive to different student populations is extremely important in terms of this particular pedagogy (Au, 2014; Aveling, 2007; Ladson-Billings, 2000). Critical educators state, "Culturally responsive approaches make the histories and views of marginalized people of color an essential dimension of curriculum" (Epstein et al, 2011, p. 4). The main reason for this is to validate and honor the student's race, culture, and ethnicity. If a teacher does not culturally respond to their various classroom cultures, then they are practicing color-blind discourse that essentially invalidates their presence/existence (Lee, 1997). Gregory profoundly states, "Know who you are. Value who you are. Knowing yourself comes from knowing what's true and accurate" (Gregory, 2018, p. 16). Young children need to be affirmed and validated. They need to see that they are worthy in the larger society, and this is directly related to how early childhood educators utilize culturally responsive history. Gregory believes that teachers need to engage the child with the reality of their own cultural history (Gregory, 2018).

As noted at the beginning of this chapter, there is a paramount need to teach Anti-Racist pedagogy in majority white settings. Many pre-service teachers believe that it is not as important to talk about race and racism in this environment because there is no need to be culturally responsive (Solomon, 2005). This is a mistake. In actuality, not covering these topics just perpetuates white supremacy and racial hierarchies that are firmly in place in the United States. If the history of BIPOC is not intentionally referred to or honored, then it is viewed as unimportant to the young children in the classroom. This is a dismissive view, one that is exclusionary and therefore it explicitly and inexplicitly perpetuates white supremacy as a "norm." White children in these environments can have little to no exposure to BIPOC's role in our American history and therefore will have a distorted view of it. Derman-Sparks and Ramsey believe that this absence of truth in a social studies curriculum can affect how young white children view their own racial identities, as being superior to marginalized populations (Derman-Sparks & Ramsey, 2005). "In short, white children, even in racially isolated areas are aware of race and without guidance and modeling, often develop stereotypes that influence their feelings about and potentially their behaviors toward people of color" (Derman-Sparks & Ramsey, 2005, p. 4).

Every day I see this in action in my higher education classroom, as most of my students have very limited knowledge of the history of BIPOC and how it is a major part of American history. Since they went to majority white schools, they were not given any information outside the standard normative "white male" historical perspective. This is clear when I introduce them to key BIPOC historical figures that they have never heard of before, like Fredrick Douglass, Sojourner Truth, Carter Woodson, Marian Anderson, and more. They also have very little knowledge about slavery, reconstruction, Jim Crow laws, and the Civil Rights movement. They have not read any biographies of BIPOC in history and they do not have any understanding of how these important leaders and movements have shaped this country. As Gregory states, this is "how white supremacy works" (Gregory, 2018, p. 245). If something is never taught or honored in any way, then it does not exist. There are no counternarratives to this "whitewashed" history of the United States. "Most curricular tools of Whiteness function to avoid teaching the history and formation of the United States accurately" (Picower, 2021, p. 27). Instead, these pre-service white teachers have a distorted view of African American history, one that does not affect their lives and that lives completely in the past. Why should they care? It does not affect them. Then as they mature and grow through their pre-service education courses, they realize that they hold biases and assumptions related to this missing history. And, honestly, most become very upset. They feel wronged by their history teachers growing up and they vow to be different when they are teachers. It motivates them in their understandings. Thus, exposure to truth in history is important and essential to being an effective Anti-Racist teacher in early childhood classrooms.

In our interview two, Ms. Verano addresses the need for white children in her kindergarten classroom to be exposed to the truth about the history of America.

Ms. V: We naturally want to reassure little ones that everything is rosy . . . that we live in a good society and people are inherently good and in this work that I am doing now I am seeing that . . . I mean I don't want to scare them and talk to them about horrible things that happen on a daily basis in our world.

R: But you want to tell the truth.

Ms. V: But I want to tell the truth and I don't want to mislead them . . . I don't want the education in the classroom to be this rosy . . . pieces of information that are misleading . . . so that when they go on into the upper grades and they really start to officially think about racism and the ways that they can interrupt it. . . . Especially the white students . . . because that is my goal . . . I want them to be thinkers and to know that they have responsibility too . . . because we are in a predominantly white area so you know . . . I am looking at . . . also educating those white students to know this is your responsibility.

R: Don't you think they need it more.

Ms. V: They do . . . absolutely . . . a hundred percent . . . anyway I want them to know that we still have a lot of work to do.

In this conversation, it is clear that Ms. Verano feels a strong sense of responsibility in the education of young white children on Anti-Racist issues. She has concerns, as do many white teachers, with scaring young children with the atrocities of our history related to BIPOC, but she believes that it is more important to tell the truth about the history from perspectives other than white perspectives in order for these children to become socially responsible adults in their future communities. To her, it is all about teaching good citizenship (one of the kindergarten standards) and thus she makes it clear to them that inequalities between races still exist and must be interrupted. This reasoning and motivation to teach about BIPOC's historical perspectives is not watered down in any way but instead is told in a straightforward manner. This takes a certain comfort level for a white teacher, and this comfort can only be achieved by constant ongoing critical reflection (see chapter 9).

All of the teacher participants in this study are bound by the social studies standards of their district and also have to meet the curriculum frameworks of the state. In discussing the standards, which are ever changing, they talk about going above and beyond what they are supposed to cover, because the standards are too broad and unfocused. The vision statement reads,

> All (state) residents will be educated in the histories of the United States and the world. They will be prepared to make informed civic choices and assume their responsibility for strengthening equality, justice, and liberty in and beyond the United States. (Mass. Dept. of Elementary and Secondary Education, 2018, p. 9)

There are many of these broad statements in the social studies standards for this state, and they are open for interpretation. In the early years, they are concentrated in the teaching of civics and how to be a good citizen in a democracy. One of the specific standards for kindergarten is about the many roles in living and learning and working together. They are supposed to be taught about classroom democracy, respect for each other, local geography, national and state traditions, and economies (Mass. Dept. of Elementary and Secondary Education, 2018). I found one paragraph in the standards that relates to diversity, "An effective history and social science education incorporates diverse perspectives and acknowledges that perception of events are affected by race, ethnicity, culture, religion, education, gender, gender identity, sexual orientation, disability and personal experience" (Mass. Dept. of Elementary and Secondary Education, 2018, p. 13). Interestingly, this sounds like any paragraph disclaimer you would find in a job posting. It is trying to be inclusive but it feels like an afterthought.

Ms. Verano was very excited about the new social studies standards for kindergarten because if finally brought up the issue of diversity and utilizing multiple perspectives.

Ms. V: Our new social studies standards are actually quite good.
R: Do they have anything to do with race? Or multi-culturalism?
Ms. V: They have . . . yes . . . they have to do with diversity and learning about others that are different than you . . . At the kindergarten level . . . that's basically how . . . they call it guiding principles . . . talks about history and how history is reported . . . the guiding principles are meant to go from pre-k to 12 but they are the same and obviously, the way they are implemented is different at each grade level but the idea that history being reported is based on the biases and background of the one reporting it . . . I was thrilled to see that finally in writing so that we don't have to talk about how Columbus discovered America.

The guiding principle she is referring to is the one I have quoted here. This, to her, is a big step forward as the standards are finally trying to put into writing that all of the standards should be related to principles of diversity and equality. Now, she feels like she has some support within the standards for her Anti-Racist teaching practices. Before it was never explicitly tied to these ideas of differences of culture and race but instead was just a stand-alone on civic engagement.

Later on, in our second interview, Ms. Verano brings up the social studies standards again.

Ms. V: Our district is really trying to work on this for our staff . . . you know work on anti-bias training and I mentioned to you our new Social Studies standards where there is a big civic engagement piece so I think a lot of grade levels are and teachers are focusing on that more now.
R: But it depends on how much they are including.
Ms. V: Right . . . they are not necessarily all including racism in there . . . that it may be other forms of civic engagement.

The standards themselves are vague enough still that they can be taught in a variety of ways. For example, in kindergarten they rarely mention the topics covered in the guiding principles (see table 6.1). Instead they focus on broader terms related to civics and being a good citizen. It seems that teachers can meet these standards in ways that do not really focus on Anti-Racist pedagogy at all. Thus, it is really up to the teacher's interpretation of these standards, in terms of what is really taking place in the kindergarten classroom.

Ms. Alice, in our interview one, talks about the broadness of the social studies standards as useful for her practices, because she has the power to interpret them any way she likes. She puts her focus on Anti-Racist pedagogy and yet is still following the standards for her district and state.

R: So, how does this relate with what you are supposed to teach in second grade? Because I know you have standards.
Ms. A: I have kinda of gotten away with it . . . I think the social studies standards might be changing so I might have to shift . . . but these are units I will not give up . . . the social studies standards in the lower grades are pretty broad so they are easy to work with which was another reason I wouldn't want to go to the upper grades because they become much more specific . . . so now I can justify what I am doing . . . within the standards.

Here, Ms. Alice likes the fact that the social studies standards are broad so that she can continue to utilize her Anti-Racist units and still meet the standards properly. She actually says that this is one of the bright spots of teaching in the lower grades because they are open for interpretation.

In the newest version of these standards for second grade, they talk about global geography, migration, and exchange of services (see table 6.1). Ms.

Table 6.1 State Standards Social Studies

Kindergarten:
Topic 1: Civics
- Understands and follows rules with minimal assistance.
- Takes on responsibilities.
- Should be exposed to a variety of biographies.
- Give examples from literature.
- Topic 2: Geography—Connections among Places
- Describes the location of people and objects.
- Explains the differences between maps and globes.
- Identify home address.
- Find state, city, or town on a map.
- Topic 3: History: Shared Traditions
- Describes civic holidays.
- Compare and contrasts traditions/celebrations of peoples with culturally.
- Diverse backgrounds.
- Topic 4: Economics—Work and Commerce
- Describe what people do in and outside the home.
- Ask and answer questions on buying and selling objects.

First Grade:
Topic 1: Civics/Community/Leadership
- Demonstrates understanding the benefits of being a member of a group.
- Works in groups.
- Demonstrates understanding of leadership in a group.
- Analyze leaders from history.
- Elections/government.
- Topic 2: Geography
- Explain maps represent spaces and locations.
- Understand cardinal directions.
- Understand capital cities.
- Locate and explain physical features.
- Topic 3: History—Unity and diversity in the United States
- Provide evidence on ways different peoples are united.
- Demonstrate understanding of the ways people show pride in belonging to the United States.
- Topic 4: Economics—Resources
- Explain the relationships between natural resources, jobs, and industries.
- Compare and contrast renewable resources and nonrenewable resources.
- Explain that people are a resource too.
- Explain employment.

Second Grade:
Topic 1: Reading and Making Maps
- Explain information provided on maps.
- Compare different types of map projections.
- Topic 2: Geography and Its Effects on People
- Locate all the continents on a map.
- Locate all the oceans.

(Continued)

Table 6.1 (Continued)   State Standards Social Studies

- Explain how the location of landforms and bodies of water help determine conditions.
- Topic 3: History—Migrations and Cultures
- Investigate reasons why people migrate.
- Give examples of why the United States is called the nation of immigrants.
- Conduct interviews with family members to discover where they are from.
- Topic 4: Civics—Countries and Government
- Recognize the difference between physical geography and political geography.
- Explain the characteristics of a country.
- Topic 5: Economics—Resources
- Explain the relationship between natural resources and jobs.
- Distinguish between renewable resource and nonrenewable resources.
- Explain that people are a resource too.
- Give examples of products people buy and sell.
- Analyze why people save or do not save their money. (Mass. Dept. of Elementary and Secondary Education, 2018, p. 32).

Alice works in global geography in her discussions of slave trading and India's peace protests. She covers migration through books on freed slaves migrating north and the African American population moving to big northern cities for jobs. All of these social studies standards are woven into her Civil Rights unit and units on freedom and slavery. Again, since they are so vague in concept, it is left up to the specific classroom teacher on how they want to meet these standards.

Ms. Broadbent, at Coltrane School, is not too impressed with the revised social studies standards and in interview one she discusses her feelings on them.

Ms. B: Yeah, so the Social Studies curriculum is uh . . . a bit disappointing but when I find out more about it . . . I really only got to hear it . . . and I need to look at it and read it.
R: Of course, and I am sure you are going to infuse your own things into it.
Ms. B: The district is sort of in charge of creating units and they were going to also create lessons and I said let's stop.
R: Create lessons? So, it's like scripted?
Ms. B: Yeah . . . Oh, you know why . . . because one of the . . . Now I can't remember what the unit is . . . but there is some . . . I really wish I had it in front of me . . . there is some unit . . . or part of a unit that talked about (pause) exploring racial diversity or cultural diversity and I was concerned about it becoming like token . . . and I said I don't want you to give me any lessons I would rather draw from . . . If I need to teach this I would rather draw from my community of learners and families . . . and make it more meaningful and connect it to who we are.

Ms. Broadbent has a valid point. She is afraid of the social studies standards limiting how she teaches Anti-Racist pedagogy in her classroom. She does not want to be told what lessons or activities to cover in specific social studies units because it takes away from her own academic freedom. Also, she is not completely sure that they will focus on pieces that are of importance. She does not want it to be a tourist approach, which happens in a lot of schools, where there is a day of culture and all cultures are celebrated through stereotypical venues (i.e., taco stands to represent Mexican culture). Her disappointment is that it can be too limiting and may not actually connect with her own families that she is serving.

This conversation with Ms. Broadbent occurred before the politicizing of the term "Critical Race Theory" and the call by the conservatives to take it out of k-12 schools. Ms. Broadbent's fears of having a scripted curriculum or telling her what she can and cannot teach in terms of issues related to race are now coming true. Does the school board of a given school district or the local legislature get to decide what should or should not be taught to young children about race and racism? This type of national pushback on teaching about race and racism will only make it harder for early childhood teachers to feel comfortable and supported in their Anti-Racist work.

Later, she refers directly to this professional development workshop the district offered on the new social studies standards and what was presented to the teachers.

Ms. B: We had a training on it (social studies standards) yesterday because there are new standards and we haven't gotten a copy of them yet (laughs).
R: So, what did they talk about?
Ms. B: They read them to us . . . so I know community is a topic.
R: Well, that's broad.
Ms. B: It's very broad . . . (the town) then and now is a unit.
R: But they are not covering any important . . . Civil Rights legislations or.
Ms. B: No . . . not in first grade . . . and everything's being pushed down . . . is what I am hearing.
R: Slavery . . . they are not talking about.
Ms. B: Second grade . . . well second grade is immigration so including forced immigration . . . um . . . but we did . . . the old standards were heroes and leaders that was part of it . . . but we had changed it to changers . . . people who have changed the world . . . who have created movements that got people on board with their ideas . . . so I am not letting go of that.

Ms. Broadbent is not going to let new social studies standards get in the way of how she effectively teaches Anti-Racist pedagogy (see table 6.1) She is dedicated to certain ideas and units, including great heroes and changers (see following text).

Another theme that several of these teachers talked about, related to standards in general, is this notion of how they are constantly being revised and revamped in order to "push down curriculum." In our conversation in interview one, Ms. Houston discusses how she feels about standards and regulations in general:

Ms. H: I think we are just getting bogged down with standards (laughs) . . . the core (referring to core curriculum) You know . . . it's great . . . it's important . . . I think it's what . . . and maybe not . . . that's just my own . . . my own . . . idyllic way of looking at . . . (pause) Unfortunately, the places that I would want to be in are so over-regulated that . . . even . . . (another town) and . . . (another town) are incredibly regulated and so you have to do certain programs . . . you know same day same page . . . you are expected to do a lot of these things or you are expected to be able to create an environment where you are still able to meet all of these expectations but also providing what you know is developmentally appropriate and.

R: You sound like a teacher who thinks outside the box (Ms. H laughs) . . . you do . . . and you do what you want to do . . . that is what I am hearing.

Ms. H: And . . . that is what is great about this district . . . because we are so small (majority white) and we don't have any programs that we have to follow.

Ms. Houston is referring to towns that are segregated with high populations of low-income BIPOC families and how they are overregulated by the state. She has worked in these towns and did not like the way they oversaw and observed everything she did in her classroom. She likes the freedom of her majority white district but misses the diversity. Here, in her "environment of privilege" she has vague standards to follow and she can just close her door and do whatever she likes.

As stated earlier, the biggest problem in the teaching of history to young children is the absence of voices from important BIPOC. Last year, John Lewis, a long-time African American senator, passed away. My first thought when it was all over the news was why didn't I know of him? I had heard of him as a senator but did not know his major role in the Civil Rights movement of the 1960s. I had never read about his peaceful protests and marches down South. I had never read a book about him in any of my classes growing up. I did not know that he had been almost beaten to death by police officers as he marched for equality. It was as if his great work did not exist. All I knew about was Dr. Martin Luther King Jr. and Rosa Parks and what they did to make change in this world. This is shameful. I never heard of Dorothy Height, Robert Smalls, Ida Wells, Vernon Johnson or Edna Lewis, and more.

And none of my white students who were born thirty-five years later have either. This absent narrative is a major part of the problem in our learning of American history.

Early childhood educators must teach a holistic view of history. They need to teach about all the great heroes and changers who made history. When talking to the participants about how they teach history, they all made a point to say that they do more than what is required of them. They go out of their way to teach about key BIPOC in history who worked for change.

Ms. B: (Going through her biography book basket) so, like Ceaser Chavez is one that we often do . . . Wangari, Ruby Bridges . . . I usually don't read about Martin Luther King because he is so overdone . . . we talk about it . . . and they know about it . . . but.

Here, you can see that Ms. Broadbent has intentionally looked for important BIPOC in history that are beyond the norms of Martin Luther King and Rosa Parks. These teachers understand that children are being saturated with just a few figures in history and are missing out on other key great BIPOC heroes and changers. It is important to note here that a lot of white teachers who teach about Dr. King are giving the watered-down version about his role in this movement. Usually, they read a bland biography on him and then ask children to write about how they would change the world. These teachers do not usually talk about his philosophical views on peace and nonviolence (as related to Gandhi) but instead only discuss his famous "I have a Dream speech." This is only giving a partial picture of this great historical figure and thus it is not acceptable.

Ms. Alice strongly believes in exposing young children to BIPOC historical figures that are not usually studied or talked about in a second-grade classroom. She also tries to broaden and deepen their understandings of leaders they do hear about, like Martin Luther King Jr.

Ms. A: I start my year with a mini-unit about Gandhi and his work with non-violence as well as his philosophy of Satyagraha. I do this so that there is a historical context and an understanding that non-violence is an active practice rather than a simple choice. This understanding is helpful when learning about events like the Montgomery Bus Boycott . . . Rosa Parks was trained in non-violence civil disobedience and the march from Selma to Montgomery.

Ms. Alice is keenly aware that young children are getting an incomplete view of great BIPOC heroes and changers they study and wants to give them a context in which to understand them better. On her wall next to the whiteboard is a poster of Gandhi, which she refers to during lessons. She feels it is important for them to understand the teachings and inspirations of these great BIPOC leaders.

Later on, in the same interview, Ms. Alice discusses the importance of teaching about the various stories that are usually left out of the classroom.

Ms. A: Over the years, I have adjusted it to try to include more current people so that students don't get that "Dr. King had a dream, Yay! The end" story that seems to be way too common. The people I currently teach about are:

- Sojourner Truth
- Harriet Tubman
- Frederick Douglass
- W.E.B. Du Bois
- Ruby Bridges
- Dr. King (might not include him because they have learn/hear/see so much
- John Lewis
- Barack Obama
- I want to specifically teach about the women who founded Black Lives Matter.

Ms. Alice, who has evolved this list over time, is very intentional in her selection of who she wants the children to hear about. Most of these figures are not usually taught in early childhood classrooms and she is determined to make them more known. Next to her Gandhi poster is a Black Lives Matter poster, and the connection is clear in her classroom discussions. She sees this present-day movement as an essential part of the ongoing history of inequality in the United States and feels that, like the Civil Rights movement of the 1960s, Black Lives Matter must be discussed and be critically reflected on in the classroom. This is especially true now within this critical time of conservative groups trying to take out as much history related to race and racism as possible.

In my first-grade classroom, I read BIPOC biographies all year round and also made an effort to include key figures that are not usually taught in the early grades. An example of this is Marian Anderson, the first black woman to sing at the Metropolitan Opera house. She is a political icon because she was the first black singer to sing in front of 75,000 people at the Lincoln Memorial in Washington DC. "Examining her heart, Marian realized that although she was a singer first and foremost, she also had become a symbol to her people and she wanted to make it easier for those who would follow her" (Ryan, 2002, p. 25). The children delight in these biographies as they start to see how she struggled in our society in order to be a star (segregated facilities, being teased and bullied,

Figure 6.1 Posters on Wall (Ms. Alice's Second Grade).

and suffering from racism). They are shocked and surprised by the brutality of this history and are interested in knowing more. This is the beauty of a good BIPOC biography. It grounds their historical perspectives and shows the truth about the past and the present in our society.

Ms. Fern, in interview two, talks about how great leaders and heroes are interconnected and that it is important for young children to see this as they learn about history.

Ms. F: when we move into the community and the world we start looking at community leaders and people who change the world.
R: Like?
Ms. F: Gandhi is definitely a character in their repertoire as a teacher of Martin Luther King . . . We also look at women from the suffrage movement because some of what Gandhi learned about non-violence . . . it all kinda of connects together and they love that . . . they love when things are all connected . . . Like when I tell them that this guy knew this guy and this woman learned from this guy and this guy learned from this woman . . . I think it is important that we learn about heroes and leaders but we also want to try and talk about the movement not just the heroes and leaders .

She is making connections between great leaders so that children understand that heroes do not occur in a vacuum. They don't just come out of nowhere. There is an historical context, one that makes sense, and this means that many great leaders, such as Martin Luther King, having studied other great BIPOC leaders (such as Gandhi) which helped to form their own philosophies based on these teachings. She is also talking about the importance of learning about movements themselves, and not just great leaders, so that there is a deeper understanding of American history.

The Civil Rights movement was a unit that these teacher participants brought up over and over again in their observations and interviews. Ms. Alice created her own Civil Rights unit and has changed and upgraded it over time. She clearly enjoys teaching it to her young children and every year has a celebration in the classroom at the end of the unit and invites all of her families to attend. They share artifacts, creative writing pieces, and other artwork to celebrate this unit. This is the unit she treasures, and as described in a later chapter, she makes it clear that she would not teach in a school that did not encourage or support the teaching of this unit.

In Ms. Verano's school, Smithfield Elementary, there is an annual Martin Luther King assembly, where each class puts on a small play about Dr. King and the Civil Rights movement for the whole school community. This can be typical in a standard elementary school, but the question is what are the teachers doing in their classrooms to really delve into this history? She wasn't sure how involved the other teachers in the school were, except for preparing for this one-day celebration.

Ms. V: So, at our school we do a Martin Luther King Day celebration where each class presents . . . it's kind of like an assembly . . . But we are in the gym and we all sit on the floor and each class presents something that they are learning about either Martin Luther King or about the Civil Rights movement or something like that . . . and this has been a tradition at our school for probably . . . I don't know . . . twelve years? Or so . . . and each class presents and it is nice because the kids get to see the older students and in some cases, they do a little you know . . . they act out a skit . . . or they talk about the time-line of his life.
R: So, are you saying that there are other teachers in this school that are doing exactly what you are doing? They are developing Anti-Racist pedagogy curriculum in their classroom?
V: Yeah . . . everyone is presenting something for the celebration.
R: Right, but that doesn't mean they are doing it all year long.
V: Correct . . . I don't know . . . I do think there may be people that do Black History Month and that's just one time.

This planned annual celebration of Martin Luther King is a way for the whole school community to connect on a specific topic of study. It is clearly a very important event at Smithfield Elementary and Ms. Verano likes being a part of it. She notes that the children enjoy seeing the various productions of other classes, especially from the older students, as it probably helps to deepen their understanding of this great leader. It is, however, important to note that she is unsure what other teachers are doing on this topic in addition to this celebration. This is just one way she teaches about the Civil Rights movement and Dr. King.

There are certain historical topics that all young children should be exposed to in their classrooms. This includes slavery, Reconstruction era, the Jim Crow era, the Civil Rights movement of the 1960s, segregation of schools, peace and nonviolence protesting, and so on. "Those who are ignorant of history can never fully understand the present" (Van De Mieroop, 2016, p. 15). For example, it is important that young children know that 40 percent of the white men who wrote the U.S. Constitution owned slaves themselves (Bigelow, 2014). They need to know that our famous first president and founder of the new republic George Washington owned a plantation with hundreds of slaves. This information is not usually taught in young grades and it is important for them to critically reflect on this irony in order to understand what the founders meant by "all men are created equal." In this case only white men are created equal.

In our conversation on these important topics, Ms. Fern makes it clear that very young children can and do understand these historical milestones. Many teachers in this country believe that kindergarteners are too young to learn about the Civil Rights marches and protests, and/or about slavery. Ms. Fern believes the opposite, stating that it is essential to their historical knowledge.

R: So, you think that kindergartners are able to learn about The Civil Rights Movement?

Ms. F: Yes . . . They come . . . in my experience they understand that there were unfair things happening . . . there were unfair laws being made and with the people who made the laws and that there were people that decided that they were going to do something about that and change it . . . I think that is really important.

Here, she emphasizes her children's abilities to understand what is unfair in our history and how great heroes and changers tried to change these injustices. She is not shielding them from their own history, but instead is revealing all of the flaws and horrors that have founded our nation so they have a more holistic understanding.

In one of Ms. Fern's observations, she reads the book *The Other Side*, by Jacquelyn Woodson. It is set in the Jim Crow era, and it is about two girls, one white and one black (the story is from the black girl's perspective) and how they become friends by sitting on a fence together. They are told to not go to the other side of the fence so they compromise by sitting on top of it and getting to know each other. The last line of the book is profound and effects young children deeply, "Someday, somebody's going to come along and knock this old fence down" and the black girl nods, "Yeah, someday" (Woodson, 2001, p. 16). This book gets the children talking about the history of race relations in our country and they see and feel the injustice. They want to know about it, and they have a right to know about it, because it is the true history of our country. Cole believes that these stories of inequality are key to learning the truth, "Such stories are important and need to be listened to in order to counter hegemonic discourse" (Cole, 2009, p. 49). This is the real way to teach children to be critical thinkers, which is essential to their understandings of American history as a whole.

We, as higher education teachers, have an obligation and a duty to teach our pre-service teachers the truth about our history, especially during these political times where certain groups of people want to censor classrooms and fire teachers who don't obey with the idea of whitewashing the curriculum. We need to expose them to BIPOC who were and/or are great leaders and changers in the world. We need to cover all the important topics and make sure that our students critically reflect on them. If we do not teach them about history and how to teach history, then they are going to continue to (possibly unintentionally) perpetuate racist discourses.

The first thing we should do at the beginning of any course is to try and assess the student's knowledges/background in social studies and history. We need to know where they are starting. This will help us to build upon or critically analyze some of the limited information they have obtained on the subject. Think of it as a KWL chart for historical knowledge. What do they know about the history of BIPOC? And how does this relate to their overall knowledge of the core history, which is based on a white supremacist lens? Do they know that there were 186,000 BIPOC fighting in the Civil War? Do they know about the slave revolts and rebellions that BIPOC participated in? Do they know about the sit-ins at the lunch counters? Do they understand the truth about Lincoln trying to make a plan to send all former slaves back to Africa? Do they know about the NAACP? W. E. B Du Bois? The song *We Shall Overcome?* There is so much content that is missing from their historical narrative when they come into our classroom and it is our job to cover it, or at least introduce them to what they have been missing. We must offer counter-narratives, new and important voices so that they can incorporate these same voices into their future classrooms.

Gregory states, "You think out of millions of blacks who were slaves, there was only one woman out there helping slaves escape?" (Gregory, 2018, p. 38). It is important that we clarify and reintroduce themes and topics that have been misunderstood over time. Here, Gregory is clearly stating that many white people think that Harriet Tubman was the only one who helped slaves escape through the underground railroad. If they are only taught about her then how would they know differently? Many of my students are surprised to learn that Rosa Parks was an activist who had been trained in nonviolence and civil disobedience way before the event on the bus. Some of my students actually believed that Rosa Parks just happened to be tired that day and therefore would not give up her seat. This is not acceptable. They need to know the whole story to fully understand the significance. Therefore, there are historical myths that need explanation and need to be fully cleared up in order for our students to understand the true history of racism in our country. Please be aware of some of the following myths that need immediate attention in our classrooms:

- Rosa Parks was just tired that day and so the event of not giving up her seat was just happenstance.
- The underground railroad was just a few stops and only a few people used it.
- In the Civil War the South had every right to fight for what they believed in.
- Abraham Lincoln was a great president and friend to black people.
- Abraham Lincoln freed the slaves making their lives far better.
- Slaves were happy and liked being taken care of on plantations.
- There was little to no resistance from the enslaved people.
- Reconstruction was a positive experience where freed slaves got their own land.
- Black men were free to vote.
- Segregation laws were short lived.

We can effectively teach about the truth of our history by using primary sources, poetry, read a louds, projects, literature circles, and so on. Students enjoy engaging activities that help them make sense of history and introduce them to counter-narratives. For example, an effective lesson in this genre would be to teach the history of the song *We Shall Overcome*. This song started in the time of slavery and was song throughout reconstruction, the Jim Crow era and the Civil Rights movement. It is still an important song, as it reveals today that there is still more to overcome (Levy, 2013). It was sung at the Obama inauguration, which many found very uplifting. In the book *We Shall Overcome*, it shows an historical timeline for this song which helps us to understand the origins and importance. "Today, people still struggle, against hatred, and for freedom, against poverty, and for families, against despair, and for hope" (Levy, 2013, p. 27). This song is a primary document and therefore it is essential to teach. It also shows clearly that the struggle against racism continues to this day and is not a thing of the past, which is very important to emphasize in our higher education classrooms. "They suffered, yet they sang—to soothe the hurt, to fight the cruelty, to declare that—yes—they were human beings" (Levy, 2013, p. 5). Students need to know and understand this struggle, the struggle to be counted as human beings (as black slaves were considered 3/5ths human). This is a good way to teach about the history of enslavement in our country, through a powerful song, one that has been sung for generations and generations.

Poetry is another good way to teach the truth about our history. I use various Langston Hughes poems, including *I too am America* and *Where is my seat on the Merry-go-round*? This gives pre-service teachers exposure to content as well as ways to use poetry related to history in their own future classrooms. Ms. Alice uses Maya Angelou quite frequently in her classroom and finds her poems to be extremely helpful in learning new content. Ms. Alice is also utilizing Nikki Giovani and Alice Walker. Using poetry with pre-service teachers gives them exposure to the beauty of new voices in history and new perspectives.

Literature circles and book groups are also useful tools in the higher education classroom. In my Early Childhood Curriculum course, I have several classes devoted to history and social studies. I find that using a good selection of books helps them to understand key concepts and be able to plan activities for young children they will later serve. I set them up in small groups and give them a pile of books to choose from. They have to read the book together, identify the themes to be taught with a certain age range (4–8 years old) and plan specific activities to go along with the book. This is not as easy as it seems as the books contain content that they are unsure about how to teach (i.e., slavery, segregation, etc.). The more you have these book groups the more comfortable the students will be in discussing how to incorporate these themes into activities for young children.

Cornell West states that slavery was a crime against democracy (West, 2020). Therefore, how can we teach to the standards that relate to civic engagement without teaching these important historical topics? Teaching about historical injustice is key to disrupting institutional racism. We must be a part of the solution and critically examine how we teach history to pre-service teachers, otherwise we do not serve them well. Just recently, the interim president of my university, who is a Japanese American, gave a talk on his boyhood in Japanese internment camps in the United States in the 1940s. Most of my college students knew nothing about this historical injustice and thus were quite shocked by his stories of racial discrimination against Japanese Americans. If they knew nothing about this atrocity, which occurred on American soil, how are they going to teach about racial injustice and historical truths? They can't. And that is why American history has to be reconceptualized to be inclusive of BIPOC perspectives and understandings.

Chapter 7

Racial Literacy

(In Ms. Fern's Kindergarten.)
Ms. F: This is my favorite book . . . I know I have said this before but . . .
WG: Yay, it has brown skin.
WB: Is that why we are reading it?
WG2: We are trying to have brown skin people books.
Ms. F: What did we notice about the library books?
Unknown child: They had white skin.
   (Ms. F explains the cover of the book. Reads the title "the other side.")
WG3: Maybe they will make friends.
   (There is a picture of a white girl and a black girl by a fence.)
WG4: Maybe a white person will be mean to a black person.
Ms. F: Sometimes there is a problem that happens . . . you are thinking that there is a problem.
Unknown child: Maybe they are already friends.
Ms. F: Should we do a picture walk?
   (Mixed responses.)
BIPOC girl: So someone doesn't cross to the other side.
WB2: (Calls out) Or for animals—so they don't escape.
BIPOC boy: Birds can fly right over.
   (Ms. Fern does a picture walk of the book—sharing each page—they look at the illustrations only.)
WG 3: Maybe they want to be friends but their moms wouldn't let them.
Ms. F: Why?
Unknown child: Because white and brown skin.
WB3: It's not fair!
BIPOC boy 2: She jumped over the fence,

WG5: *(Loudly)* I think the fence is there . . . because the two girl's moms don't want them to be together.
Unknown child: They want to be together but their moms don't.
   (Ms. Fern reads the book.)
WB3: Because they don't want them to go to the white people's house.
Ms. F: Why is it not safe?
WB4: Because they don't like her.
BIPOC girl 2: I think I noticed the white girl was sitting on the fence and the brown girl had her had on the fence and it looked like she would get up there with the other girl.
Ms. F: Do you think they want to be friends?
BIPOC girl 2: She just wants to be on the other side.
BIPOC boy 3: I think after the white girl climbs the fence, she is going to climb up the fence and sit there.
BIPOC boy 4: They are being brave with each other.
Unknown child: Is this a real book?
WB5: It sounds like an old book.
WB6: It used to be white and black not together . . . but now they can.
WG6: I think something similar from this book is happening now.
Ms. F: Can you say more?
WG7: White and black person could be becoming friends . . . not other things I am thinking when walking on sidewalk and mom says don't stare is not happening now.
   (Ms. Fern reads again.)
Ms. F: Here's our last page.
   (She reads it.)
Ms. F: Why do they want to knock the fence down?
WB7: Because they are tired of jumping over the fence.
Ms. F: I like all the thinking and talking about the book . . . what do you think is the most important part of the book? We will make some pictures of the most important part because there is a fence in the book why don't we use popsicle sticks to make a fence.
   (Children rotate to the art table to make their pictures of the characters on the fence.)

All of the participants in my study use read alouds as a way to build content knowledge with young children. This is their primary strategy or tool in their effort to teach Anti-Racist pedagogy. Each book is picked with care and is used to scaffold previous knowledge on the subject. In this chapter, I will delve into the world of read alouds, and how they can contribute to combatting racism in early childhood education. How do these teachers consciously use multiple texts to deepen understanding of racial literacy? How do these

Figure 7.1   Other Side Illustrations (Ms. Fern's Kindergarten).

specific books make a difference in children's growth/knowledge of topic? I will explore several key elements of read alouds and racial literacy, as well as interdisciplinary approaches to using texts across the curriculum. Teachers in the field need to understand the politics and history behind the texts they teach (Souto-Manning & Martell, 2016). Understanding that black is beautiful and is a positive attribute is also key in the analysis of text selection for teachers. Later, I will delve into how this can be translated and utilized effectively in the higher education classroom.

Ms. Maltes defines read alouds as the primary tool in scaffolding critical knowledge for young children on racial literacy. In interview two, she states:

> The primary tool we use is children's literature. . . . Both through using books that represent children across life experiences . . . and across racial identity (loud speaker sounds) but we also make sure to look at the diversity of our authors and viewpoints and that kind of a thing.

Here, she is talking about the importance of intentionally picking the right read aloud for her class. This is the key way she teaches Anti-Racist content and she wants to make sure her books are representative of all experiences related to the topic, including the viewpoints of BIPOC populations.

Actually, all of the participants made it very clear that the selection of texts was a key strategy in their efficient use of teaching Anti-Racist pedagogy. As noted earlier, this is something they use all year long. Hearing books on the same theme helps young children to delve deeper into complex topics and really question the world around them (Souto-Manning & Martell, 2016). They search carefully in libraries, online, and in bookstores for the latest fiction and nonfiction texts that will complement their pedagogy and practice. It seems that all of the participants in this study have something in common, in that they are very intentional in their text selection. This is a hard balance, as the books need to be on topic and yet understandable to young children (see appendix A). Teachers in general search high and low for the right books for their units as a rule, but these teachers are committed to finding texts that are meaningful in their depiction of race and racism in the world. There are more and more children's books on this topic (especially since I was teaching six years ago) but there are still not enough. Therefore, they have to search very hard to find texts that will work all year long for their specific grade level. It was clear during the research that the second-grade teacher had more books to choose from than the kindergarten teachers, as most books on topic are long and have more text per page. I noticed that a few kindergarten teachers still read these books but abridged them as they read, skipping pages and long sentences but still giving them the important content by reading it aloud.

Ms. Alice, in her second-grade classroom, used a read aloud in both of her observations in order to teach key concepts related to race and racism. She makes it clear, much like the others, that she is very intentional in her choices of books and specifically looks for literature about and by BIPOC authors.

> Throughout the year, I include read aloud books by and about people of color. My library grows each year in this aspect. Last year I purchased a bunch of books by and about Native Americans . . . I can always do better, though, and plan to continue to grow my knowledge and my library.

Interestingly, this is one of the few times the teachers brought up indigenous people and including them into their Anti-Racist work in their classroom. Ms. Alice was concerned that she was missing a whole point of view within her classroom library and was reflecting on how to solve this problem. To her, introducing a population that has historically and is still marginalized brings another dimension to the study of racism in our country. Thus, she was on the hunt for more books from this point of view to share with her students.

Ms. Fern also laments on the lack of availability of books on this topic for very young children and is always concerned about having access to enough texts that portray a variety of black/brown experiences.

> (Talking about Thanksgiving) this book told more than one side of that story and one of the sides of the story told was about some indigenous people who protest the holiday and they saw the the picture in the book of people protesting the

holiday so I do think this year in terms of where I want to grow . . . this year the second grade teachers did a unit dispelling the thanksgiving myth . . . which was great . . . What they found is that our kids didn't have an understanding of the myth to begin with . . . Yeah so, I feel there is a gap there . . . and I feel like there is an invisiblization of native people in a lot of Anti-Racist work . . . but in my own . . . so I would like to think about how to help . . . I'd like more resources around five year old kids and how they can come to their understandings.

Here, Ms. Fern is reflecting on how she can utilize books from different points of view that are not traditionally used in the classroom and she sees a gap in her knowledge and use of books on indigenous populations. Therefore, similar to Ms. Alice, she is actively looking to expand her knowledge and text selection to include books from the viewpoints of indigenous populations in America.

Ms. Fern uses children's literature as a key way to start her children to think about their racial identity. In her kindergarten classroom, she uses up to ten books at the beginning of the year as a way to introduce them to this topic.

Ms. F: We start with a focus on the self because they are five and they are completely self-centered (laughs) little beings . . . So, we kinda of start with an understanding of ourselves and our own racial identities and we do that through activities. . . . We do that mostly through stories and children's literature . . . some of them more explicitly talk about skin colors . . . shades of hair . . . different kinds of hair . . . or eye color . . . um . . . so we start with that . . . Coupled with books just exposing them to children's literature that feature a variety of different kinds of people . . . All year we use a lot of books . . . but books at the beginning of the year tend to be targeted to racial identity so the topics that the books are covering are directly bringing their attention to similarities and differences.

R: So, how many books would you say you use every year . . . in that.

Ms. F: In that part of the year? I'd say there are maybe ten different books.

Ms. Fern believes that key literature read alouds help children to develop a deeper understanding of important concepts related to Anti-Racist pedagogy. Her strategy of utilizing at least ten books on the topic of racial identity at the beginning of the school year gives her students the foundation necessary to explore this topic later on. Therefore, she is utilizing key read alouds at the start of the year in order to build knowledge and continue their critical reflection on racial identity. This grounds them in the work of Anti-Racism and helps build a safe community for later discussions on this topic.

These committed teachers use mentor texts often. These are books that they can come back to at any given time of the year. They are referred to and reread on an ongoing basis so that children have a reference point of understanding. In most rooms, these mentor texts were on display all year long. In our second interview, Ms. Houston and I have a conversation on this particular point.

> *R:* Some people use read alouds and they don't have an activity that follows . . . do you have follow-up activities?
> *Ms. H:* Sometimes . . . sometimes we will base it on that for the following . . . following day . . . we have been reading about this . . . like when we did this how can you make the world a better place . . . it was based on . . . I said "Remember when we read this book?" So, it is almost using them as mentor texts for their ideas . . . not necessarily the logistics of the . . . the mechanics of the book . . . the books drive my curriculum.

While observing Ms. Houston, I realized that she and the others constantly referred to books that they previously had read in the classroom. This is how a mentor text works, it is always on display and referred to during a variety of lessons, even much later on in the year. Later on in our discussion, Ms. Houston makes a point to tell me that she displays some books (referring to them as mentor texts) all year long so children have unlimited access to these texts.

> I kept up the books I did earlier in the year about everyone belongs and the skin you live in . . . Like all my ones that specifically talk about skin tone and multiculturalism . . . I have kept those up all year . . . I usually rotate the books I keep up but I kept those books up all year . . . because I want that to be visible . . . This is important . . . I want you to see these . . . I want your eyes . . . if they absorb these images.

Here, Ms. Houston intentionally displays certain mentor texts on this subject all year long so they "are visible" to the children. This shows that she is infusing this curriculum all year long as she wants children to always think about this pedagogy and why it is important. She also is emphasizing the importance of children actually seeing important mentor texts on display so they can continue to critically analyze these visual book covers.

In Ms. Broadbent's first-grade classroom, children ask for books to be read over and over and she is happy to read them again and again. An example of this is when she reads a Wilma Randolph biography and the next day, as I am observing, many children are asking when she will read it again to the whole class. They clearly know and understand that she will reread certain texts that are important to them, on a specific subject, again and again. She promptly responded that she planned to read it again real soon and this made her class very happy. She also brings up certain texts related to this content as a way to relate to past content while introducing a new book. The more they read it, with her and without her, the more familiar they are to the topic and the more interest they have in it overall.

Experts agree that rereading books is a very good idea for young children. This is so they get many chances to absorb important details as they analyze the text (McGee and Schickedanz, 2017). Researchers claim that rereading the text a few days later is essential for developing long-term understanding of the topic (McGee and Schickedanz. 2017). Mentor texts are often referred to and reread multiple times, as in the case of *Wilma Unlimited* in Ms. Broadbent's class and *The Other Side* in Ms. Fern's classroom. "Repeated interactive read-alouds, a systematic method of reading aloud allows teachers to scaffold children's understanding of the book being read" (McGee & Schickedanz, 2017, p. 1). Rereading helps the child to fully understand the complexities of a topic and reengages them with the text and its content.

When schools went remote (in March of 2020), teachers had to be resourceful in how they read or presented books to their class. Ms. Fern recorded herself rereading important texts that related to Anti-Racist pedagogy so that they could reread the book by watching a video. She found this tactic helpful especially to parents who had questions about George Floyd's horrible murder and the racial injustice that was prominent in the headlines at that time.

Ms. F: And then I think this pandemic and going online . . . I think that . . . I went back . . . when we went online every-thing kind of hit the fan after George Floyd was murdered and families were wanting to know what to do and they understood that their kids had this base from kindergarten so I went back and I basically . . . I use a platform called Class Dojo . . . they are asynchronous . . . I record a story of a read aloud . . . and they watch it . . . I went back and re-read a lot of books we already read online to the kids and encouraged their families to watch them together and talk about it . . . At the beginning of the year a lot of the books I read just have black characters first of all . . . so that it is not just a white heteronormative family . . . so we go back and read a lot of those . . . like *Jamari Jumps* . . . so some of them were just sweet stories about kids and the kids were of color and I was able to expose that idea to a parent to look at their own libraries . . . what books are you choosing and reading? I did a parent zoom . . . just to see how it was going . . . they talked for maybe ten minutes about remote learning and then the rest of the hour they wanted to talk about racism and how they can talk about these things with their kids . . . it was really powerful . . . so at that point I read . . . *A Kid's book about Racism* . . . and I think that was really helpful . . . That book is a nice bridge . . . actually between the multicultural and the racism and I think it has helpful language that kids can understand and grown-ups can understand . . . you know when you read a book with a kid . . . they are just talking about it . . . you don't have to sit down and say "can we talk about . . . Some people have light skin and some people have dark skin" You know you just read a book and there are questions and thoughts that come up . . . I choose to do only books that we have already read . . . intentionally for that reason . . . kids already have the background . . . we have already had group discussions about it . . . They could sort of continue the work . . . rather than read something new and have their parents unpack it.

Ms. Maltes believes that children's literature frames content such as Anti-Racist pedagogy in a way that young children can relate to it. In interview two, she sheds light on this topic:

Ms. M: (reading books) . . . Really trying to say to children (pause) that you are not alone . . . that we appreciate who you are . . . we appreciate where you are coming from and also to just give language around it so that kids don't ever feel like just because they are different in some way that it is something that they need to hide from the rest of the group . . . But certainly, as social situations come up, I feel like children's literature often frames it in such a way that other kids can relate to it.

Clearly, Ms. Maltes feels strongly that utilizing a variety of read alouds that focus on differences and similarities in identity can be a helpful tool for children to truly examine their own feelings related to racial identity.

One of the most important aspects of a good read aloud is the questions a teacher poses during and after reading a text. The right phrasing of a question on the text helps children dig deeper and critically reflect on the variety of content within the text. Reading books aloud is a dialogical process, together the teacher and the students coconstruct knowledge from a given text (McGee and Schickedanz, 2017). This usually only occurs by asking questions. Open-ended questions are key to this process so that children are not just searching for the answer the teacher wants. Yes and no questions are not as helpful, for example, Is the character angry? Good open-ended questions get children thinking critically and help them to place themselves within the context of the text. "Research has demonstrated that the most effective read alouds are those in which children are actively involved asking and answering questions and making predictions rather than passively listening" (McGee & Schickedanz, 2017, p. 2). It also helps them to understand key vocabulary words in order to understand the topic more fully. An example of a good open-ended question is, "What are your thoughts about the characters actions?" or "What did you notice about this particular setting and how does it impact the storyline?" In terms of Anti-Racist pedagogy, asking appropriate open-ended question is a powerful tool in helping young children understand and engage with the content of the text.

In Ms. Broadbent's first-grade classroom, she is very thoughtful in her lesson plans and tries to come up with key questions before she introduces a book.

> Most of what we do when we do read a louds are . . . There are questions that I plan before we do the read aloud so kids can talk and be sort of held accountable for the information.

She wants to make it clear that she gives them essential questions before and during her read alouds so that they can get a deeper understanding of the complexities of the content. Through rereading and posing critical questions she sees that they are more engaged with the text and thus are more motivated to learn from it. Furthermore, she can assess their ongoing scaffolding of knowledge on a topic through open-ended questioning. This means that she assess their growth and progress related to the material through this questioning process. She, like the others, utilizes turn and talks or think pair shares with her young children so they can talk through their understandings of the questions she is posing.

Another important thing to consider during read aloud time is how these particular texts that a teacher selects can challenge common perceptions related to race and racism, such as the notion that the color black or brown is not beautiful. It is important that early childhood educators actively read and discuss books that honor and value BIPOC children and counter this normative discourse. This is essential for a BIPOC student in the classroom, as representation and honoring their skin tone is crucial to their feelings of being valued. Yet, it is also equally important in a class with an all-white population as well, so that they recognize the beauty of different skin tones and honor and respect people that do not have white skin. In my higher education classroom, I make sure to include lots of picture books that are positive portrayals of BIPOC children and that elevate the notion that black is indeed beautiful. This is usually contrary to what pre-service teachers have been taught or been exposed to over the years and thus it is essential for them to critically examine the deficit binary of white = good and black/brown = bad. They are usually surprised to find out that they have been socialized by society to make negative associations with the color black/brown. And they won't always admit that this is the case, but after much examination of their own biases and assumptions, they realize that they were never exposed to books that portray black/brown people as beautiful. (See appendix A.)

In Ms. Verano's kindergarten, she spends a lot of time appreciating and honoring black/brown skin tones and black/brown people's unique hair through the use of different literature. An example of this is during observation three when she read the book *Hair like Mine* to her class.

Ms. V: I have a brand new story . . . I just bought it . . . so excited to share it with you . . . perfect for before we do our portraits for March . . . It's about a little girl . . . about five or six . . . she is feeling kind of sad because she wants to find somebody that has hair like hers.
   (Holds up book *Hair Like Mine*.)
   (Ms. Verano starts to read.)
   (She reads a page about two children that do not look alike.)
WB1: But they could change their hair to be the same.
   (She reads a page about twins.)
Ms. V: Can you tell . . . and . . . apart?
WG1: . . . and . . . are also twins (names two boys in the class.)
Ms. V: Not identical twins though (she explains the word "identical") This is a story about how people look . . . how no people look exactly the same . . . I want to read my favorite page again (Reading) "You are Unique and beautiful—just like all of you."
Ms. V: (Stops reading) I want you to focus on your hair and face . . . you can even look at the book we read yesterday (*I am Not Enough*) you are not drawing your clothes . . . focus on shoulders and up . . . not your body . . . if you notice the picture just shows from the shoulders up (holds up book). Focus on your beautiful unique face and hair.
   (Ms. . . . (the paraprofessional) draws her face and hair on chart paper. She is modeling how to draw for the students.)
   (Ms. Verano gives directions.)
BIPOC boy1: I can't draw that good.
Ms. V: She (the paraprofessional) has been practicing a long time.
   (The paraprofessional explains how to draw the face and hair.)
Para: I'm done (she stops suddenly)
Class: NO!
   (The paraprofessional puts in eyes and ears—she role models thinking aloud as she does this.)
Para: What shape are my glasses?
WG2: Oval
Para: What should I do next?
WB2: (shouts) Hair!
   (The paraprofessional draws her hair in braids.)
Ms. V: You can do loops or circles to make curlies around the face. Add as many details about your beautiful unique self.
WG3: Eyeballs.
   (Ms. Verano talks about pupils in the eye.)

BIPOC BOY 2: What's a pupil?
   (She explains the word to the class and has the paraprofessional draws it in.)
WG3: Eyelashes.
WG4: Eyebrows.
BIPOC boy 3: I think you forgot one thing (he gets up and points to her button on her shirt.)
Ms. V: I love that you are giving details but I want you to have enough time to draw your portraits . . . if you raise your hand, I will come by with a handheld mirror.
Ms. V: (pointing to the model portrait) Notice . . . she didn't color it in . . . you need to color your own hair . . . the color it really is . . . you can use skin tones to make your hair color.
   (Children get called to their tables to work on their own self-portraits.)
   (Ms. Verano walks around the room.)
Ms. V: If you are missing teeth . . . don't forget.
   (She rings the bell and the children freeze.)
Ms. V: Kindergarten, I want to remind you . . . you have a unique smile because some of your teeth are missing . . . you can leave a space where they are missing . . . raise your hand and I will come over with the mirror.
BIPOC boy 3: (to me) My mom said I have chocolate-covered eyes.
Ms. V: If you are mixing skin tones . . . not too hard.
   (The children continue to work on their self-portraits—some go to the easel and pick up the book she just read—others look at the book from yesterday. They are all talking and excited. They ask me to take photos when they are done.)

This book *Hair Like Mine* is a perfect book to use with young children to show them that brown and black hair is beautiful. It values and honors the hair of this girl and tells them that she should not feel sad about her hair, but instead should be proud. The pictures/illustrations in this book show that by the end she is very pleased with her hair, even though she cannot find others nearby who have the same kind of hair. She has a natural look that is beautiful and the children appreciate her hair and understand and can relate to her insecurities of looking different. Ms. Verano has read several books and poems already at this point that celebrate different hair and skin tone and so the children are inspired and motivated to draw their own self-portraits.

During interview two, Ms. Verano talks about how she introduced Langston Hughes poetry to the children in order to continue the theme of black is beautiful.

Ms. V: We are memorizing *My People* (a poem by Hughes) . . . so in teaching *My People* it talks about . . . the night is beautiful . . . so the faces of my people . . .

the stars are beautiful . . . so are the eyes of my people . . . beautiful also is the sun . . . beautiful also are the souls of my people' . . . so I talked to them about it . . . he (Langston Hughes) wanted to write a poem so that other people could know that black people are beautiful . . . that they are . . . and this is a way to make people feel good about themselves but also to have white people know that. . . . You know . . . because a lot of times people were being unfair or unkind were looking at somebody who had dark skin as not as pretty or not as . . . so we talked about that with this poem.

Ms. Verano selects books that counter the good white, bad black binary so that children can appreciate and value BIPOC populations. She is not just exposing them to different types of skin tones and hair types but instead is actively trying to give a counternarrative to the societal standard of beauty, which is usually presented as white people with straight blond hair. She is giving them options to see themselves and others with brown skin and curly, curly hair as beautiful too. It was clear when I was in her classroom that this was especially important for the BIPOC students in the room who were excited to see hair just like them represented in a book.

Part of honoring the concept of black and brown as beautiful is being open to learning about a given text from a child in the room. Children like to see themselves represented in books and come to a text with their own sets of knowledge which help to inform the teacher and the other students about the text (Souto-Manning & Martell, 2016). An example of this happened in Ms. Broadbent's first grade and she recalls it in our interview one.

R: So, do you read biographies?
Ms. B: We are going to read one next week on Wangari.
R: Yeah . . . the trees (it is about a woman in Kenya who plants thousands of trees as they were being chopped down and it was affecting the environment.)
Ms. B: And a student of mine told me today that I have been pronouncing her name wrong.
R: It's not Wangari.
Ms. B: No, it's Wangareee.
R: Oh, Wangareee . . . so I have been pronouncing it wrong as well.
Ms. B: Because he told me that it's a Jamaican name and he has a Jamaican aunt and she knows how to say the name right.
R: Interesting.
Ms. B: So, I thanked him because I have been pronouncing the word wrong all the time.

This is powerful as a lot of white teachers mispronounce important names of BIPOC in their classrooms. Part of honoring and respecting different populations is responding to critique and reflecting on our own mistakes, including pronouncing names of BIPOC correctly.

It is important to note that all of the participants utilize key read alouds across many disciplines. They are very aware of the power books that convey in other subjects such as history/social studies and science. Souto-Manning and Martel state, "Read alouds can serve as a way to introduce topics in other content areas such as social studies, and make the curriculum more inclusive and representative" (Souto-Manning & Martell, 2016, p. 94). In the following observation, Ms. Verano delves into skin tone through a scientific lens by reading a book on Melanin to her kindergarten class.

(At rug holding up book in English and Spanish—All the Colors We Are—The Story of How We Got Our Skin Color.)
    (Ms. Verano reads the English page and her paraprofessional reads the Spanish translation on the opposite page.)
Ms. V: Remember we talked about how we all look different different hair . . . different skin color . . . this book is an information book and it will teach us how we get our skin color.
WB1: There is something called Melanin that makes it look darker or lighter.
Ms. V: Give me a thumbs up if you remember doing this when we mixed paints to make our skin tone.
    (Thumbs go up.)
Ms. V: What color would you call your skin?
    (Students call out all at once.)
    Tan.
    Black.
    Rose.
Ms. V: How do we get our skin?
WB2: From God.
WB3: (screams) DNA.
WG1: Depends on if we live in a shady place or a sunny place.
    (Ms. Verano continues to read.)
Ms. V: From our ancestors . . . can you say it?
Class: Ancestors!
Ms. V: One way is from our parents and families. . . . From the sun . . . we all have melanin in our skin.
WG2: I have light skin.
Ms. V: Thumbs up if your skin gets darker in the sun.
    (Some thumbs are up.)
Ms. V: This is the science part which may be new to you . . . What are three ways we get our skin tone?
WG3: (screams) Parents.

BIPOC boy 1: DNA.
Ms. V: Book does not mention that . . . what's the other one?
WG4: From Melanin.
BIPOC boy 2: From my brother.
Ms. V: What are the three ways?
Unknown child: The sun.
Ms. V: I want you to think about your ancestors . . . do you think they lived in a place with a lot of sun? Or less sun that gives you lighter skin? Your ancestors lived a long time ago and lived in other places. Not in this area . . . unless you are Native American . . . the ancestors came from other places because they wanted to or they were forced to.
WG5: Why forced to?
Unknown child: Slaves.
WG5: What are slaves?
Ms. V: They came and worked for no money.
WG5: No money?
Ms. V: Some of your families are from Puerto Rico and came here because they wanted to . . . some came from Europe . . . Some from South America . . . places like Columbia . . . Some places are warm and some are cold.
WB4: My auntie lived in Ireland.
Ms. V: But we are talking about a long time ago.
WG6: A long time ago my grandmother lived in Italy . . . now we are going on vacation there.
Ms. V: I like how you are looking at your skin tone . . . think about whether your ancestors came from a cold or warm place.
  (She takes out a map inside the book and points to it.)
  The dark spots on the map are hotter . . . where the sun is the strongest . . . places that are lighter are colder.
  (They discuss melanin and how it affects skin tone. Then Ms. Verano asks them to draw an accurate representation of their family's skin tone and all the children happily run to their seats and start drawing.)

This observation is a good example of the way these Anti-Racist early childhood educators utilize read alouds across many different subjects. In this case, Ms. Verano was trying to explain the scientific differences in their skin tone, by utilizing geography and social studies/history. This gives children a deeper understanding of skin tone in general and helps them to see how they have different shades/skin tones.

Husband states that "Anti-Racist ideas (curriculum) should permeate all areas of the early childhood classroom" (Husband, 2011, p. 369). This is important because it helps them have a deeper connection to the topic. Books can be utilized in all key areas of the curriculum including math. Chao and

Jones talk about the importance of utilizing key social justice topics through read alouds so that children understand math concepts (Chao & Jones, 2016). One activity they recommend is a bodily kinesthetic activity that relates to Harriet Tubman's travels up north. In this activity, the teacher asks a child to pretend to be Harriet Tubman, take three steps to the right, over a bridge and five steps north following the north star. The teacher then asks them to crawl under a table to the other side take three more steps to freedom. How many steps did you take altogether to reach freedom? This type of activity, according to Chao and Jones, creates agency and helps children relate the subject of math to important Anti-Racist history (Chao & Jones, 2016).

How can we teach this important concept of using read alouds to further students learning of Anti-Racist pedagogy in the higher education setting? Well, overall, it is important to realize that using children's books within the higher education classroom is essential, for role modeling purposes. Teacher education students need to see, sort, and read a variety of books and it is important that we intentionally find the right books to share with them. By right books, I mean books that will broaden their views and perspectives and challenge their own biases and assumptions. As a professor, our selection is key, because it demonstrates the thought and care that comes into play when looking for books that can be effectively used in the early childhood classroom.

Reading books aloud to college-age students may seem strange or inappropriate but it is essential for their understanding of how to do this on their own in their classroom. Plus, they usually enjoy being read to. I model how to hold the book, to show the pictures to the entire class and I read it in an engaging voice, stopping to ask questions along the way, much like we do with small children. I do this a lot in my Early Childhood Curriculum and Early Intervention classes. I think it is important to model the read aloud on an ongoing basis and then utilize different activities that go with it. Sometimes, I have them read aloud in small groups to each other and then create their own activities that can go along with the text. This process helps them to see that there are many possible ways one can actively engage with the literature. It also aids them in thinking differently about books and how to use them in the classroom to cover important content.

Giving students time to explore and examine different books is also important. I dump bins of books on their tables and ask them to work together to look and review the books in front of them. Sometimes I ask them to sort and classify these books. For example, I may ask them to put the books in different piles, according to stories with and about BIPOC people and books that depict white people only. This gives them a clearer idea of the lack of books on or about BIPOC for young children. I have also asked them to order different picture books by the skin tone of the main character. They spread the books out on the table and work together placing them in order from lightest to darkest skin tone. They have to open the books and identify the main characters and decide who has darker skin. At first, they seem uncomfortable with this project but after they finish and we discuss their process of ordering the books they understand the usefulness of the activity and see how it can work with young children as well. Here, they are being asked to think about books in a different way. Who is being represented and who is not being represented? And this brings up biases within themselves that they have never really thought about or unpacked before related to their own racial identity (see chapter 9). "Teaching effort needs to be redirected toward identifying early childhood texts to use with children, that helps children to engage with how whiteness operates as a position of privilege in their lives" (Davis & MacNaughton, 2009, p. 62).

It is also important for them to critically reflect on any given book, as not all books with BIPOC populations are representative of good books to use with young children. Analyzing and examining a book is essential before incorporating it into your curriculum. And they need to practice this with intentionality. Some books on the surface seem like they will be good examples of promoting Anti-Racist pedagogy in the classroom, but actually they may have the opposite effect and may just reinforce stereotypes and biases in children. Some books, like *A Fine Dessert* and *A Birthday Cake for George Washington* are good examples of books not to use in your classroom, as they are glorifying slavery, depicting enslaved people as happy in their life as slaves. Therefore, it is essential that you really examine a text before you use it in order to critically reflect on how it depicts certain topics.

It is also important to utilize books in teaching other subjects outside of English Language Arts. As stated earlier, it is very helpful when teaching social studies, science, and math content. We need to help pre-service teachers see the importance of using many read alouds a day within a variety of subjects. I use book groups and literature circles with my students so they can review several books on a theme (i.e., skin tone, civil rights issues, slavery, and so on). I usually provide a two-part prompt: find examples in the text that illustrate that it is a good book to use on this theme and then reflect on their biases related to the text. They usually have the most trouble with the reflection part of the prompt and this is where it is helpful that they are in small groups so they can openly discuss their own issues/assumptions about the text. Most of the time they talk about how they feel the content is too heavy or not appropriate for little children, especially when it comes to slavery. This is their own bias and it is usually based on the fact that they really didn't learn much about slavery until middle or high school and even then, it was limited (see chapter 6). They need to work through this bias in order to present read alouds on these topics in their own classrooms and therefore, book groups can be helpful for their understandings.

I think it is key to set up play centers and areas of the room so that they can rotate or wander around and explore materials, just like they would use in their own classroom. Books can be included in these centers, especially board books. You could also have dolls with different skin tones, art materials with books on skin tone, picture cards of diverse people, or costumes to examine. In my early childhood curriculum course, we do a lot of hands-on learning, essentially to help them see how to use these materials in their classrooms themselves. Having them play with materials and books related to Anti-Racist pedagogy really helps them see that it is possible to incorporate them in their daily teaching. Play is how young children learn new concepts and therefore you must practice play in group settings in the higher education classroom as well. The following materials would be helpful for play centers in your higher education classroom:

- Play-do in different shades of brown, tan.
- Clay.
- Paints.
- Multicultural crayons/markers.
- Dolls with different skin tones.
- Puppets with different skin tones.
- Paper with different shades of brown/tan.
- Artifacts of different cultures.
- Picture cards.
- Games that are multicultural.
- Board books related to skin tone that include BIPOC.

As pre-service teachers explore different materials and read a variety of books related to this content, they can actually see what it looks like and how it can be modeled in their future classrooms. It gives them a sense that it is doable and thus not this unknown concept that they have no idea of how to translate into their daily teaching lives.

Again, role play is also helpful with read alouds. You can have your students dramatically reenact a scene from a book and then have the other student guess which book it comes from. For example, they could be on the bus in *Last Stop Market Street* and talk about the world around them they observe during this bus ride. Or you could have them act out *Freedom on the Menu* having them pretend to be protesters sitting at the lunch counter refusing to move when told they won't be served because of their skin color. Reader's theater is a good way to get your class to really understand the complexities of important books. It helps them to synthesize the information and understand their own biases and misconceptions about different topics (such as Civil Rights, Jim Crow era, slavery, and so on). The use of drama and reader's theater can be a great way to teach about racism and how to be an Anti-Racist (Husband, 2010). It is certainly a useful tool for the higher education classroom.

Clearly, literature is key to effectively teaching the complexities of race and racism with young children. Thinking about engagement levels, questioning techniques, rereading of texts, utilizing mentor texts, and providing appropriate activities are all essential to this process. Pre-service teachers need to be exposed to a variety of texts that are representative of BIPOC populations and they also need to be able to think about how to be intentional in how they use these texts. This is the only way they can become racially literate themselves.

Chapter 8

Teaching Activism

(Ms. Verano introduces book—Child of the Civil Rights Movement.)
Ms. V: She was a little kid during that time and we will find out what she does
 (Holds up a picture).
 What does that look like a picture of?
WB1: People marching.
 (She continues to read the book.)
Ms. V: Read what that sign says *(points to picture in book).*
WB2: *(Screams)* Whites only!
Ms. V: They weren't allowed to go there.
BIPOC Boy1: Why?
 (Ms. Verano explains Jim Crow Laws.)
 (She then explains next picture of Freedom Riders.)
WG1: But is she a baby?
Ms. V: No, she is a kid. Why do you think they wouldn't let them in?
BIPOC boy2: I think it's whites only.
WG2: There is a sign on the page—it might say white only.
BIPOC boy2: I think it is for blacks only.
Ms. V: But they wouldn't let blacks in.
 (She explains the concept of sit-ins.)
Ms. V: Back then they were saying this is the only pool blacks could go in . . .
WG3: It looks nice.
Ms. V: It's the only one—is that fair?
Class: *(shouts in unison)* No!
 (Ms. Verano explains voting—blacks are not always allowed to vote.)
 (She is abridging pages as there are too many words on a page.)
WG4: Is he in jail right now?
Ms. V: Might be.

WG5: Some of the white people didn't want to make other people's choice.
MS. V: It wasn't just black people participating.
Unknown student: They were being nice.
BIPOC boy1: When my grandma didn't have a car, she could sit in the back.
BIPOC boy1: I can go to the front too.
Ms. V: But that's the difference back then . . . There are still things that are unfair today—there are marches that happen.
BIPOC boy2: I can't look (talking about a picture of a person with one leg marching).
Ms. V: Why aren't you looking?
BIPOC boy2: It's too sad.
Ms. V: What's sad about it?
BIPOC boy2: Oh, because he has one leg.
Ms. V: Even a person with one leg was there to march.
    (She explains the word Lei—a necklace of flowers.)
    (Students are all calling out—cross talk.)
    (Some students are off topic.)
Ms. V: (calmly) We are going to keep talking about the story—we are getting distracted.
    (She explains that televisions were black and white back then.)
    Do you remember the video of Martin Luther King in Black and white? There are laws that are not okay . . .*
BIPOC boy1: Stealing—red lines—crossing the line. Not stopping when you have to stop.
WG6: You can't cross a red light.
Ms. V: So, there is still a lot of work to be done—people today march and protest that things are not fair—for people with dark skin . . . if people who have dark skin or are new to the country who are discriminated against it's called . . .
WG4: (calls out) Racism.
Ms. V: Not getting a good job—not treated fairly or getting arrested for something a white person wouldn't . . .
    (She brings out another book.)
Ms. V: I want to show you pictures of protesters.
WG7: (quietly) Today?
    (Ms. V shows pictures of marchers and signs.)
BIPOC boy1: I am going to make a sign.
Ms. V: If you were going to make a sign today about people being treated fairly with dark skin . . .
    (She reads protest signs in book.)
WB3: Those are some big words.

Ms. V: What do you think your sign is going to say?
   (A small girl speaks in low voice—inaudible.)
WG8: (screams) Don't back down.
Ms. V: We have to make a sign that shows we are fair to everybody.
WB4: You need to make more fair rules.
WG9: (Calls out)I love my friends.
WG1: I love my friends and the whole wide world!
WB5: No more slaves in the world.
BIPOC girl1: Be nice to all people.
Ms. V: Grown-ups will help you spell the words.
BIPOC boy1: Keep the city safe no matter what.
WG: People can have peace and love.
BIPOC boy2: No more racism.
BIPOC boy3: What's racism?
BIPOC boy2: It's like whites only ... like blacks as slaves.
Ms. V: There is racism today ... racism is when people with dark skin are treated unfairly—when there is not fair treatment.
WG7: (shouts) Don't be mean to other people.
Ms. V: You can work with a buddy or alone ... make the letters big. You can draw pictures too.
   (Another teacher is handing out big white paper—as Ms. Verano calls people to their seats.)
   Think of a sign you would write to bring to a protest.
   (All children are working at their tables on signs—I walk around to help—as do all the teachers in room.)
   (Some children are struggling with spelling—we help them sound out words.)
   (The period ends soon after and they leave the room for recess with their finished and unfinished signs spread out on the tables).

According to Ms. Fern, "engaging in Activism is the anecdote to the despair." Teaching about activism in early childhood is essential to the child's understanding of democracy and being a good citizen. Cornell West refers to it in terms of justice. "Justice is what love looks like in public." (West, 2020)

Children, even at a young age, are aware of issues related to fairness and justice. They engage in this type of talk early on (as noted in this chapter) and are profoundly motivated to understand these concepts. In this chapter, I will examine issues of activism and justice in the early childhood classroom, including fairness/equality, play as a political space, and how to be an ally and stand in solidarity. All of this relates to Anti-Racist pedagogy and other social justice topics. At the end of this chapter, as in the others, I will delve into how higher education teachers can incorporate activities and practices in

Figure 8.1 Poster (Ms. Verano's Kindergarten).

Figure 8.2 Poster (Ms. Verano's Kindergarten).

their college classrooms that relate to topics of activism and justice related to discourse on Anti-Racism.

It is important to note here that young children are obsessed with the notion of fairness. Most teachers hear "that's unfair" several times a day in their early childhood classroom. They are highly motivated to understand what is fair and/or unfair in the immediate world around them. And this is the seeds of activism. Ms. Fern infuses lessons on activism into her kindergarten classroom throughout the year:

Ms. F: I kinda of always come back to well if you tell kids the truth and you give them the tools to analyze the truth . . . it is not up to me to tell you what to think or feel . . . they figure it out and they know what's fair . . . and not fair is like hot in kindergarten . . . they are ready to talk about what is fair and unfair and I don't have to.

Several of the teachers in this study agreed with this sentiment. Fairness is a hot topic in the early grades, because young children are very aware of what is fair or unfair in their immediate circles. It can be a small topic, like children complaining about a change in schedule or it can be a larger issue, like the boys racing the girls on the playground. This was actually an issue in Ms. Fern's class at Coltrane School:

Ms. F: Last year for example the kids would go to recess and the boys would yell boys vs. girls race to the playground and they would run to the playground . . . well the girls organized a protest against this because they felt it was unfair that they were separating boys from girls and two, that it was unfair that the girls weren't always . . . and I can't . . . I wish I could remember the words they used . . . girls weren't always prepared because girls were asked to wear different kinds of shoes than boys were so they couldn't run as fast . . . even though they really could run fast . . . probably faster.

Ms. Fern is actually very proud of the girls for protesting the unfairness on the playground. She sees her children critically thinking about the concept of fairness and is pleased that they are considering an activist approach to the issue. Kissinger states, "Fairness is a concept that children seem to innately programmed to understand" (Kissinger, 2017, p. 42).

In Ms. Houston's kindergarten at Longwood Elementary, she hones in on the issue of fairness by actually demonstrating it in the classroom. She believes that by focusing on the issue of fairness, which is paramount in young children's minds, she can introduce terms like inequality, related to her Civil Rights unit.

Ms. H: As I was first introducing about how he (Dr. King) was fighting for this (civil rights for all) . . . how it's just not fair . . . the unfairness of it all and I do my read alouds right before we go out to recess and so I said . . . Instead of calling them by rows as they are seated on the rug . . . Instead of calling them by rows to go and get ready for recess . . . I looked at them and without any kind of background . . . I didn't preface it with anything . . . I just said "so and so and so and so . . . you all have light eyes so you go get ready for recess . . . oh no you have brown eyes . . . Actually you . . . you . . . you . . . you are staying in for recess . . . "

R: They were freaked out.

Ms. H: They were kinda of freaked out . . . I was like "What? What is wrong?" and they said "that is not fair." And I was like "Why? I like blue eyes."

R: So, do you do activities on fairness?

Ms. H: I do activities on fairness . . . I do activities on peace and love and what can I do to make the world a better place? Again, I prefaced that with Dr. King who worked to try to make this world a better place amongst other important people we will be learning about as the year goes on.

In this case, Ms. Houston is using the concept of fairness to help her demonstrate the inequalities in our society both past and present. She introduces her civil rights unit with this concept of fairness as all young children seem to be very engaged in this ideology of what is right and what is wrong. This specific demonstration of blue eyes versus brown eyes is a class method or way that teachers have illustrated unfairness to their young children. This comes from Jane Elliott in 1968 and later in Toni Morrison and her book *The Bluest Eye* (Bloom, 2005). Oprah used this as a classic demonstration on national television back in the 1980s. The idea is for young children to connect the concept of fairness with discrimination and inequalities related to race.

Ms. Verano uses the book *Say Something* by Reynolds to connect this concept of fairness with inequality and discrimination. In the following conversation, she describes the book and how she utilizes it with her kindergartners:

Ms. V: So, it (the book) talks about that when you see something that you have the power . . . so it's like the world needs your voice . . . mine . . . yes, yours . . . so it doesn't need to be perfect but you need to speak out and it basically talks to kids and that's something that I 've done in the past and the focus has been around bullying and not being a bystander . . . by speaking up for something and fairness . . . but I am adding in the race piece in there to have that be an anti-racist.

R: To stand up for racism?

Ms. V: . . . that you are standing up for fairness and equality and equity for everybody . . . right . . . so the idea that I want them to look out for . . . if you see something that's not fair . . . if you see something that is not okay that you speak up about that and in a developmentally appropriate way.

Ms. Verano, as noted in the read aloud chapter, is using certain books as a strategy to connect their previous knowledge of fairness with the inequalities related to the Civil Rights movement. She realizes that children need help connecting this overall concept with racism and forms of oppression. She is also making them aware of how one can respond to unfairness. "If you see an injustice, say something peacefully . . . inspire others to do the same" (Reynolds, 2019, p. 21). She is giving children agency to say something to stand up for what's right, to be heard and listened to. She is advocating for activism in her kindergarten classroom, but on her terms, in a "developmentally appropriate way."

Ms. Maltes, another kindergarten teacher at Baker Street School, also reviews the concept of fairness in relation to her lessons/activities on Dr. Martin Luther King and his activism.

Ms. M: So, around Martin Luther King Junior's birthday we can really talk about his famous speech and what he wanted from the world and then we start thinking about how we might want to make the world a better place and then from there we also look at the concept of fairness and treating people equally or equitably . . . we will look at what it means . . . to treat people better or not allow them access to things based on their skin color or some other defining feature.
R: So, do the terms like racism come up? Intolerance? Prejudice?
Ms. M: They do, but sometimes it is not always the focal point of the lesson . . . we start broaching that . . . whereas, I personally might use those words more in first or second grade but we talk more from the standpoint of inclusion or being fair or unfair or not having access to things.

Once again, Ms. Maltes, similar to the other kindergarten teachers in the study, is starting from the premise of fairness, what is fair or unfair, when teaching about larger issues of discrimination and racism. Like Ms. Verano, she understands the important role that the concept of fairness plays in a young child's mind and uses that to make a connection to the study of Dr. King. Interestingly, she says that even though she uses terms like intolerance and prejudice, she feels that these terms are more appropriate to really delve into later on in first or second grade. She is laying the foundation for these later discussions by making connections to the concept of fairness with inequality related to the Civil Rights movement.

Teaching children the issues related to social justice is crucial to their understandings of activism. They know what is fair and unfair and now they want to speak up about it. They want to make a difference in the world and speak their truths. In order to do this, we must teach children how to be an ally to others. They need to feel so strongly about injustices in the world (including racism) that they want to work toward critically responding and being part of the process to help bring about fairness. Kissinger states, "To be an ally means that you are already familiar with anti-bias or anti-oppression education and that you want to do more. You are willing to step up, speak out, support and challenge yourself and others" (Kissinger, 2017, p. 2). These teacher participants are already allies in the cause of fighting racism, but they feel that may not be enough. They are interested in teaching about allyship and making young children critically examine their own identities as emerging activists. Ms. Fern actively cultivates activism in her classroom and encourages her young students to be allies to causes that are related to issues of social justice.

Ms. F: I like that they get it as a strategy for engagement when something is unfair and it is also literacy wise . . . making signs and posters is right up their alley.
R: So, your book selection is important.
Ms. F: Yeah . . . and my goal is to not like skew them toward the left or whatever . . . my goal is for them to understand their place as citizens in a democracy.

Teaching about citizenship is in the kindergarten standards and therefore is the main objective of these teachers. Yet, they go above and beyond other teachers by incorporating activism and allyship into their curriculum.

In Ms. Verano's kindergarten, she makes it clear that either you are an ally or you are a part of the problem in terms of activism. Since she has a majority white classroom, she believes it is even more crucial to build on concepts related to allyship so that these young white children will speak out against any injustice they encounter. She consistently points out to her class that some white people made a choice to be actively fighting for justice during the Civil Rights movement. And this is crucial in the understanding that white people can be allies in the cause of racial justice.

Ms. V: the idea of white people having to be involved in order to make those changes because if no one . . . if the people that were making the laws weren't listening to black people then they are not going to listen to change those laws . . . that they are only listening when it becomes.
R: When it becomes powerful.
Ms. V: When there is more people involved.

Ms. Verano is talking about white supremacy and that the power is and has always been in white people's hands, as they create and judge what is right or wrong in our society. She is basically saying that white people have no choice but to be involved or else there will be no change in the laws or the actions of the institutional racism that is America. When discussing Martin Luther King and the Civil Rights movement, she talks about how white allyship helped the movement progress. To her, this movement, and or any movement related to issues of social justice can only work if there are more people involved, including members outside of the oppressed group.

Saad defines the term "allyship" as "it is a lifelong process of building relationships based on trust, consistency and accountability with marginalized individuals and/or groups" (Saad, 2020, p. 125). Clearly, if it is a lifelong process it must start young, like in kindergarten. Teaching very young children to be allies, and stand up for what is right is crucial to the growth of a social justice movement. They are becoming more than just good citizens, they are united in a cause of justice and are building a foundation of knowledge that is related to this purpose of righting an injustice in the world. It lends itself to future activism and participation in all issues related to justice. Children need to learn about being good allies and standing up to injustice, as that is really the only way, they will be an active participant in our democracy.

During the 2016 election, Ms. Fern, along with the other participants, talked about the election and the civic duty and responsibility of all citizens to vote. Ms. Fern held a mock election that was emotional and difficult for some of the children.

Ms. F: We did a mock election that year at school and in kindergarten they got pictures . . . and circled the one they were voting for and I literally had kids that . . . we do mock elections all the time . . . you know Obama/McCain was a somewhat big election but not nearly like this . . . I had kids literally fist their pencils and scribble Trump's face out . . . draw little horns and angry eyes on him . . . they were crossing out the one they didn't want . . . it was 100 times . . . They were crossing it out.

R: They were upset?

Ms. F: They were . . . it was really . . . hard . . . a lot of kids voted with their parents . . . a lot of kids were ready to wake up to Hillary Clinton being president and a lot of kid's parents were visibly upset in front of their kids . . . .we did have to talk about it . . . what we always try to come back to is that the grown-ups are here to help you and we live in a democracy and we have systems in place that we are going to hold to make the president accountable (Ms. F. laughs) . . . I say this is as we are in the midst of an impeachment trial.

This scenario illustrates the political trauma that impacts children. Politics is never neutral in the classroom and students, even young ones have thoughts and feelings about political justice. They see this time, the election of 2016, as an unfair or unjust period and they were expressing themselves accordingly. Later, some of these same children were actively involved in protests and marches that directly targeted the new president's policies. They were learning to be activists and allies in the world and wanted their voices to be heard. A colleague of mine documented young children in various protests between

2016 and 2019, in order to show that young children needed the agency to act and be heard. She wrote a paper for AERA (American Educational Research Association conference) and presented it in 2019, showing slide after slide of photographs of children with their own protest signs at different rallies for justice (Peters, 2019). These young children were activists in their own right and were proudly participating in the resistance to discriminating policies during this time period. And the point is that these children's voices matter.

Play and pretend activities are ways that young children explore issues related to fairness and inequality practice. Rosen believes that active pretend play is a political space for young children (Rosen, 2017). It is a space that gives children the freedom and agency to explore issues related to fairness. He states, "Play is not just fun and games but is very 'real' in experiences and effect, and as I will go on to suggest, intricately bound up with questions of the political or indeed the political economy" (Rosen, 2017, p. 4). Play, in this aspect, is seen as a form of activism, a way of being in the world.

Play, according to Rosen, is a way to overturn the status quo (Rosen, 2017). All forms of pretend play can be utilized to be methods of counter-narratives that critically question political spaces/ideas or it can be a space that reinforces and perpetuates stereotypes. Rosen states, "Insights therein provide the basis for rethinking the relationship between play and the political, and even play and activism, given play's possibility for imaginary and enacting new ways of being" (Rosen, 2017, p. 3). Play is a way, a form for children to explore their knowledges of the world, which includes political spaces. Children like to role-play what they see and know about the world around them, including practices of fairness and unfairness. It is their method of agency, free of limitations and constraints, to interpret their worlds. It is how they position themselves in relation to others as well (Rosen, 2017). They are learning through their pretend play. "Playing is learning," as my now nine-year-old always used to say to her second-grade teacher who only gave them limited time to play. Children act out concepts, like fairness and inequalities, in order to better understand them. And this is a part of activism.

At the same time, it is important to note that children need space in order to play. They need time and agency in order to explore different concepts and really delve into their meanings. This is easier to come by in kindergarten classrooms than in higher grades where play is pretty much nonexistent due to the high demands of the core curriculum (Tager, 2017). When I was teaching first grade, over six years ago, I was the only teacher on my grade level that had blocks, Legos, costumes, and other play materials in their classrooms. I actually got most of my materials through the years from other first-grade teachers who felt the pressure to give up time for play for more "instructional time." I remember my principal being upset that I still had a playtime (or center time) in my classroom as it was cutting into my instructional minutes.

Time for pretend play is not valued in early childhood classrooms like it used to be and therefore it is harder for teachers to give children the time and space to explore important concepts, like fairness within play venues.

I believe play is an essential activity for young children in order for them to actively engage with the world and their knowledge of the world. Teaching about activism at an early age lends itself to pretend play. Thus, it is key to discuss this in the higher education classroom as well. Pre-service teachers need to feel that play is essential to a child's learning, otherwise they will cave into the demands of their district and give less time for pretend play. This implicitly effects how we teach activism and fairness in terms of racial equity.

How does this all translate in the higher education classroom? It is important that we empower pre-service teachers with all the possibilities available in teaching social justice issues and activism. There are a variety of ways to include this idea of activism and allyship with new teachers, including the following:

- Role-play different scenarios related to fairness.
- Utilizing persuasive writing.
- Brainstorming ideas to protest within your own college campus.
- Creating protest signs.
- Reenacting important Civil Rights moments.
- Teaching about biases and assumptions.
- Encouraging a child's agency and voice.
- Writing letters to key government officials.
- Modeling units on peace and/or fairness.
- Writing lesson plans that relate to activism/justice issues.

Role play is key in student's understanding of how to present activities related to the concept of activism and social justice. As previously stated, role play helps students to understand the political position of marginalized and discriminated populations of their own future students. Teaching empathy helps them be a better teacher, as they have more understanding of what their students go through in their young lives. Some role-play scenarios could include sit-ins; rallies; lunch counter protests; integrating schools, pools, parks, and other recreation areas; and more. Pre-service teachers need to practice these role-play scenarios so that they can understand how to utilize them in their own classrooms. Some students genuinely like these activities as they need to move about the classroom as well and learn best through bodily kinesthetic activities. It also brings out their creative spirit and is helpful in their thinking about the history of activism.

Ms. Verano utilizes persuasive writing in her kindergarten classroom in order to get children to critically reflect on their own racial identities and allyship to just causes. She does this unit in April because students are just learning how to create their own sentences and it is more developmentally appropriate to write in full sentences toward the end of the year. Before the unit, they focus on protest signs, as it is easier for them to write phrases and use single words to express their feelings about injustice. This helps them to get ready for the persuasive writing unit later on, because they understand that their voice is important and should be a part of a larger conversation. Some of these protest signs included *No More Racism*, *No More Slaves in the World*, and *Please Be Nice to Other People*. They are then ready to write sentences about injustices that mean something to them. For example, in Ms. Broadbent's first-grade class they wrote letters to a publishing house expressing their dismay that there are not enough books that showcase BIPOC children. They had a whole discussion about the injustice of the types of books found in most classrooms and then went through each bin in their own class to sort and classify books about BIPOC children.

In a higher education classroom, I utilize persuasive writing in terms of what my students feel are pressing issues on campus. Writing letters to key government officials can be a great way to combine honing writing skills and encouraging activism with students. They write letters to the president, dean, or provost commenting on issues that directly impact them. For example, I had students who were upset by the racial slurs on campus and wanted the administration to be more active in combatting the racism around them. They asked for more inclusive courses to be required for all students, even outside of the education department. They felt strongly that more exposure to how racism deeply affects BIPOC individuals would help correct the backlash of racist events on our campus.

Creating protest signs is a very simple way for students to understand the importance of doing this within their own classroom. Again, it is critical that you let the students brainstorm the issues of injustice that are important to them first. Have them utilize the popcorn method of calling out their ideas, or have them write an idea on a piece of paper, crumple it up and throw it into a box (or can). Afterward, you can have a student read out all of the crumpled-up ideas and list them on chart paper or whiteboard. From this list, you can have students creatively make their own protest signs, either with paper and markers or cardboard and paint. When they have words and pictures to illustrate their social cause, they can attach their signs to a ruler or long stick. To take this a step further, you can bring the class outside and have them march around campus with their protest signs.

In order to reenact important moments in the Civil Rights movement, it is important to state that this is not just a thing of the past. Protests and marches are happening right now, today, related to racial injustice. As talked about in the chapter on characteristics of an anti-racist educator, it is essential that you, the professor, clarify daily that racism is not a thing of the past. When you are reenacting history you are also reenacting the events of today. Some of these scenarios that can be reenacted, discussed, and or related to writing assignments are the following: sit-ins, lunch counter protests, civil disobedience, entering a school for desegregation, and so on.

Teaching about biases and assumptions will be covered in-depth in the next chapter on reflection, but it is important to keep this in mind when teaching about activism and social justice. Students must be open to critically reflecting on their own biases and assumptions on topics related to race and racism. This is particularly essential in the teaching of activism. If students are not open-minded to issues related to social justice then they will push back on incorporating any type of activism into their classroom community. They may say things like "What does this have to do with teaching 1st grade?" or "This is not developmentally appropriate." However, if they are constantly reflecting on their own biases and assumptions, especially on what a young child can or can't understand at this age then it follows that they will be more inclined to be open about sharing these specific activities in their future classrooms.

Encouraging a child's agency and voice can only happen if you, the professor in the classroom, encourage student agency and voice. Activism can't be encouraged in a room where agency is limited. Thus, it is essential that you share the power in your higher education classroom. The students need to feel that they have agency to explore materials and critically reflect on issues that are presented. Setting them up in small groups and pairs is helpful. This encourages them to share their thoughts without you hovering nearby. If it is a true democratic space where all students are valued and respected, you will have a much easier time modeling and doing different projects related to activism. They need to feel motivated and that comes with giving them some degree of agency. The hard part is qualifying this process, by only giving it at certain times and/or not letting views that differ from you come out in a safe space where they can be reflected on and discussed without judgment. If it is a true safe space, students will feel better about taking on their own agency and sharing their true thoughts on controversial topics.

Every semester I teach Early Childhood Curriculum to seniors in our early childhood program. My job is to prepare them for practicum (student teaching) the following semester. They need to write and teach a 6–8 lesson unit plan that includes a big idea, essential questions, and an instructional sequence, including the implementation of Universal Design for Learning. Most, if not all of my students, have never written this many lesson plans or have taught a whole unit before. They have taught a couple of lessons that were supposed to be in sequence from an earlier course but lacked experience with building and designing their own unit for an early childhood classroom. Therefore, it is always crucial that I model how to effectively create their own unit so they can do their own independently. Their units are expected to include social justice elements so I usually model a second-grade unit on either fairness or peace. Here, as a class, we construct a big idea and an essential question for the unit and then we plan the culminating activity before we go back and brainstorm different possible activities related to these topics. Modeling the process is important to their understanding of how to create their own unit and it helps them to think outside the box when connecting social justice topics/ideas to their unit activities. I believe that "the aim of anti-bias education is inclusion, positive self-esteem for all, empathy and activism in the face of injustice" (Lin et al, 2008, p. 189).

One of the most important parts of being a higher education teacher is to be a good role model. Students look up to their professors to see what is right and what is wrong. They look to us to see what we will stand up for first, before they consider standing up on their own. That is why it is crucial that we are practicing what we preach. We need to talk the talk and walk the walk when it comes to issues related to social justice and racial inequality. In the fall semester of 2017, my education department staged a walk-out protest that was in reaction to the recent racist events campus-wide. There were reported incidents of racial slurs written on dorm room doors and a series of issues related to harassment of BIPOC students in the dining hall. The education department (and others who followed suit) took our classes outside onto the nearby college commons and held a rally that was planned and organized. Each of the education faculty made remarks criticizing the role of the administration's handling of the current racist atmosphere/events. We then turned the microphone over to the education students who spoke their truths and let their voices be heard (especially the BIPOC students) so that all who were present would understand their plight for justice on campus. The administration was treating each racist incident on campus by punishing individuals involved instead of trying to fix the inherent problem of racism within the institution itself. The BIPOC students were not having it, they told stories of despair, wanting to transfer, feeling alone, and generally upset by the lack of support from the college. These were powerful statements, ones that were deeply moving and memorable. It was also activism and a way to give voice to students who were not being seen or taken seriously. Therefore, it is crucial that you support your own department in their quest to support BIPOC students on your own campus.

Freire believes, "Developing cultural consciousness and an understanding that we have the power to transform reality must begin at the earliest stages of education" (Lin et al, 2008, p. 188). This is key to professors of early childhood education. We need to cultivate social justice intelligence. "To be an activist means that you have put working for social justice at the forefront of your lives" (Kissinger, 2017, p. 2). Pre-service teachers need help to see how to do this on their own and we need to be there for them and guide them through a process in which they feel comfortable actively teaching about social justice and activism. This is our responsibility, and our duty as professionals. When discussing sit-ins and other protests during the Civil Rights movement, Gregory states, "They first had to learn how to do it" (Gregory, 2018, p. 80). And that is why we must teach it in our higher education classrooms.

Chapter 9

Critical Reflection on Biases

R: How do you . . . how do you work with families of color in your classroom? I mean how is it different from working with white families in your classroom?

Ms. F: Well, I think I am aware of my own sort of racial Identity . . . or my perceived lack of racial identity.

R: (Interrupts) Actually, that's the next question.

Ms. F: (laughs) Excellent . . . I am jumping ahead.

R: Describe your reflection of your own racial identity and how this impacts your teaching.

Ms. F: So . . . yeah, clearly, I am a white woman and I present to the world . . . you know as white . . . I receive white privilege . . . um I live in a town where lots of people have that privilege . . . lots of people have that "woke" awareness.

R: Liberals.

Ms. F: Yeah, you know I live in a great place where there is lots of great dialogue and discussion but then . . . you know . . . and this has come up in my class . . . from kids that even though we live in this great town where we talk about these things . . . where are the families of color? Where are the people? . . . like I mean I think five year olds recognize that.

R: So, they say that to you?

Ms. F: They did.

R: Where are the families of color?

Ms. F: They will . . . last year a student in my class . . . um got upset . . . Got like physically upset . . . was crying . . . and you know when I talked to him about what was going on for him he said, "It's Just really hard because" I think he recognized that

R: (interrupts) That there is nobody looking like him?

Ms. F: Nobody looking like me and my family and that's hard.

R: So . . . let's go back to your own personal racial identity . . . when did you realize that you were white and had white privilege?

> Ms. F: *I don't think I understood the concepts of power, privilege and oppression until much later . . . until I was older and kinda did reading and got this idea . . . but I think when you are young, in school . . . and you are in a community where there is not a lot of kids of color . . . and the kids of color that are there are often kids who are having behavior problems or are targeted as such . . . I remember those experiences very clearly . . . they were always getting yelled at . . . the ones going to the principals . . . it made me uncomfortable I remember feeling uncomfortable and I don't know . . . you are like at this age . . . naturally inclined to wanting justice and fairness so I think as soon as somebody (an English teacher) planted that seed of we create others to maintain power structures . . . it was sort of like oh . . . I don't know that I would have had the words to say that back then . . . it was just this is so wrong . . . this is so unfair . . . I remember she (the teacher) had us journal as we read books and I can remember writing in my journal about how upset I was . . . um . . . like a betrayal or something to learn these things about the world and these people I cared about.*
>
> R: *How does this impact your teaching?*
>
> Ms. F: *Well I think an awareness I guess is probably the biggest impact . . . an awareness that . . . I think part of the problem with privilege is there is just this undercurrent that if you keep going about your life receiving things and you don't think anything of it . . . I think when you have an awareness about your own power and privilege you can be more mindful about trying to interrupt some of these systems when they are in place.*

Critical reflection is the ability to look inward and really consider internal biases and assumptions that we as educators bring into our classrooms. In this chapter, I will examine how and why critical reflection as a practice is essential to preparing Anti-Racist pre-service early childhood educators. Key researchers in the field believe that critical reflective practice, which includes examining and uncovering one's own biases, is the only way to move forward in combatting racism in schools (DiAngelo, 2010; Jewell, 2020; Lawrence and Tatum, 1998; Lin et al, 2018). Jewell, an educator and author in this region, states, "Everyone has prejudices or bias . . . some of our prejudices are conscious and some are not" (Jewell, 2020, p. 33). It is important to note that this fact has to be accepted as true by a person before he/she can unpack their own biases and assumptions. Therefore, it is paramount that early childhood professors utilize the practice of critical reflection in their classrooms. Later on, I will specifically discuss how to implement this in the higher education classroom in a very intentional way. But first, we will examine why this practice is essential to the future of Anti-Racist pedagogy and we will also examine the concepts of White Savior Industrial Complex, racial identity, and racial humility.

There are several reasons why we, as early childhood, educators need to practice critical reflection, look inward, and unpack our own biases and assumptions. The main reason is society itself. We are, like everybody else, a product of the society we live in (Lea & Helfand, 2004; Maxwell, 2004). Thus, what we read in books/newspapers/magazines, view in the media, and see in everyday life affects how we perceive others. Di Angelo firmly states that "all people have prejudice; it is not possible to avoid absorbing misinformation circulating in the culture about social groups" (DiAngelo, 2010, p. 5). DiAngelo believes that all humans possess some forms of bias (DiAngelo, 2018). On the first day of my classes, I start with this premise, we all have biases and assumptions. It is a given. Now we must spend the semester unpacking these biases in order to be a more conscious and intentional educator. It is important to note here that there is always some pushback on this idea within my classes, as many young white women (who are in the majority in teacher preparation programs) have a very singular view and don't always want to admit to some or any personal bias. This has to be handled effectively within the classroom (see the section on higher education at the end of this chapter). No one has actually revealed this to them before, and they are afraid that self-examination will cause them personal discomfort (Gay & Kirkland, 2003). These white students, and white people in general, do not want to confront the possibility that they are part of the problem.

The true concern is that white pre-service teachers do not believe that there is even an actual problem (Segall & Garret, 2013). Racism does not affect them (or so they believe) and therefore why should it be discussed? Saad makes a great point when she writes, "But not looking at something does not mean it does not exist. And in fact, it is an expression of white privilege itself to choose not to look at it" (Saad, 2020, p. 38). I remember one former student of mine who insisted to me and our class that the problem was actually talking about race and racism and that if we did not discuss it then there would be no real problem in the classroom. This kind of logic just does not make sense. Racism and prejudice exist. If you do not talk about it at all, it still exists. It is actually a very bizarre argument and one that is used by white people to deflect and in turn gaslight others (Saad, 2020).

White Saviorism is not new, in actuality it has been a big part of our American culture for a long time now. Just look at the movies. Some of the biggest hits and award winners over the years involve white characters who help or save BIPOC people from their "inferior lives." This includes films like *The Blind Side, The Help, Dangerous Minds, Driving Miss Daisy,* and so on. Saad refers to this as an attempt to help white guilt (Saad, 2020). According to her, the concept of White Saviorism is patronizing and is a form of continued colonization (Saad, 2020). This is so common within our society that we don't always recognize it as a problem. For example, at my university, the website is full of pictures of white students involved in some kind of peaceful work in foreign "underdeveloped" countries. This means that there are continual displays of white people helping brown people in their own lands.

Teju Cole coined the term "White Saviorism" in 2012, specifically looking at how white people used their images with brown people in foreign countries to show that they are "good" white people (Aronson, 2017). According to Aronson, these white people are rewarded for saving others from themselves (Aronson, 2017). This complex has been co-opted by white teachers, here, in America, teaching in predominately BIPOC schools. "The white savior narrative is indoctrinated in many of our pre-service teachers and educators who remain a predominately white and female teaching force" (Aronson, 2017, p. 3). Oftentimes in my classes, white students say that they want to give back to inner-city school children and help them, which on first glance is a nice thought, but they do not understand the white savior complex and the deficit discourse that it entails. They want to see themselves as heroes, helping those who are suffering under the weight of poverty and food scarcity. These white females see it as a mission, a way to carry out good work and services to others that are deficient. This feeds into a deficit construct that empowers white supremacy. It is the false narrative that brown-skinned people need saving by white people (Aronson, 2017). "How do we get them (white teachers) to see that saviorism is racist in and of itself?" (Aronson, 2017, p. 18). It reveals the underlying assumption that white teachers have that brown-skinned children need to be saved from their own so-called deficient lives and families.

This relates to the Theory of Cultural Deprivation, created and subscribed to in the 1960s, that later became the narrative for discourses on the "at risk" student and the concept of the "achievement gap." It continues the theme that BIPOC students are inadequate and do not compare to that of white students (Pennington, 2007). "Black children are also often pitied in the white imagination, with white people wanting to 'save' them, whether from their own blackness, from their black parents" (Saad, 2020, p. 102). Randolph believes that white teachers intentionally or unintentionally are trying to save BIPOC students from their own environments (Randolph, 2013). It is important that we, as higher education professors, be clear about the deficit effects of this complex and that we encourage our white students to critically examine this notion in their everyday practices.

This relates to the concept of racial identity. Most white people, including pre-service white female educators, do not consider their own racial identity at all. Actually, they have never thought about it or reflected on their racial identity before being asked about it in a higher education setting. They have never been confronted about their race, asked to explain about their backgrounds, as they are part of the dominant structure of white supremacy. Most of my students hail from segregated white neighborhoods/townships and have had very little interaction with BIPOC populations in general, so it is not surprising that they are unaware of race and the power dynamics involved. It is important to note that their lack of understanding about race and their own racial identity is a major factor in maintaining white supremacy. "White denial of ourselves as socialized group members, deeply affected by images and discourses that circulate in the culture, is also necessary to hold domination in place, for it ensures that these discourse will remain unexamined" (DiAngelo, 2010, p. 12). This means that it is not in their best interest to examine and reflect on their own racial identity as it will just cause them discomfort and will force them to face their own privilege in society. BIPOC people, on the other hand, have no choice, but to examine their racial identity as they are constantly reminded of it, just being in the world. For example, my wife is constantly being followed in stores, because she is black and yet, I have never been followed around or racially profiled for the possibility of shoplifting. This is called shopping while black, or there is driving while black, hailing a taxi while black, and so on. Thus, BIPOC people are confronted with the difference and deficit views of their race daily. My white female pre-service teachers have never had to look at their own racial identity and that is white privilege in of itself. "When white adults have not thought about their own racial identity, it is difficult for them to respond to the identity development needs of either white children or children of color" (Tatum, 2017, p. 37).

In Ms. Verano's interviews, she reflects on her own racial identity and her discomfort with it, which evolves over the course of this research project. When I first interviewed her, she was more uncomfortable, as it was clear that this was one of the first times someone asked her about her racial identity. Here is a discussion we had on multicultural education and Anti-Racist practices.

Ms. V: And I feel like my own tendency was towards Anti-Racist work or I should say anti-bigotry . . . I guess because it wasn't necessarily about . . . it wasn't necessarily about race per say and I still have a problem with the term race I think (laughs a bit) and I don't know if.

R: (interrupts) What is your problem with the term?

Ms. V: Because I feel like people . . . I feel like the shade or the tone or shade of our skin whether it's dark or light does not make us a different race . . . I feel like we are all . . . like I think of race as a species . . . I feel like we are all humans.

R: But that would work but our society has constructed this notion.

Ms. V: Correct.

R: of race.

Ms. V: Yes . . . right that's upsetting to me (laughs).

R: So, it exists.

Ms. V: It does exist and I don't mean to say it doesn't exist . . . I feel like in my own cognition . . . in thinking about it . . . it inherently bothers me because I feel like that makes it as if this is a different part of a human . . . like a different kind of human . . . if you are a different race . . . It's almost like.

R: But there are hierarchy of races.

Ms. V: Right that's true . . . but is it . . . should it be called white supremacy?

R: Yes, you can call it that.

Here, you see that this white teacher is uncovering some of her own discomfort on the topic of race and espouses color-blind discourse without even realizing it. This is par for the course in the beginning of discussions on racial identity. Later in the same interview, she discusses, for one of the first times, her thoughts on her own racial identity.

Ms. V: So, my family is Sicilian from Italy and we have . . . some Sicilian and Calabrese. . . . My aunt is very dark . . . her skin tone . . . and her hair is nappy . . . she is darker than me. . . . I will never forget this . . . when we had a birthday party for my dad and you know . . . my extended family . . . they all came to my dad's house for his birthday and my daughter, who was seven at the time, and so this is the first time meeting my aunt and uncle and cousins and their children. . . . So, I was there with my children and they were there with their children and all of them are pretty dark and my daughter said to me, "Mom, I didn't know we were black" and I thought . . . and I was like "Oh, well."

R: What did you say to that?

Ms. V: "What do you mean?" and she was like "well, those are your cousins and that's your aunt and they are black" and I am like "Well they're Sicilian and yeah I guess we are dark . . . I guess it depends on what you mean by black . . . because certainly in the summer I get pretty dark and my family is dark" and that was interesting for me . . . hearing that because I never really thought about it . . . somewhere way back in history . . . the Moors from Africa invaded Sicily and had colonized part of Sicily for a while and so, for me . . . I remember hearing about this as a young kid . . . I feel like I always thought to myself there is definitely some African in there . . . I guess I wouldn't identify as white.

R: But you don't identify as black?

Ms. V: No, I definitely don't . . . correct . . . I do not . . . and if I write it down you know if they ask for your ethnicity, I write Caucasian . . . but for me . . . if you said to me . . . what's your nationality? What's your background? I would say Italian . . . and for me Italian isn't really white . . . like it's almost like . . . white is more eastern European.

This argument is not uncommon for people with strong connections to their ethnic background. Here, Ms. Verano is stating that she does not consider herself white, but instead is Italian. She later goes on to talk about the discrimination her family faced as immigrants coming to America and this makes her feel that she is more Italian than white. To me, this just continues her own thoughts of discomfort on the possible identification of being white. Yet, later she concedes to her own white privilege, so in this interview, her first real foray into discussing her own racial identity, she does not want to be perceived as white. It is interesting to note that my mother, who is currently eighty-four, has also always contended that she is not white but is instead Jewish, which she considers a race. And yet, she is, like Ms. Verano, viewed as a white person, with all the privileges it entails. Later, in the last interview, this perception changes again, after the project and after much outside reading, including the DiAngelo book *White Fragility*. This is important to note as racial identity is not static but develops over time.

In the next interview with Ms. Verano, her thoughts on her racial identity had shifted somewhat.

Ms. V: At the time I was just starting the book (*White Fragility*) and so I hadn't read much of it and we hadn't had any meetings yet and in between the time of that interview and when I got the transcript of the interview I had read part of the book and already had one of the group meetings and so it was interesting to me because I realized that in my interview and in my own thinking that I had a lot of the . . . I had some of the characteristics that DiAngelo is talking about in her book when it comes to identifying oneself as white and because in my interview . . . and I remember you asking me about how I identified and I said I identified as Italian . . . and like she literally pretty much quoted my own experience or my own thoughts in her book as being a problem for white people . . . she refers to people saying "when my people came here they were discriminate against as Italians" which is partially somewhat true . . . but that's not my own. . . . Like I don't in anyway deny my own privilege in that . . . but the fact that my first instinct is not to say I'm white . . . my first instinct is to say I am an Italian from New York . . . by me saying I am Italian or in somehow in not identifying as white I am perpetuating that bias that is in society . . . I am perpetuating my own privilege . . . and that is a problem . . . and it is something I want to learn more about and I want to continue the conversation and continue talking with POC so that they can educate from their perspective . . . because it is something that I can try to understand . . . I feel like I have to consciously work at that and it really opened my eyes.

As you can see, the process of unpacking and examining your racial identity is ongoing and evolves over time. Thus, it is critical to engage in discussions of racial identity early on in one's life so that a person can continually reflect on it and see how it affects their own world views. Therefore, it is essential that the first or introductory phase of this critical reflection process happens within the higher education classroom, otherwise young teachers are entering into the teaching force without even considering or reflecting on their own biases. This, in turn, effects how they interact with BIPOC students and how they present materials and/or create activities in their classrooms.

How can we effectively and efficiently engage in discussions on racial identity and critical reflection of our own biases and assumptions in the higher education classroom? In this section, I will examine a variety of methods/strategies that can help pre-service teachers to critically think about themselves, so that they can become more aware and understanding of what they need to work on as a teacher in training. Cornell West states, "I care about you and your formation and need to unsettle each and every one of you" (West, 2020). Caring about our students is the first step. Unsettling them is the next and less obvious step toward the transformation of the reflective process. I always say to my classes that I want them to feel some discomfort, some uneasiness during our discussions on race, otherwise they are not actually involved in the critical reflection process. Being unsettled, as viewed earlier, in some of the interviews with participants, is crucial to understanding our views of the world. These views and perceptions greatly impact our teaching. If the teacher is not aware of their own biases and assumptions in terms of race, privilege, and oppression then they are unwittingly involved in the perpetuation of white supremacy and institutional racism. Therefore, encouraging open dialogues on racial identity is essential in the higher education class.

The following ideas will hopefully help higher education professors utilize critical reflective practices in their classrooms:

- Using open dialogues.
- Creating safe spaces.
- Adding language on critical reflection on biases and assumptions into your syllabi.
- Requiring journal entries on racial identity awareness.
- Teaching empathy.
- Giving space for development of racial humility.
- Disrupting discourses on deficit constructs.
- Having them reflect on videos related to examining biases.
- Conducting implicit bias testing.

Having ongoing in-depth discussions on race and our biases and assumptions related to race is critical to transforming awareness. In the beginning of the semester, I set up a safe learning environment that is mutually designed and coconstructed with the students. In the first class, instead of spending a lot of time reviewing the syllabus, we discuss one paragraph in my syllabus:

> Note on biases and assumptions: The Education Department is committed to working on challenging our own biases and assumptions through our coursework. In this class please be prepared to honestly reflect on your own biases and assumptions on race, class, gender, disability and etc. This is an important part of becoming a practicing teacher in the field.

When we discuss this passage, I ask them to come up with rules for our class discussions on critically reflecting on our own biases. They then turn and talk to discuss possible written strategies and then share them with the class. I write down all suggestions and hang them up on experience chart paper so they are visible for the whole semester. This is like setting up rules in the classroom with young children, but it is specifically designed to create an environment of safety so that students feel a bit more comfortable delving into their own biases and assumptions. The given, that is accepted before they design the rules, is that we all have biases and assumptions that we have not yet examined and that they must be explored in order to become a proficient teacher in early childhood. Students need to be prodded into trying to be open about exploring their own biases and they need a safe space to do so. Some of the rules they generate include respecting other people's opinions, being open and honest, and be willing to look at other points of view and more. This really helps them to define how these discussions will work within the classroom. The parameters are set up by them, which helps them to feel a part of the process. It makes them feel more at ease in an uneasy situation and more willing to be vulnerable and reflect on how they think about their own beliefs. In her dissertation on racial identity with Asian teachers, Lee states, "Understanding identity means making sense of positionality" (Lee, 2018, p. 9). If students do not understand their positionality in a given conversation, especially on race, then they will continually be unaware of their own identity and how it affects others.

Facing our own biases and assumptions is essential to any teacher education course, because that is the only way pre-service teachers will be able to grow into Anti-Racist educators. St. Denis and Schick state, "By requiring our students to examine their dominant identifications and the power relations through which they are produced, we see students engage in a difficult but necessary process in challenging the assumptions that normalize and naturalize inequality" (St. Denis and Schick, 2003, p. 67). Open and honest dialogue can only be a part of a classroom environment when the critical reflection process is laid out and defined in the very first-class meeting. This transparency makes it easier for students to accept and to engage in the critical reflection process because it is designed to be a central component of the classroom.

In my courses, I assign online reading responses to articles related to race and racism in early childhood schooling. They have to read the assigned reading and respond to it in a specific way. I give them a rubric that helps them to understand the process of responding to the material that is rated from 1 to 4. It includes

1. Response is vague and does not cover any specifics within the text. It is scattered and unorganized. There is little to no insight or personal connection or reflection on biases.
2. Response covers the main points of the text but does not delve into specifics. It shows a superficial understanding of the text and involves a summary.
3. Response contains references to specifics of the text and uncovers at least one insightful understanding. There is a personal connection that relates to modern-day practices.
4. Response includes insights, deeper understandings of the text. There is a solid connection between the text and personal practices. Included in the response is a critical look at the knowledge presented and an acknowledgment of biases and assumptions on the topic.

I review this rubric carefully with them before their first reading response; however, it usually takes a couple of responses for them to really be able to achieve the highest score. And this is because they are not used to it. No one has ever asked them to make a personal connection to a text that unpacks a bias or assumption they may have. I make sure to give them very specific feedback in their scoring so they understand how to revise it and make it better the next time. The more you review and give examples of biases and assumptions, we all have the more they are able to critically reflect. One example that I use frequently is the assumption some teachers have that boys should not be playing in the dress-up area because of their gender, which reveals gender bias. Another good example of a bias a lot of teachers in training have is that they think multilingual learners are not as capable in the classroom. It is important that you provide many examples and share reading responses from students that really understand how to critically unpack their own biases.

Teaching empathy is a key component in this work. First, it is important to model empathy within the classroom so that they can, in turn, do this in the future with their young children. The other reason it is essential to teach empathy is that it is the heart of where critical reflection lies. Seeing and trying to understand the perspective of others outside of your own race helps you to be more aware of your own biases and assumptions. "The truth is for most of my early life I had too little consciousness about race, and I didn't have any deep personal empathy. It was just the way things were . . . it was just a fact" (Rather, 2019, p. 21). Rather states that examining one's own racial identity or understanding other racial identities relies on the concept of empathy. Empathy is not necessarily understanding how others feel, as white people can never truly understand what BIPOC populations go through on a daily basis. It is more about listening and being made aware of your own biases and thoughts regarding people of other races and trying to delve into unpacking them over time. "It is uncomfortable to be confronted with an aspect of ourselves that we don't like, but we can't change what we refuse to see" (DiAngelo, 2018, p. 42). Rather, who grew up during the Jim Crow era, has a similar answer to the question of biases and assumptions as present-day white pre-service teachers. Not much has changed. He didn't think about race at all, he was not confronted by it nor asked to challenge his own biases growing up. My students, some sixty odd years later have the same issue. They were not asked or taught how to critically reflect on race and how it affects others and themselves. Thus, they don't understand that there is even a problem. Yet, when they walk into the higher education classroom, they lack empathy and understanding, because this is what happens without a foundation of empathy.

In Ms. Houston's kindergarten, she is constantly teaching and reteaching the concept of empathy with her children. She uses her own personal experiences of feeling excluded from gender normatives, as she talks about how she is harassed for looking different than the gender normatives of a woman. Reflecting on this and talking to her kindergartners about it helps her in her own understanding of empathy and how she can empathize with BIPOC.

Ms. H: I mean, there are parallels to whole gender non-conformity and sexual orientation . . . being passable or not.
R: They are social constructs.
Ms. H. All social constructs . . . and so I think that's why I do a lot around that . . . but race is so important cause I guess you can change how you look . . . you shouldn't have to . . . for gender non-conformity . . . you shouldn't have to . . . but I did this with myself when I went to Texas . . . you are going to dress a little more of what is expected of you . . . you can do that . . . but you can't do that with race . . . this project has really caused me to just look harder at what I am doing.

Here, Ms. Houston is modeling empathy, by discussing differences in how people look and present themselves in society and at the same time is gaining a deeper reflection into her own personal biases and assumptions on race. She realizes that although she has no choice in her sexual orientation, she has choices in how she appears to others and can change that appearance to fit in and yet BIPOC cannot change their look in order to fit into a dominant white society.

How can we teach empathy in the classroom? Model first and then do activities related to empathy each week so that over time they are reflecting on empathy and building more skills within it. If you are constantly asking them to write or speak openly on their own biases it helps them to look at their own levels of empathy or lack thereof. Role play, which I will go into later, works well in this case, acting out scenarios in small groups, and having others critique them. You can also utilize the fishbowl technique, where one small group acts out a scenario related to empathy in the classroom and the other students gather around to view it, as if looking at a fishbowl.

Another important issue to examine in our quest for critical reflection on our own biases and assumptions related to race and racism is racial humility. DiAngelo and others believe that racial humility is essential to confronting white pre-service teachers' biases and assumptions (DiAngelo, 2010; Saad, 2020). In higher education classrooms, it is important to stress racial humility and to provide space within classroom discussions for students to practice it. They are so used to their own privileges that they don't even question it. Having humility is a part of critical reflection, as the person undergoing it is constantly thinking about how they can better themselves and their everyday practices. We want our students to consider other points of view, even if they make them uncomfortable because that is how they confront bias. What we don't want is pre-service teachers to go into their practice without being aware of their own biases. This lacks humility and critical reflection. Racial humility can only be practiced through the process of critical reflection. And this is very important as we cannot grow and learn more about ourselves and who we are in this world without humility. Being open-minded and willing to take a long hard look at oneself is the key to making this happen.

White privilege is a major part of why white students resist examining their biases and assumptions. First of all, they don't want to be considered racist or biased in any way, because this makes them a bad person in their eyes. Yet, they also don't want to believe that they receive special treatment, because that would tear down their notions of color-blind discourses, that we are all treated the same. It is not uncommon for a white student to feel or react in a fragile manner when trying to discuss their own white privilege. Many students want to believe in meritocracy and the power of the individual, so that they can continue to reap the benefits of white privilege and not challenge their own thinking or lack of awareness.

In the classroom, it is important that the professor calls out white privilege on an ongoing basis. Just calling attention to it, from my own experiences, helps the students understand how it operates in the world. For example, I will explain my privileges as a white teacher or parent, alluding to times where I can effectively navigate and negotiate services for my daughter who is learning disabled or when I have responded differently to concerns from BIPOC families and white families. I talk to them about my privilege as compared to my black wife and biracial children and how it is easier for me to be in the world. Sharing these stories and experiences helps them to understand better, as they are real-life situations and examples of how I benefit from my white privilege. Since the majority of higher education faculty are white (over 77 percent), then it should be easy for them to disclose their own privilege and relate experiences that they have had that have been favorable (Picower, 2021).

Some of the skills that will help you with this transformative process of critical reflection include role play. Role play is a useful tool in teaching critical reflection and awareness of biases and assumptions. Again, like empathy, it should be modeled in the higher education classroom and then practiced throughout the semester. Role play can develop cultural competence (Lin et al., 2008) and that is exactly what is needed with young white students who have never before given thought to their own racial identity or to their own biases. It is also key in the teaching of empathy, as demonstrated earlier. "Role play provides opportunities for teacher candidates to develop a better understanding of how other person might think or feel" (Lin, et al., 2008). Sadly, most college professors do not do a lot of role play in their classrooms, but in early childhood it is a key method that works well and should be utilized often. For example, you could act out real scenarios that students brainstorm from their own lives. Generating a list would be helpful. The list could include scenarios such as having only one BIPOC student in their classroom and how the teacher relates to that student, students sitting at their own lunch tables segregated by race, having conversations with their parents about treating all people the same (while living in all-white neighborhoods), going to history class in high school and not learning any black history or learning about important BIPOC. All of these scenarios and others are directly from my student's own personal upbringings. Through constant critical reflection, they are able to examine and unpack scenarios that they never even thought twice about before and this is essential for their growth.

Drama can and should be utilized in the classroom as it also represents teaching multiple intelligences, a theory by Howard Gardner. Young adults, like children, have different learning styles and focusing on bodily kinesthetic activities, where they are getting up and moving around is really helpful in higher education classrooms for absorbing content. Sometimes they are shy when it comes to performance, so it is important not to force it upon them often, but some students really have a better understanding about content when they are acting it out. Sometimes you can provide scenarios, like the following:

- You are the teacher in a parent-teacher conference and a parent complains about another young child in the class trying to wash off his child's dark skin and saying mean things about his dark complexion.
- You are a teacher in a conference with a parent/child and principal as the black parent is unhappy with how much you are punishing his child in the classroom.
- You are a parent who is upset about your child (a boy) who is wearing tiaras at school and playing princess.
- You are a teacher who is having trouble with a black girl in your class who you feel is constantly rolling her eyes at you and you feel is disrespectful.

You can also have the students create their own scenarios, but this takes practice, as you do not want them to act out anything offensive or racially insensitive. You must review all scenarios before they are acted out to make sure they are not just perpetuating stereotypes. Then after the role play, it is important to critically reflect on each scenario. How would you respond differently if you were the teacher? Parent? Principal? Child? Have students ask questions about the scenario, possibly write about it and then examine their own thinking on the situation. All of this preparation helps the student to more critically reflect on their own biases and assumptions and it also effectively teaches them how to utilize role play in their future classes.

Call outs and call ins are another effective tool for this topic (Saad, 2020). Professors need to decide at a specific moment and time in a given class discussion whether they should call out a student or call in a student. It is important to feel comfortable doing either/or at any moment in time. Call outs are essential for overall student understanding but should be utilized carefully. White students can be very defensive and part of their privilege is feeling uncomfortable when being called out. Yet, it is crucial, especially when there are BIPOC students who call out things that are deemed unacceptable in this process. An example of this is something that I do on a regular basis. Many of my white students use inappropriate words in the classroom and it is important that other students hear your call out on this. Some of the following words have been used in my classroom: colored people, at risk students, culturally deprived students, oriental students, and more. Students need to know what is acceptable language to utilize and what is not so it is important you call them out on it continually. You also want to call out misconceptions, stereotypes, and other languages that if not called out will continually stay in their discourses. For example, "We are all the same" or "I don't care if the child is blue or purple, I treat them the same." It is also important to note here, never put a BIPOC student on the spot, as if they can explain everything you need to know about their race. This is called "emotional labor tokenism" and puts the burden on the one or two BIPOC students in the classroom (Saad, 2020).

Call ins are when a professor or teacher waits until later to talk to the student privately. This can also be done through written feedback while grading critical reflections of students. This works well when someone, perhaps unwittingly, says something that reveals bias. You address it briefly in class but then call it in later when you speak to them in private. This, be warned, can lead to tears, as whites can be very fragile and emotional when confronted in private.

Critical reflection is essential in the process of becoming an Anti-Racist early childhood educator. Students that practice this will be better overall teachers. It is important to note that most states require proficiency in critical reflection of student teachers, although it is usually in terms of how their lessons went and what they could improve on. A good program supervisor (who grades/observes student teachers) should also be looking for critical reflection as related to biases and assumptions. This should be a part of the grade. How can you effectively grade a student teacher without examining their own critical reflection process? This should also be an important part of the philosophy of your education department, otherwise students are getting mixed messages in different courses, which leads to less critical reflection on the whole. In my department, we have worked hard to change the language of the syllabi so that it includes critically reflecting on one's biases and belief systems. We also have included it in our five educational pillars which drive all of our courses. An example of this is:

Reflective Practice: Critically self-reflect on own biases and assumptions to guide and change your practice.
How does critical reflection on our biases and assumptions become a habit of mind?

This is directly in the syllabus and is discussed in each education classroom. It should become a habit of mind for all students, so that they are more prepared to enter their future classrooms.

Cornell West, who recently came and spoke to a packed house at my university, talked about critical reflection eloquently when he said that biases must be reflected on, in order to die within a person so that the person can live (West, 2020). This concept had a great impact on my students as they then thought about biases, and the unpacking of one's biases is essential to their future living. The biases must die so that you can live. A powerful theory, one that needs to be explored in every higher education classroom.

Chapter 10

Dealing with Administrators and Parents

Ms. A: *Okay, I had this awful experience . . . I had an interview in . . . (white suburb) and you know it?*
R: *Yes, I do.*
Ms. A: *And so I was excitedly telling them about this unit I teach (on the Civil Rights Movement) and the principal . . . who by the way has won all sorts of awards and everyone thinks she is so great except maybe me . . . um . . . she said to me in the interview "well, you know . . . (her district) is a very different community than . . . (nearby inner city district where Ms. A used to work)." And I wish that I had the confidence to . . . what was going through my head which was Yeah, I think that . . . (suburb) is exactly where this needs to be taught . . . more so than (inner city district) . . . Actually but I didn't say that but I knew I wouldn't take the job . . . I left the interview and I called . . . (her partner) and I said honestly they could offer me anything and there is no way I will work at this school.*
R: *That's a very white district.*
Ms. A: *But also, that attitude is not okay . . . and then I went to my interview at Packard (her school) and I actually told them in my interview what had happened and I said that I am very passionate about this unit (on Civil rights). It's really meaningful to me and they were much more excited about it . . . so I was like, yeah . . . this is . . . also white . . . but.*

Ms. Alice, who had been teaching first grade for years actually was looking for a new job in another district that was open to her units on Anti-Racist pedagogy. To her, it was important that the principal and the administration were on board with her ideas on teaching her well-designed Civil Rights unit. She had a bad feeling in an interview with a renowned principal in the area, just because her unit was dismissed as not important to that district's agenda.

Husband believes that engaging and discussing Anti-Racist pedagogy to certain administrators can have a negative impact and thus deter teachers from moving forward with this work (Husband, 2010). In this case, Ms. Alice just avoided taking a job in a district that did not support her Anti-Racist pedagogy practices.

In this chapter, I will delve into administration and parental response to teachers who are strongly involved in teaching Anti-Racist pedagogy/activities. First, I will explore parental support systems and then go into how parents can sometimes pushback on this work, in an early childhood setting. I will also discuss the administrators of these specific participants and how they supported or needed to support their work further. At the end of this chapter, I will give specific advice to higher education faculty for ways to incorporate positive partnerships with parents and administration centered around this topic.

Both Ms. Alice and Ms. Fern have reputations as teachers who center their curriculum around Anti-Racist pedagogy. This reputation is positive, in the sense that parents know what to expect when they get to that class level and most are quite happy to get these teachers for their children. In our interview one, Ms. Alice confirms this idea:

Ms. A: The parents kind of know that (she teaches Anti-Racist pedagogy) when they come to second grade . . . and a lot of them will say I am really excited about . . . yeah, they are excited.
R: They are excited that their kid is going to learn all about this.
Ms. A: Yeah.
R: Okay . . . sounds like you have a reputation . . . and it's a good reputation.
Ms. A: I am sure some people don't like it (laughs) Luckily, I haven't had to hear about it . . . I am sure there are some families . . . in their minds . . . were probably not into it but all I have received is appreciation . . . you know parents being really happy that this was happening.

In interview two, Ms. Alice expands on this concept of parental support by stating,

> I have had many parents tell me that it (the Civil Rights unit) has opened up conversations in their households . . . conversations that I strongly believe need to be happening in households with white parents/guardians and white children.

Ms. Alice makes it clear that the majority of her parents actually love her unit based on the Civil Rights and are happy to attend a Civil Rights unit celebration every year. "I have gotten numerous emails of thanks along with one sent to the superintendent of schools," she states. She wasn't sure if she would be as accepted as she was in her previous district and school (majority black) but was very well received in both districts by parents. "In . . . (majority Black school) I worried about being the white teacher, the only white person in the room, teaching black history, but families loved this unit."

Ms. Houston, who also teaches in a predominantly white district, has only received positive parental feedback for her Anti-Racist work. In interview two, she says "I make it a point to really have a good rapport with my families." This is a characteristic that all the teachers in the study displayed, as they intentionally made efforts to build positive relationships with all of their families in their classroom.

Ms. H: I haven't gotten pushback . . . but again I really try to send that message to the parents as well in my newsletters of . . . here's exactly what I am teaching and here's why and here's why this is so important.

R: So, did anybody get upset about how you taught Thanksgiving? (She taught it from indigenous perspective.)

Ms. H: No . . . I got nothing back which I was wondering if I would and I didn't . . . I have gotten . . . with my family of color . . . I did get positive feedback of this directly . . . of the kinds of things that I teach around the holidays . . . it was at an open house . . . early on . . . but I was specifically asked about what I teach around Multi-cultural issues and diversity so I said, yeah . . . Thanksgiving . . . Columbus Day I don't acknowledge what it is for . . . so by the time conferences (parent-teacher) came around in December I got positive feedback from them . . . they really appreciated that.

In this case, her one and only BIPOC family (at the time) was very appreciative of her style of teaching critically around traditional holidays. There are very few BIPOC families in her school and thus, it was important to her to put them at ease and highlight her Anti-Racist approach to the kindergarten curriculum. This is how she garners their support and appreciation.

Ms. Fern, who also has a long-term reputation of being an Anti-Racist educator and is well-liked at the Coltrane School, believes that this is also related to the reputation of her school as a whole.

R: Well, do you have a reputation as a teacher who does this?

Ms. F: I think so.

R: So, a parent knows that if they get you, they are going to expect this? (Anti-Racist work.)

Ms. F: Yeah . . . I think so . . . And I think most of the parents that come here . . . I shouldn't say most of the parents . . . I think a lot of the parents come to this school expecting that . . . from everybody at this school.

R: So, they are excited by that in kindergarten?

Ms. F: Yeah, they are excited by that . . . so . . . they are passionate about that themselves . . . I think we live in an interesting town where you have sort of . . . it is a very white town . . . very politically progressive . . . which is great but then you have this void of People of Color . . . of diversity . . . so I think you have people that want to try and fix things and try to be part of the solution.

In this case, Ms. Fern believes that it goes beyond her own personal reputation as a teacher who is passionate about this work, and instead is about the positive expectations of the white progressive parents. They are eager to have their children learn about race and racism and therefore have specifically selected this school for their child (there are five schools to choose from in this district). Ms. Maltes, also a kindergarten teacher at Baker Street, in this same district, agrees with Ms. Fern's theory. She also states that parents are looking for and expecting discussions on diversity and race in her classroom.

Ms. M: I think it is sort of understood or easily accepted that affirming racial identity would be a part of our classroom conversation . . . I have only worked in early childhood where there is a high expectation that you include . . . um . . . diverse . . . for lack of a better word . . . especially in play areas . . . I haven't run into people with strong white nationalist identities that I have had pushback but I have also been pretty careful and fortunate to choose communities that are progressive.

Ms. Maltes, like Ms. Fern, is referring to community parental support, one that comes from being in a progressive community. Ms. Maltes believes that parental support is part of the expectation for her to cover the exploration of racial identity with her young children. The expectation of her families is that she will include discussions on diversity, race, and racism. They both feel that this is important in their continuation of this work as the expectation from the community propels them even farther in this work.

Ms. Verano, also a kindergarten teacher at Longwood, in this same district, feels lucky that she has always received parental support for her Anti-Racist work in her classroom. In interview two when asked about parental pushback, she states,

Ms. V: No, and I feel really lucky for that . . . I haven't . . . I have not.
R: Not even in the subtlest of ways?
Ms. V: No. I think that there might have been questions in the sense of wanting information but I always . . . I think that when I explain the parts of the curriculum that they are okay with it . . . and I have never heard anyone say "Oh I don't want you to teach that" . . . you know people may say . . . if there was

questioning about it . . . I tend to present it in a matter of fact way of like this is what we do and nobody has questioned it.

Ms. Verano prides herself on building trust with families at the beginning of the year and continues the process throughout by sending home newsletters, like the others, and keeping them informed of what topics she is teaching in the room. She is a straight shooter, so parents know what to expect. There is no hidden agenda, as it is all out in the open. She thinks that this approach helps prevent any negative feedback from families and keeps them actively engaged and excited by what is occurring in the classroom. Like the other teachers in this study, Ms. Verano believes that good communication and building of trust brings about parental support, for any topic she covers, including Anti-Racist pedagogy.

Sometimes there are issues related to parents and family support when teaching this topic. When I was teaching fifth grade in Brooklyn a long time ago, I ran into some parental pushback related to this work. I was in one of the only truly diverse schools in Brooklyn where half of my children were white and privileged. I was doing a unit on slavery and the historical aspects of it and decided to show sections of the classic mini-series *Roots*. One of my white parents was very upset about this prospect. She contacted me and said she wanted her daughter to opt out of this viewing as she believed she was too innocent and it was not appropriate for her to learn about the horrors of slavery. Mind you this was fifth grade, so I was completely taken aback by this request. I proceeded with the unit and this particular fifth-grade girl had to go work in the hallway every time we showed a section of the mini-series on slavery. What I learned from this episode in my teaching career is that there may be moments of parental pushback that are inevitable, but it is important to proceed anyway. I believe that a teacher must be true to who they are as a teacher, and I was a teacher who valued telling differing perspectives of history. I still feel that it is important to be on the right side of history as a teacher and as a scholar. And in this specific case, the right thing to do was to teach about the horrors of slavery so that history does not continually repeat itself and so that my students fully understood oppression and the marginalization and dehumanization that perpetuates racism and white supremacy in this nation.

In Ms. Fern's kindergarten, she has encountered several incidents of parental pushback, but she has held firm in her beliefs and commitment to her Anti-Racist work. When discussing one father's strong reaction to her approach to teaching about good citizenship she stated,

> I think he thought I was too far left and that was going to influence the things I was going to present to them . . . and I wasn't . . . I never presented anything

or said anything about Trump . . . what I ended up saying to him was you know . . . the anger that he sounds like when he speaks on the radio or the news . . . kids feel that . . . even if they have no idea what he is talking about . . . they are scared of him and they identify him as a bully . . . we did a mock election that year at school and they got pictures . . . and circle the one they are voting for and I literally had kids fist their pencils and scribble Trump's face out . . . draw little horns.

Here, Ms. Fern is pushing back on a father's comments on her "left" policies and thoughts on what makes a good citizen. The important thing for her was that she be clear that she is not trying to indoctrinate children but is instead trying to encourage them to be a part of the democratic process and care about other citizens. This dynamic, including her focus on teaching activism to young children, as noted in chapter 8, reveals her commitment to racial justice. She knows that children are understanding more about the world around them than even their parents think, including how the president of the United States comes across as a bully and seems angry most of the time. A lot of parents have this strange notion that teachers may be indoctrinating their children by literally teaching them who to politically align with and so on, but this is far from the truth, as young children are more aware of what is going on than we think. They are interested in justice and fairness and that is what teachers, like the ones in this study, are focused on, and this is a big part of racial injustice work. Ms. Fern states, "what we always try to come back to is that the grown-ups are here to help you and we live in a democracy and we have systems in place that we are going to hold to make the president accountable." Ironically, she is saying this in the midst of an impeachment trial of the forty-fifth president of the United States.

In another instance, Ms. Fern received negative feedback from a parent related to a poster she had displayed on her door.

I had a poster hanging on my door that was maybe like a "we all belong here . . . everyone is welcome" sort of poster . . . and those were the big words and the poster was distributed by Move On (an organization that is liberal) . . . so that meant that I was 'left' and in all honesty I had no idea it was a Move On poster . . . I told him . . . I said I can honestly tell you that the little Move On symbol on the page was not what I was wanting anyone to notice or focus on . . . it was the "Everyone is welcome here" . . . and he was actually willing to reach a compromise with me that if I cut off the Move On tag that I could leave the sign . . . that is eventually where our conversations got . . . that I want the children in the class to get that this value of we are all welcome here . . . he agreed that was what he wanted as well but he thinks the talk about politics should be out of school so we did have some moments about agreeing to disagree.

Interestingly, later that same year, this same father made a stink about her Black Lives Matter sign, where again he believed it to be too political for a kindergarten classroom, and once again they agreed to disagree. It is important to note that this father was white and although he did not like her to display anything related to politics in her classroom, he was not classifying himself as a conservative. Again, like the experience I had with supposedly very liberal white parents who did not want their child to learn about the horrors of slavery, these are white parents asserting their privilege and their discomfort on topics that need to be reflected on. This is clearly on display currently in many states as white families testify against teaching of Critical Race Theory in their school districts. This national debate is not really on Critical Race Theory but instead is focused on teaching about truth and history related to racism.

In Ms. Verano's and Ms. Houston's kindergarten, they have not had any direct negative pushback from parents, as of the date of this writing, but were clearly ready to address it if needed. In Ms. Verano's second interview, she described a time when she thought she may get negative parental feedback from one of her lessons, but she did not. She was reading about Martin Luther King's assassination and the children were visibly upset about the event.

> So I was prepared . . . I thought in my head and I basically thought that if somebody (a parent) questioned me about it I would just say I think that it is important in our Anti-Racist education . . . that it is important for us to know that many times black leaders are often injured or in this case killed because of the work that they did . . . and I feel like when I present it that this is just the way it is . . . that I think parents respond to that because I am lucky that I have their respect so when I say something . . . I do think that I build that trust.

Ms. Verano made it very clear in this instance that she was expecting many emails from parents questioning why she read and discussed the violent assassination of Dr. King, but she did not receive any pushback. She was, however, prepared for how to respond if needed. She had critically reflected on the lesson and how it had impacted her students, as they were very emotional and shocked by the assassination of a well-known historical figure, and yet she was convinced that it was best to tell her students the full truth. Therefore, she stood by her decision to tell them the entire story, as opposed to a sanitized view, of the legacy of Dr. King's life and work.

Ms. Houston also had a similar response to this question of parental pushback.

R: Well, what would you do if a parent did complain to you? About this? Say they emailed you about the way you are teaching the Civil Rights Movement and they think they are too young to learn about this?

Ms. H: If that happened, I would be honest . . . I would say that this is a very important part of history and it is still very relevant and I am sorry that he/she felt that way (laughs) but this is important.

Ms. Houston's approach, similar to the others in the study, is that as a teacher it is critical to be true to the facts, to the history of what really happened and is happening here in the United States. There is no sugar coating it. To her, children deserve the truth and she could care less if it is offensive to teach the truths about racial inequality and our white supremacist history. She feels that even if a parent approached her, she would still continue to learn and grow in this field and continue to teach it throughout her year.

It is important to note here that we, as early childhood educators, can't always steer clear of negative feedback from parents and families. Many students of mine worry about how to respond to parents that give them negative feedback about their lessons and units and this worry is important to address. They need to feel empowered and able to rightfully respond in a genuine and clear way, one that does not further complicate the dynamics of their relationships with their families. Since they are usually in a public school environment, I make it clear to them (through various role plays) that responding honestly is key. They have the right to teach historical truths and social justice topics as every young child has the right to know and understand the world they live in. A public school is a space where teachers have an obligation to teach the truth, even if it includes topics we may feel uncomfortable teaching.

Having a supportive administration is very helpful when teaching Anti-Racist pedagogy with young children. Early childhood educators proceed in this avenue with or without support from their administrators but it is much harder without their encouragement and backing. Getting an administrator that has your back and wants you to do your own thing is a tall order. I have had many different principals over the years and some have been more supportive than others. Some I built fantastic mutual relationships with that helped me as a teacher with my classroom and yet others were actually thorns in my side. My last principal, in fact, was one of those administrators that professed support and concern but whose actions said otherwise, another common practice among principals and vice principals. Like teachers have two sets of lesson plans, one for the administrator to review when they randomly entered the classroom and one that teachers actually follow, administrators could present as supportive and encouraging but in the end are neither. My final principal was a frustrated actor, who did not want to be a principal, but instead went to many auditions in nearby New York and tried to guilt his teachers into coming to his productions. He was of Latino descent and therefore everyone assumed he was supportive of Anti-Racist pedagogy and teachers who believed in these practices, but he was not. On many occasions, I would have heated debates with him about play and the importance of teaching multicultural education and Anti-Racist pedagogy to young children. He was a bottom-line guy, you either got the part in the production or you did not. Similarly, he was more interested in instructional minutes that prepared children for standardized testing than in teaching issues of social justice.

In Texas, there was a research study on how administrators responded to teachers actively teaching Anti-Racist pedagogy and other multicultural topics. This study included four different districts, including some schools that refused to relinquish their data (Khalifa & Briscoe, 2015). The findings revealed that these administrators responded in the following ways:

- Avoidance of issue.
- Use of bureaucratic systems.
- Protected their own interests (including testing). (Khalifa & Briscoe, 2015)

As they collected data, including interviewing principals and vice principals they concluded that "educational administrators largely shy away from controversial issues such as discussions of race or racism" (Khalifa & Briscoe, 2015, p. 2). They looked at the data revealing high suspension rates of BIPOC students and compared it to the rising rates of BIPOC in prison. These researchers believed that the problem was deepening and not getting better (Khalifa & Briscoe, 2015). The suspension rates in all four districts showed that 90 percent of all students suspended were Latino. "We found that districts are constantly attempting to challenge, make excuses for or avoid discussion of any racism problems within in their organization" (Khalifa & Briscoe, 2015, p. 17). Part of the problem, they concluded was the overall bureaucracies of the districts, and how they were not practicing culturally responsive pedagogy. BIPOC students in this study were excluded from their own learning, through suspensions, being classified as special education and/or not being heard. The administrators were part of the problem and as such, these districts were not practicing funds of knowledge or any cultural understanding of their different populations of BIPOC students.

Many teachers, like me, and the ones in this study, just close their doors and do their own thing with or without the principal's consent. And yet, this move in itself can be seen as afront and can be detrimental to the teacher's livelihood. Ms. Houston, in interview one, states:

Ms. H: Even in . . . (another town) and . . . (another town) are incredibly regulated and so you have to do certain programs . . . you know same day same page . . . you are expected to create an environment where you are still able to meet the expectations but also providing what you know is developmentally appropriate.

R: You sound like a teacher who thinks outside the box (Ms. H laughs) you close the door and you do what you want to . . . that is what I am hearing.

Ms. H: Asking forgiveness (laughs) I do what I do and I ask for forgiveness later and I can back it up.

R: Who are you asking forgiveness from? From God?

Ms. H: No (laughs) from administration.

Ms. Houston is a known rebel, which is common for teachers that practice Anti-Racist pedagogy. She does what she wants in her kindergarten and asks for forgiveness later. And sometimes she gets it, like in her new school, and sometimes she does not, like in a past school that let her go, even in the face of parent protests.

The teachers in this study continue to do their own thing, regardless of whether they have full support. This takes a strong presence of mind and a feeling of security in your own abilities as a teacher. Ms. Broadbent, in interview one, talks about her own autonomy as a teacher and why this is important:

R: And are you allowed to do anything you want in this school, administration wise?

Ms. B: I want to say yes, because it really feels like that . . . um . . . (Coltrane School) has a reputation of doing it their way . . . but we do follow the curriculum . . . but often are the ones that pilot projects and spearhead new ideas . . . generally not around curriculum . . . more about policy and procedure . . . but I do have a lot of autonomy.

R: That's really good . . . so your administration trusts you.

Ms. B: The current administration really trusts us.

R: Okay, but that's changing.

Ms. B: It's changing (laughs) so we will see.

Here, Ms. Broadbent is referring to her long-term principal's upcoming retirement. She was a huge supporter of Ms. Broadbent and Ms. Fern and their Anti-Racist classrooms and there is concern that she will not have the future support that she needs to continue to commit to her work. Later on, in interview three, which is at least ten months later, she has a new interim principal, a former teacher from her school, who is very supportive of her work.

R: And the other participant in this study (Ms. Fern) said that the new principal was open . . . is open to this work . . . correct?

Ms. B: Yeah . . . like very much . . . like will advocate for us . . . in the district . . . or just building wise to get the kind of training that we want . . . that she feels is necessary . . . we are in good hands there.

Ms. Broadbent's worries of lack of future support are no longer a concern as the new interim principal, who comes from within the school, understands what she and Ms. Fern are trying to accomplish in the early grades and is very encouraging and responsive to their work. It is important to note here that although she finds what she needs in terms of support from her new principal, she is still unsure of the support from the district office.

Ms. B: Well, some things are already happening . . . but not quite enough . . . the district's union already put out an Anti-Racist training . . . that I wasn't able to go to but I am hoping that they are just going to repeat it . . . the district is thinking about adding it into their curriculum but not to the degree that the teachers want. . . . I heard they think one lesson a year will do it.

R: What?

Ms. B: Yeah.

R: That's offensive actually.

Ms. B: It is . . . it came from our current principal . . . interim principal . . . who went to a meeting . . . she went to another meeting to make the point that was not enough . . . and that it was insulting . . . and I just feel like . . . given the current situation of the world . . . well at least here . . . as a topic in education that has just risen to the surface . . . and I feel like opportunities are going to be endless . . . . I hope they are and our union is under negotiations right now for re-opening . . . and one of our things is Professional Development on Anti-Racist education . . . so we are kinda of putting that into our negotiations.

This discussion took place in August of 2020, when all school districts across the country were deciding how to get back to school in the middle of a worldwide pandemic. I think it is interesting that although she is pleased with the advocacy of her interim principal she is not as satisfied with the overall district's support on this topic. She and others at Coltrane School, including Ms. Fern, were not happy about the prospect of teaching the topic one day a year or that the district expected that this was enough time to cover such a complex topic of study.

Ms. Verano, who is in fact the teacher's union leader for the district, also made it clear that the district must be overall more accountable in their practices of supporting Anti-Racist work in early childhood classrooms. She is presently advocating for more professional development district-wide on this topic and has already brought in speakers (remotely) for teachers to learn more on the topic. She also put this work in the teacher's negotiations for returning to work during an unsafe time so that the district could not just dismiss it.

> I feel that the union has a responsibility towards dismantling the systemic racism that is in our schools and so we have a power because of our collective bargaining for the common good, right . . . we have the power in our districts to negotiate things that can help dismantle systemic racism that is within our schools and I think that is a big role of unions everywhere . . . we put an Anti-Racist statement up on our website about our position . . . so I think that is another big piece . . . so I think supporting teachers in their professional development, but also dismantling the systemic racism that is in our schools so things like the school to prison pipeline and having school resource officers in buildings and all of those things that perpetuate racism at the systemic level.

Here, Ms. Verano is making it clear that the teacher's union plays a powerful role in keeping the district level in check in terms of teaching Anti-Racist pedagogy. She is also talking about the larger issue, about the school system, and the district, even in a progressive area, that is actually perpetuating systemic racism. She believes that teachers' unions must advocate for their teachers and their right to continue to do their work on this topic in their field. Honestly, this is the first time I heard this perspective and it was truly powerful. I never considered the union's role in the quest for Anti-Racist pedagogy until this conversation with Ms. Verano, and now I see just how important it is in the transformation of a district and their role in this continued work. Ironically this district prides itself on being progressive and would be aghast to hear a teacher infer that they were perpetuating systemic racism, or that having one day a year marked out as the day you discuss Anti-Racist pedagogy and practices is acceptable. This is much like the culture fairs that take place once a year in certain schools that just continue to perpetuate different stereotypes of certain cultures, giving a tourist viewpoint.

Ms. Fern, on the other hand, is working within the district guidelines to further her knowledge on the topic. She decided, even before I asked her to be a part of the project to have her annual SMARTGOAL be centered on improving her Anti-Racist pedagogy in her classroom. She was actually documenting her progress on working with young children on their acceptance and discovery of their own racial identity. I thought that this was ingenious to work on furthering her own practice in this field by documenting the progress children were encountering while engaging in her Anti-Racist course work. She had full support of the principal, the one that was a long-term advocate and was retiring soon after. It is clear that this would have been harder to do if she did not have the administrations' full support as she had to meet with the principal at least twice on the topic of her SMARTGOAL and show her documented progress as a teacher of Anti-Racist pedagogy. In interview three, the following summer, Ms. Fern discusses her SMARTGOAL for the past year and how it turned out:

R: Wait, didn't you do a SMARTGOAL on this?
Ms. F: Yeah . . . I did.
R: Tell me how that worked out.
Ms. F: Well, you know the SMARTGOAL sort of fizzled a little bit (laughs) . . . what my goal was . . . I was using the kid's artifacts as evidence of their work and growth . . . their development around their racial identity . . . I think at the kindergarten age . . . I think that that piece on identity and community and belonging is sort of where we focused.

Ms. Fern's SMARTGOAL "fizzled out" due to the pandemic and going remote in the spring of that year. Yet, it is important to note that the principal was supportive of her SMARTGOAL and that is why she could pursue it as a way to improve her teaching. In a lot of cases, a principal would not support this SMARTGOAL and would push the teacher to do a more traditional SMARTGOAL centered around how to improve in teaching academic skills such as reading and writing, and math. I had many SMARTGOALS over the years, none of which were on Anti-Racist pedagogy or related as I knew that this would not be formally sanctioned by my principal. Thus, it is a feat in itself that she had a supportive principal, one that not only encouraged her to continue to grow in this area but also completely understood Ms. Fern's need to continue to transform her work. This is true administrative support and is sadly not always the case in the field of early childhood.

The question becomes then how do we, as faculty in higher education programs teach young pre-service teachers how to deal with their administration on this topic of Anti-Racist pedagogy? I think it is very important, first of all, that we make sure to expose them to different possible scenarios of support or lack of support so that they are initially prepared to respond to the administration and their concerns. A good way to do this is to show videos of different situations and how teachers can or should handle them. This could include videos on how to approach administration when encountering issues with students or parents and so on. Role play is another way to get pre-service teachers more comfortable with possible scenarios and encounters with administration. Conducting pretend job interviews is also very helpful as most pre-service teachers are anxious about this and need extra support and guidance. I think modeling the exact same situation that Ms. Alice encountered with the principal who said they don't need to do this work in her school and that it was different than schools in inner cities is a good way to expose pre-service teachers to the possibilities of encountering negative feedback in an interview. How would you respond? Or would you just not consider taking this job as Ms. Alice did? I think building their confidence will help them in these awkward situations. Telling pre-service teachers over and over again to be true to their teaching style and to embrace it in an interview is essential to them finding a school that fits their needs and for them to excel in.

Providing books that highlight teacher's independence and autonomy are important as well. Students need role models to feel as though they can stand up and advocate for themselves, that they have a right to be firm in what they believe and what they want to teach. A good example of this is Mary Cowhey's book *Black Ants and Buddhists* which I use in my Early Childhood Curriculum course. This book empowers students to think outside the curriculum box and bring social justice issues front and center in their classrooms. The title anecdote centers around the children's understandings of ants and whether they should step on them or try to kill them. Ms. Cowhey, the teacher in this scenario, had them spend a great deal of time thinking about this and had them consider a Buddhist approach, which was based on the reverence for all life, including the life of an ant. She brought in books and experts to speak on the topic, introducing Buddhist concepts and thinking to help them understand the importance of honoring life and thinking of other animals in the world (Cowhey, 2004). I find that using this as a text for this early childhood curriculum course helps students to understand that they too can be teachers that are committed to teaching about social justice, that there is a place for them in the traditional public school or nearby early childhood centers.

As higher education faculty, how do we support pre-service teachers in their quest for good working mutual relationships with parents and families? As stated earlier, one of the key characteristics of an effective Anti-Racist educator is to have trusting relationships with families. Mutual trust and utilizing the practices of Funds of Knowledge, which means that teachers treat parents/families as experts and invite them into the classroom to share their wealth of knowledge, is an essential tool within this work. "This approach calls for more parent-centric practices that empower parents in the school's decision-making process and educators will need to view black parents as capable collaborators, advocates and decision-makers" (Allen & White-Smith, 2017, p. 19). An early childhood educator who is dedicated to teaching Anti-Racist pedagogy must be invested in dialogical relationship building with all parents and families. Furthermore, it is important that pre-service teachers feel comfortable relating to all types of families, including BIPOC families. The following are ideas that you can cover in the higher education classroom that will help build mutual relationships of trust with families and therefore make it easier to teach Anti-Racist pedagogy:

- Home visits—walk them through a possible home visit in their future community.
- Explore different possible communication tools (i.e., newsletters, memos, websites, etc.)
- Being transparent with curriculum to families.
- Include families in classroom discussions and events.
- Prepare possible community visits/field trips.
- Actively work within the community.
- Contact different community organizations to see how you can integrate community work with classroom work.

In conclusion, it is important that we, as faculty in teacher education programs, infuse ideas related to both administrative and parental support on our Anti-Racist practices into our own curriculum. Pre-service teachers need to know how to advocate for their continued work on this topic and need to be able to effectively navigate how to interact with both administrators and families within this process.

Chapter 11

Get On Board

Ms. F: *I think that over the course of this year and sort of the unfurling of events in our world... I have been surprised that these findings (this project) are not as common in other people's classrooms... so I think it is surprising to me in general about the differences in work and how hard it is for other folks to understand how to get on board with this happening in their lives... "Oh, okay... you are not all doing this... What's going on?" It is just so interesting to see work you have been doing... and prioritizing... and all of a sudden to see everybody saying "Oh my gosh... we have to get on board with this..." that is interesting to me... It is a compelling time right now to try and make change... and then we have the pandemic... right... where it reveals everything that is inequitable about schools... it is either the opportunity to freak out or wait let's re-envision this and really do some amazing radical change... Well I just hope... like everybody is seeing it and everybody is wanting to engage... I hope that passion and those feelings stay with us and that people will continue this work... I hope more educators feel compelled to raise their own consciousness around these issues and bring this into the classroom more.*

In this final chapter, I will critically examine what it means to *Get On Board*. By this I mean how do we, as higher education faculty, get on board with the ideology of Anti-Racist pedagogy. First, we need to acknowledge that this pedagogy is not new and that it has been around for many years. This idea of nothing new will be examined and highlighted here, as well as the conversation spaces that we need to have within our departments and in the community at large. I will also look at how teachers need to commit to this work and be provided with crucial Anti-Racist professional development workshops that will actually help them move forward in this quest. Furthermore, there will be a discussion on the need for BIPOC early childhood educators, faculty, administrators, and program supervisors. Diversity and inclusion cannot be just buzz words in policy but must be actualized. This will then lead into the topic of solidarity and the need for working together, both white and BIPOC faculty and educators toward the same goal, Anti-Racist pedagogy. Finally, there will be an in-depth look at how we must change and reform our higher education department from within, including policies, practices, groupings, meetings, course structures, and more.

Kendi states that "the only remedy to racist discrimination is Anti-Racist discrimination" (Kendi, 2019, p. 19). We can't work together toward the same goal if we all do not agree with this statement. This is not a new concept in the United States; instead it is as old as our country itself. The problem is that we, as a nation, do not believe that this is a long-standing problem that needs to be addressed. An example of this racist discourse was revealed recently during a reality television host giving a candid interview regarding a white female contestant proudly going to antebellum Southern parties. This host (of a popular dating show) said that there should be no issue with her past, and he defended her social media posts related to confederate flags and Antebellum Southern parties, where societies and fraternities celebrated the Old South. He said that he thought that this would be no big deal in 2018 (when the posts and parties occurred) but that now, because of the heightened awareness of racism it was all of a sudden a problem. The interviewer (who was a black woman) responded that it was never okay to attend these types of parties and that it was never the right thing to do. The white male host went on to state that he didn't want the "woke police" to hurt the reputation of this young white woman. This was so controversial and in the news that the host (who had been with the franchise for twenty years) was asked to take a leave from the show, even after he made a public apology. The comment about the "woke police" is common language nowadays with white Americans as they continue to downplay race and racism as an issue in our society.

In my third interview with Ms. Fern, she talks about her fears that early childhood educators will just read one book on Anti-Racism and be done. She is concerned that the commitment and passion for integrating Anti-Racist pedagogy will fade as times change and issues like Black Lives Matter and police shootings disappear from the front pages of the newspapers.

R: Sounds like you are afraid this is just a trend and that it is a fad that may disappear when people realize, "eh, it is not important anymore."
Ms. F: Yeah, I read a book and good . . . I read *White Fragility* . . . check . . . I am good to go . . . because it is ongoing work and work is hard and it is hard work . . . this is my life too . . . it is not just at school . . . If I learn a new way to teach

addition . . . I might be like . . . "Oh God, this is so annoying . . . I like the old way better." It is not going to impact my life and the life of other people in the same way.

Ms. Fern is making an important point, this is her life's work, and she is worried that other educators are not going to be as committed to this hard work when issues of racial inequality are not flashing in the headlines.

The only way to combat this issue and get everybody on board is to have open and honest conversations about race and racism and how it affects us all. "There is always a chance for conversation—a chance for people to believe that there is hope for the future and a meaning to a struggle" (West, 1993, p. 18). In March of 2020, just days before the pandemic shutdown, the education department at my university sponsored a speaking engagement with Cornell West. He spoke to a crowd of a few thousand (mostly white) and was very well received. Students emailed me weeks later telling me how much his words affected them and how they learned so much from just a 1.5-hour speech. In his speech, he talked about many topics related to race and racism, but one that stood out for me was his candidness about the need for ongoing conversations. Critical conversations regarding race and racism need to occur everywhere, including on college campuses.

The only way to have these important conversations is to create a warm and safe environment, so that people feel a sense of belonging. Spaces for conversations need to be respectful, thoughtful, and vulnerable places. Even with this idea of a safe space, many white people will feel uncomfortable engaging in discussions related to race and racism, and that is okay. Change of ideas and thought start with conversations. Many people do not want to have these conversations but that is all the more reason to have them again and again. If white people are surrounded by these conversations, they will have no choice but to listen and reflect on their own biases and assumptions.

Jewell, an Anti-Racist educator, believes that all teachers should learn to interrupt (Jewell, 2020). Interruption is an important part of the ongoing conversation. People need to be interrupted at times so that they can really examine and reflect on what they are actually saying, especially if the words are harmful. She talks about making the choice of calling someone in (talking to them privately) or calling someone out (in public) (Jewell, 2020). This is a choice that every teacher needs to contemplate. There must be an interruption of some kind otherwise the teacher, whether early childhood or higher education, will be seen as dismissing the topic as not relevant. Silence is the opposite of a conversation and that must not be an option for educators. Jewell states that it is important to call out people when they say harmful things such as "I don't see color" or "I don't think people should use the race card," and so on (Jewell, 2020). This can be hard for most white teachers as they do not necessarily want to confront other people in regard to race. Sometimes, and this has happened to me, white students will cry or get emotional when interrupted, as they think they are being called "racist." This is a distractor and a part of white privilege. It is used to keep the silence. Many white teachers will drop the subject or deliberately not interrupt controversial statements because of these dramatic responses. White people do not want to be called out as racists. Actually, even the most racist people do not agree with this label and do not accept it. "Whether you choose to call someone in or out, know that it will feel messy" (Jewell, 2020, p.114). And this messiness will not end anytime soon, unless we have more and more conversations about race, racism, and Anti-Racism.

Many critical BIPOC scholars have written about how to have conversations about race and racism (Jewell, 2020; Oluo, 2019; Saad, 2020; Tatum, 2017). They agree on some fundamentals that need to be adhered to when the topic emerges within the classroom or any workplace. First, it is important that if you are white you try to decenter your voice and give space for BIPOC students or colleagues a chance to speak. White teachers should not be interrupting BIPOC students within their classrooms. Ms. Fern is a good example of an early childhood educator who does this consistently in her kindergarten classroom. She actively listens to her young BIPOC students and aggressively shuts down any white guilt that presents itself within their conversations. She, along with Ms. Broadbent and others, has created a "dialogical safe space for children" (Husband, 2010, p. 73). This means that the teacher is not talking at the child but with them as they co-construct and make meaning of the topic. "By opening and providing space for students to ask questions or have their assumptions challenged, teachers may also have been implicitly communicating to students that questions about race are acceptable to ask" (Lee, 2018, p. 100).

Another issue that comes up when having these conversations is the need to check yourself, as a white person and be sure not to be a part of "tone policing." This is something that I personally have had to address in my own conversations with others. Sometimes when we are heated, we "tone police" other people (especially, BIPOC). We tell them that we do not like the way they are talking and/or we label them as being overtly angry in our conversation. This is very harmful, and even if it is unintentional can shut down a conversation about race before it even really begins (Saad, 2020). When calling out a student, it is important that you think carefully about how you address them. If you sound righteous about something, or come across as a know it all, then you will have effectively hurt the climate for honest discussion. Humility is important here, especially for white people, in conversations about race, as conversations are about listening too and not just talking. There is a back and forth, a dialogue that must be honored and respected, otherwise it becomes a heated argument and not a conversation. It also will not decenter the white person who is speaking (the teacher in question) and therefore will be detrimental to the conversation.

A good way to have open and honest dialogues about race and racism is to have them in small groups. This could be done in classrooms as well as in faculty meetings/professional spaces. These can be set up as affinity groups (which I will go into later) or diverse groupings. It can also be good to have these conversations with a partner so that it is an even smaller group and both parties have to work on listening to the other. You can practice conversations that interrupt as in Tatum's exercise or you can have specific topics to address per group. The more you have these group conversations, the more comfortable and free colleagues and students will be to really reflect on issues related to racism and Anti-Racism. Oluo has various tips about how to conduct these conversations, which include stating your intentions clearly, doing your research on the topic, trying not to be defensive, making sure you do not "tone police," and trying to reflect as you speak, so we can do better (Oluo, 2019). The most important thing to remember is to not dismiss the openings of conversations that naturally occur in classroom settings. The biggest issue is silence, not having these conversations at all. This is very harmful as it perpetuates myths of a color-blind discourse. "If you do not see yourself as part of the problem, you cannot be a part of the solution" (Saad, 2020, p. 43). Complacency is the opposite of having key conversations about race and racism and it is not acceptable anywhere, especially in the classroom or the education department of your university.

Higher education professors of early childhood education must be committed to becoming Anti-Racist educators. This is the only way to challenge the pre-service teacher's struggle to teach Anti-Racist pedagogy in their own future classrooms. Commitment takes courage (Kendi, 2019). "We have to commit to the process if we want to address race, racism and racial oppression in our society" (Oluo, 2020, p. 6). Commitment means taking the time and the effort to really dedicate your work and life to a cause, to a movement, such as combatting racism within our early childhood programs. Saad refers to this as "truth work" (Saad, 2020, p. 17). White higher education professors need to commit to this idea of "truth work." Much like our commitment to being great teachers and role models for our student population, and to our research, we must commit to being an Anti-Racist educator. This does not happen overnight, it is a long journey, one that takes years and years of dedication and service. Commitment and dedication require the ability to be open to lifelong learning, something that each of the six teacher participants values. It is not enough to be aware of racism, to be so-called "woke." It is essential that we commit to acting on this ongoing commitment and really focus on how we can be a part of this movement.

One of the ways to dedicate ourselves and commit to this important work is to hold and/or attend professional development workshops (virtually and in person) that address this topic. "Believing in the importance of social and personal change is one thing. Doing it is another" (Derman-Sparks, 1997, p.126). We must be actively engaged in the work. If we are attending workshops, we need to listen, learn, and take note of what we should incorporate into our daily work lives. If we are a part of Anti-Racist education committees in our departments then we need to be fully committed to learning and working with our colleagues, especially BIPOC colleagues. We need to join book groups, sponsor important events/speakers, and even be facilitators within these events and workshops. We need to be humble and be clear in our intentions to learn more about Anti-Racism each day.

We need to advocate for more professional development in the school districts within our communities. Jewell states, "If you do nothing, everything stays the same" (Jewell, 2020, p.94). Professional development opportunities should be mandatory so that there is no choice for teachers, otherwise some will just not seek it out. It is important that it is accessible and well-crafted so that teachers really reflect on this practice. Ms. Fern speaks to the need for professional development in her interview three:

Ms. F: Well, I think there needs to be a lot more professional development around these issues and I think . . . again . . . because everything came to a head . . . George Floyd's murder . . . It really created an atmosphere where people were 'getting' on the bandwagon but Anti-bias and Anti-Racist work is not a bandwagon . . . I think the training initially is supposed to start with self-awareness . . . and not necessarily . . . here is the right book to read with your kids . . . go and do it . . . or here's a lesson to do with your kids about whatever . . . I think teachers need to have a lot more diverse books . . . I think it is pretty simple that most teachers can do is looking at the diversity in their classroom library and read alouds . . . but I think that in order to manage the dialogue that you need and want to get from kids . . . from the text . . . activities that you are doing . . . you have to reflect on that . . . yeah, so I think teachers need more training in their own reflection.

Ms. Fern feels strongly that in order for professional development workshops to be effective they must be centered around the work of reflection on biases and assumptions and ideas on racial identity. She makes a good point when she states that learning about books and activities to do with young children should be negotiated with the teacher taking the time to critically reflect on their own perspectives/racial identity. She is worried about school districts forming their own curriculum related to Anti-Racist pedagogy as it may be superficial or not worthy of the work. In the same interview, she addresses this issue:

So, now that districts are talking about . . . you need Anti-Racist curriculum . . . it's interesting because it feels a little backwards . . . I want Anti-Racist curriculum in schools but there has to be work with educators. . . . Especially white educators on themselves before just opening a canned curriculum book and doing a lesson.

Ms. Fern is worried about "canned" curriculum centered on Anti-Racist pedagogy. She does not want to be forced to do it the district's way. And this happens a lot in school districts, they take a topic and make a curriculum out of it that can be limiting and not developmentally appropriate. Or it could be questionable as a whole if it is laid out as a tourist approach that is superficial at best. Ms. Broadbent responds to this in her interview:

Ms. B: The district's union already put out an Anti-Racist training . . . that I wasn't able to go to but I am hoping that they are just going to repeat it . . . the district is thinking about adding it into our curriculum but not to the degree that the teachers want . . . I heard that they think one lesson a year will do it.
R: What? That's offensive really.
Ms. B: It is . . . it came from our current interim principal . . . who went to a meeting . . . she went to another meeting to make the point that was not enough . . . and that it was insulting . . . and I just feel like . . . given the current situation of the world . . . well at least here . . . as a topic in education that has just risen to the surface . . . and I feel like opportunities are going to be endless . . . I hope they are and our union is under negotiations right now for re-opening . . . and one of our things is Professional development on Anti-Racist education . . . so we are kinda of putting that into our negotiations.

Part of our commitment to this work is advocating for the hiring of more BIPOC teachers in our higher education communities and within our pre-service populations. It is clear that we need to mobilize as a nation to address this inequity in teaching as we continually maintain a very high percentage of white teachers (usually female) in early childhood, holding steady at around 85 percent. In my conversations with Ms. Broadbent, who was a part of a recent hiring committee in her elementary school, she made it clear that it is hard to find BIPOC teachers. And yet when school committees do find qualified candidates they don't always end up with the job.

Ms. B: There was one little thing that happened . . . I mean it wasn't great but . . . we did some hiring over the summer (2020) for a first grade position at our school and there were 1000 applicants and of them . . . so five of the . . . the five we decided to interview . . . two of them were people of color . . . and I thought "Okay, we are moving in the right direction" . . . we didn't end up hiring them

... but at least they were at the table and represented ... and I am just thinking ... I don't think I have seen this in a long time ... I don't remember the last time I was on a committee and it was ... we had a diverse committee as well ... a racially diverse committee.... So, that felt encouraging. ...

R: So I am assuming that you hired a white teacher.

Ms. B: We did (laughs) Yeah ...

R: A white female? Another white female?

Ms. B: Yep ... And you know what? I knew one of the candidates and she was a POC and she was our second choice and she was so strong and it was really, really frustrating that it was so close ... it was close but it was not ... there were things ... you know ... but I was only one voice on the committee and she was a friend ... so it was really tricky ... but she got a job somewhere else ... not in our district.

I found this tale disheartening. Even with a diverse hiring committee, they chose another white woman out of 1,000 applicants. Yes, it is important to have more diversity at the table but I question why one of these two BIPOC finalists was not picked, especially in a town that defines itself as "liberal" and striving to be Anti-Racist.

This is a problem in higher education too, as the majority of professors of early childhood education are white as well. Only 4.5 percent of faculty nationwide are BIPOC (Marx, 2006). This means that white faculty are over 90 percent of the population in higher education. This is why it is crucial that you join hiring committees at your institution so that you can work toward hiring more BIPOC faculty and staff. The population of pre-service teachers is predominantly white too, which means we need to create new avenues to encourage BIPOC students to major in early childhood education. We must continually work hard at trying to change these numbers. "If you are a college student in a historically white college, you must raise hell to change your college; you must organize to change the racial climate and demography of your college" (Bonilla-Silva, 2006, p. 214). This is stated in a book from fifteen years ago, but it still holds true today. We need to actively engage in this change. This is not only because it is a crucial way to combat racism and encourage more possibility for Anti-Racist pedagogy within the classroom, it is also because the demographics of the United States are changing. In the next twenty years, we will have a predominantly BIPOC student population, and as we have more and more BIPOC children in our early childhood classrooms, it is essential that we have more BIPOC teachers as well (Phillips, 2016). Representation and role modeling are important for a young child. This is not to say that with more BIPOC teachers we will automatically get teachers who are more dedicated to Anti-Racist pedagogy and the work it entails. However, this chasm of a predominantly white teaching force is part of the overall problem and has to be challenged as such.

Solidarity and the building of solidarity are crucial to the commitment of this work. "Working in solidarity with others is an incredible way to take action and build collective power for change" (Jewell, 2020, p.110). All movements for change need solidarity. We need to work together in partnerships and groups in order to make change. Anti-Racist work is no different. It thrives on solidarity. Love and solidarity go hand in hand, according to West, and they are both needed in this case (West, 2020). At a conference a few years ago, I ran into a legend in the field of Critical Race Theory, Zeus Leonardo and after I saw him at an event, I asked him for his autograph. To me, it was like seeing the Beatles in person. I had read all of his books, and they had changed me and changed my world for the better. I was expecting just a signature but he wrote, "I look forward to our future together, sometimes bright but certainly filled with love and solidarity" (Leonardo, 2019). This statement is profound to me as it makes it clear that we are all in this together, whether we embrace it or not. This encourages me daily, to do better, to be more committed to this work, and work harder at solidarity than ever before. Without solidarity, we are lost. We need to ban together in love and solidarity in order to make change. MacNaughton, one of my favorite critical early childhood researchers states, "Learning with others can lessen the challenges of change" (MacNaughton, 2005, p. 200). This makes total sense. We need to work in solidarity with others at all times, otherwise, the challenges are too daunting and can seem insurmountable.

Being an ally is key to the concept of solidarity. White teacher educators need to strive for this goal. It can be messy at times and you will make mistakes (Jewell, 2020). You will say the wrong thing, you will apologize for not understanding something and you will be caught off guard in conversations centered around race. However, you need to be open to all of this and embrace it. This is part of being an ally. Jewell makes it clear that we all need to find our people, people who share our vision, in order to engage in Anti-Racist work (Jewell, 2020). Our white privilege should be used for the good of humanity, and that includes working with others in combatting racism. It is important that we, as white educators, are mindful of the white savior complex and do not try to use this tactic in our quest for allyship. We are not trying to save BIPOC from themselves or from the world. To be a true ally and work in solidarity with BIPOC colleagues, white teacher educators should be committed to the cause, to the injustice of racism. We are not here to take charge or control of this work, we are here to work together, side by side with our BIPOC colleagues and friends. This is very tricky, and should be critically reflected on regularly by white teacher educators. The world does not need more white people taking charge, but we must be in this fight for the long haul.

What can be specifically done within our higher education departments? Well, there is a lot to do, and every early childhood faculty member must get on board and help drive this bus. The first thing we can actively participate in is changing our own courses and help in reshaping the department as a whole. Teacher educators have the responsibility to go over their syllabi with a fine-toothed comb and revise their courses (Sharma, 2005). Be sure to infuse your course with this work. Do not just add to it, piling on more work instead of making it a focus in each and every class. Like Black History Month, this should not be an additive activity. Look carefully at your fifteen-week semester and examine each class, looking for the right materials to insert and shift the focus.

After you have revised all of your classes and syllabi, it is time to advocate for changes in your entire program of study. "We believe that teacher education students need not just one course in Anti-Racist education but a series of courses where Anti-Racist and multicultural concepts build upon one another" (Lawrence & Tatum, 1998, p. 10). When I came to my institution, I noticed that there was only one class centered on this topic, *Multicultural Education*. Over the years, as we developed an Anti-Racist education committee, this shifted. We started to work together as colleagues to redesign all of our courses, aligning them with our new and improved dispositions and pillars so that Anti-Racist pedagogy was front and center. Since then we have redesigned each of our programs of study, including early childhood education with a focus on Anti-Racism. We revamped the entire course structure and are presently going through governance to get our new programs approved. Our course in Multicultural education is now one full year long and has a critical approach. It is also tied to a field placement in diverse schools so that students can apply these new theoretical concepts to real-life classrooms. I should note that in this case "diverse" placements refer to de facto segregated schools largely populated with BIPOC students. Before this shift, students were only required to do one semester in a "diverse" environment. Now all field placements are centered in "diverse" schools, so they are actively involved in BIPOC communities for four full years.

It is important for the higher education institution to be actively involved in the communities that surround them, with a focus on BIPOC communities. Students need to be aware of their local school communities and be actively involved in local groups that are fighting racial inequalities (Cole, 2009). Schools of Education need to also actively recruit BIPOC students from these communities so that there are more BIPOC pre-service teachers in their programs. Set up a program in your institution that connects BIPOC communities and schools to your university. In my school, we have a program called "Reach to Teach," which honestly still needs work, but is centered around encouraging young BIPOC students in the area to come to our education programs and be pre-service teachers. We offer financial and emotional support so that BIPOC students will excel in the program. It is fair to note that retention of BIPOC students is problematic in my institution, and in most institutions, mainly because there are not enough BIPOC students and or support for them. Thus, it is important that education departments actively seek out spaces for BIPOC students, with mentors (BIPOC faculty) and support groups. It is essential that we make sure that there are student affinity groups, where every BIPOC students feel supported (Derman-Sparks, 1997). We need to actively recruit students from within our classrooms to help run these support groups. Ask white students to be allies for these groups, but be sure to leave space for BIPOC students to congregate and support one another. This requires physical space in your department too, like an empty meeting space or an unused office that can be used to house meetings and support groups.

The only way to really carry out this work is to form a committee. I know that the word "committee" is dreaded by most higher education faculty, but here it has a real purpose. An Anti-Racist education committee was formed in my department six years ago, the year I came to the institution. Clearly there were people who were actively fighting for the inclusion of Anti-Racist pedagogy before I arrived, including Robin DiAngelo, who was a department member before I came. She left suddenly, probably because she was frustrated, as most can be, with how slowly the department was moving on this work. In my first year, another critical scholar arrived to take her place, teaching multicultural education, and he, along with other BIPOC faculty, proposed a committee that would effectively work at dismantling racism within our program and school. We set up a co-chair system where two faculty members took turns leading this committee. At one point I was a co-chair of this committee, and believe me there was a lot of work involved, but it was worthy work. The purpose of our committee was to infuse Anti-Racist pedagogy within all of our education programs (special education, elementary, secondary, and early childhood). We set up meetings to plan and then we approached the chair of the department in order to utilize some faculty meetings per semester. We now have three faculty meetings devoted to this work each semester, along with a spring annual retreat. These sessions are all mandatory for faculty and therefore they must be a part of the work. At first, there was some resistance and there were a few faculty members who left these meetings early or went into the hallway to look at their cell phones. But years later, with each meeting, these same professors are more involved and interested in the work.

What do we exactly do within this Anti-Racist committee work? First, we took the time to provide readings, such as Kendi, Tatum, West, and so on, that would inspire our colleagues to make changes in their syllabi and course work. We utilized affinity groups, placing white faculty together and

BIPOC faculty together, to discuss issues related to privilege and racism/discrimination. I am not going to lie, some of these group experiences were not pleasant. I had to sit through some white colleague tantrums and rants on their privilege. At one point several of us had to convince another white female faculty member it was never okay to read a book in class that used the "N" word. There are always going to be uncomfortable moments in this work, especially within white affinity groups. Yet, we had to provide these spaces, so that our colleagues could critically reflect on their own biases and assumptions on race. We also worked together as a faculty planning events (i.e., Cornell West, Shaun King, Beverly Tatum, Nicole Hannah Jones, Tim Wise) for our students and for ourselves. We set up Town Hall events each fall that focused on one important topic related to Anti-Racist pedagogy, such as school to prison pipeline, segregation, and desegregation of schools, lynching, and violence against BIPOC, and so on. We specifically picked a section of a documentary to share with all the students of the education department, making it mandatory for attendance. They would come to one of the nine sessions (run by our faculty), watch a part of a documentary, and talk about the issues involved. We set up exit tickets, compiled data with student questions and concerns and then brought the data to faculty meetings to share. We found that students were confused about certain historical events and that helped us to incorporate more of these topics of concern into our individual courses.

It is important to note that this Anti-Racist education committee is a work in progress. We (including five faculty members) work hard to help educate our colleagues and ourselves on the importance of this work. Yet, we are making progress. Just last year the dean of our school of education, health and human services approached us to extend our work to other departments on campus. This is when you know that your committee is making an impact. However, we realized that there was still so much work to be done in our own department that it was not a good time to expand into other departments. We needed to stay focused on the education department. I think this is an important point for all of us, don't expand too quickly, even if things are going well. Keep your focus on your department at first, and this can take many years. Change the policy, challenge the dynamics and work on your goals of transforming your department little by little over time. Later this can then lead to change in policy in your institution as well. "There is no such thing as a nonracist or race neutral policy. Every policy in every institution in every community is producing or sustaining either racial inequity or equity between racial groups" (Kendi, 2019, p. 18). The committee collectively decided that to combat institutional racism it was important to keep our focus and not spread ourselves too thin. This is a problem that every faculty member faces as we are constantly asked to give more and more service to our institution with little in return. It should be noted that this is especially true for BIPOC faculty members.

One of the committee's focuses is on reflection. We try to set up spaces in our work where faculty members can critically reflect on their own biases and assumptions. After we discuss a chapter or article, spend time in groups reflecting on it and how it impacts our work we then give ten minutes for each faculty member to free write a reflection in their own journals. We don't share these reflections as they are intended to be for our own personal growth. However, we have gotten a lot of feedback from other colleagues praising this task as they never get the chance to actually reflect on the ongoing work of Anti-Racism.

I think it is crucial to let everyone, including yourself, have the space to process what you are experiencing. Yes, we need to talk about important books/articles/videos related to this topic but we also need to make that personal connection to ourselves, our own racial identities, and how we fit into this fight. One important exercise that you can use is the written reflection on our racial identities. We have done this multiple times over the years and our colleagues find this very helpful. As noted in chapter 9, most white people do not spend time critically reflecting on their own racial identities. They do not even question it as they do not see themselves as the "other." It is important that white people examine the history of their racial identity. Do they see themselves as belonging to ethnic groups? Do they consider their own privilege? Do they deny being part of white supremacy? Again, this exercise is private and does not have to be shared with the whole group, but sometimes faculty want to share their perceptions of their racial identities. BIPOC faculty also can be conflicted with their racial identity and need to work through issues of colorism, and or being from other countries that are predominately BIPOC (i.e., Jamaica, Haiti, etc.) where racism can take other forms. This is a complex topic, one that needs to be reexamined over and over again, much like kindergarteners drawing a new self-portrait monthly. As professors, we are in process, a lifelong process of becoming and identifying as Anti-Racist educators. This does not happen overnight.

The work in an education department needs to be done from the inside out. Yes, you can get experts to come in to help once in a while, but the process as a whole works better when there is a committee of diverse faculty dedicated to this work. Remember it is a process, one that takes time and commitment, by everyone in your department. Oluo states, "It's the system, and our complacency in that system, that gives racism its power, not individual intent" (Oluo, 2019, p. 28). Thus, in order to take a stand against racism, we must be actively working together to become Anti-Racist in our practices. Complacency is the fuel to the fire of racism and that is an issue in many early childhood education departments. It all starts with us, the faculty and staff of a higher education department. My feeling is that there is no time limit or restriction to this work, it is ongoing and never static. We are still working on it and we are six years into the process of Anti-Racist work, and yet I feel as though this is something I will be involved with during my entire time at this institution. There is no ending to this work.

One of my graduate students, a kindergarten teacher in the area, wanted to do a research project on Anti-Racist curriculum/pedagogy in early childhood education. She looked high and low for resources and could find very little that actually related to this topic. She approached me and asked me for advice. Was there anything out there? Was she missing something? Honestly, I was not surprised she could find so little on the subject, and that is one of the main reasons I started writing this book. We need to have more resources/materials that will help us to explore Anti-Racist practices in the early childhood classroom, and this has to start in teacher education programs. We are the ones who are training early childhood educators. We are preparing them for a complex career, one that already is overloaded with standards, core curriculum, and test preparation practices. Early childhood educators are tired, disrespected, and not given enough accolades for their tremendous work. And now, I am asking you to rethink how we are preparing our early childhood pre-service teachers. This can be seen as overwhelming, but it is crucial to our jobs. We have no choice but to do this. We must recenter our work and commit to teaching pre-service teachers Anti-Racist pedagogy and we need to do it now.

Just last year, at the Democratic National Convention, which was virtual due to the pandemic, Kamela Harris, the soon-to-be vice president, stated, "There is no vaccine for racism. We have to do the work" (Harris, 2020). Higher education professors are key players in this work. We have to get on board right now. I look forward to the day when there are tons of resources for early childhood educators and for teacher preparation programs to use in their continued practice of Anti-Racist pedagogy. I am hopeful that we are on the road to achieving this and I am genuinely thrilled to be a part of this process. I hope you are too.

Appendix A

RESOURCES/MATERIALS TO USE IN HIGHER EDUCATION CLASSROOMS AND PRE-K-2 CLASSROOMS

Board Books (Pre-k-1)

Browne, M. (2018). *Woke baby.*
Tarpley, N. (1998). *I love my hair.*
Lee, S (2006). *Please, baby, please*
Membrino, A (2019). *I look up to . . . Misty Copeland.*
Kendi, I. (2020). *AntiRacist baby.*
McQuinn, A. (2006). *Lola at the library.*
Hooks, B.(2017). *Skin again.*

Books on Celebrating Black/Brown Skin

Brown, K. (2020). *I am perfectly designed.*
Diggs, T. (2011). *Chocolate me!*
Diggs, T. (2021). *Mixed me.*
Beaumont, K. (2004). *I like myself.*
Katz, K. (1999). *The color of us.*
Tyler, M. (2005). *The skin you live in.*
Rotner, S & Kelly, S. (2010). *Shades of people.*
Byers, G. (2018). *I am enough.*

Chapter Books (Read alouds)

Clements, A. (2002). *The jacket.*
Woodson, J. (2016). *Brown girl dreaming.*

Williams-Garcia, R. (2011). *One crazy summer.*
Craft, J. (2019). *New kid.*
Levine, K. (2013). *The lions of little rock.*
Reynolds, J & Kendi, I. (2021). *Stamped for kids.*

Organizations/Online

Embracerace.org
Raceconscious.org
www.tolerance.org
Rethinking schools

Picture Books (Pre-k-2) Fiction

Woodson, J. (2001). *The other side.*
Woodson, J (2018) *The day you began*
Woodson, J. (2013). *This is rope: A story from the great migration.*
Grimes, N. (1997). *Wild, wild hair.*
Farugi, R. (2015) *Lailah's lunchbox: A Ramadan story.*
Penfold, A & Kaufman, S. (2018). *All are welcome.*
Steptoe, J. (1987). *Mufaro's beautiful daughters.*
Gaiman, N & Mckean, D. (2009). *Crazy hair.*
Ringgold, F. (1991). *Tar Beach.*
Ringgold, F. (1992). *Aunt Harriet's underground railroad in the sky.*
De La Pena, M. (2015). *Last stop on market street.*
Choi, Y. (2003). *The name jar.*
Joy, A. (2020). *Black is a rainbow color.*
Mora, O. (2019). *Saturday.*
Levine, E & Nelson, K (2007). *Henry's freedom box: A true story from the underground Railrood.*

Picture Books (Pre-K-2) Non-fiction/Biographies

Pinkney, A. & Pinkney, B. (2002). *Ella Fitzgerald: The tale of a vocal Virtuosa.*
Thomas, V. (1997). *Lest we forget: The passage from Africa to slavery and Emancipation.*
Ryan, P. (2002). *When Marion sang.*
Bridges, R. & Maccarone, G. (2003). *Let's Read about . . . Ruby Bridges.*
Coles, R. (1995). *The story of Ruby Bridges.*
Adler, D. (1994). *A picture book of sojourner truth.*
Kamma, A. (2004). *...If you lived when there was slavery in America.*
Celano et al (2018) *Something happened in our town.*
Giovanni, N. (2005). *Rosa.*

Asim, J. (2018). *A child's introduction to African American history.*
Woodson, J. (2005). *Show way.*
Kaiser, L. (2016). *Little people, big dreams, Maya Angelou.*
Kaiser, L. (2017). *Little people, big dreams, Rosa Parks.*
Reynolds, P. (2019). *Say Something.*
Weatherford, C. (2008). *Before John was a jazz giant: A song of John Coltrane.*
Kissinger, K. (2014). *All the colors we are: The story of how we get our skin color.*
Shelton, P. & Colon, R. (2013). *Child of the civil rights movement.*
Spilsbury, L. (2018). *Racism and intolerance.*
Memory, J. (2019). *A Kid's book about racism.*
Sand, B. (2019). *A kid's book about white privilege.*
Lester, J. (2008). *Let's talk about race.*
Mochizuki, K. & Lee, D. (2018). *Baseball saved us.*
Weatherford, C. & Nelson, K. (2006). *Moses: When Harriet Tubman led her people to freedom.*

Poetry

Roessel, D. & Rampersad, A. (eds). (2006). *Poetry for young people: Langston Hughes.*
Michelle-Baron, L. (1995). *The sun is on.*
Greenfield, E. (1991). *Night on neighborhood street.*
Wilson, E. (ed) (2013). *Poetry for young people: Maya Angelou.*
Gorman, A. (2021). *Change sings.*
Grimes, N. (2017). *One last word: Wisdom from the Harlem Renaissance.*

Songs

Levy, D. (2013). *We shall overcome: The story of a song.*
Sly and the Family Stone. *Everyday people.*
Sam Cooke. *A Change is gonna come.*
John Coltrane. *Alabama.*
Stevie Wonder. *Living for the city.*
James Brown. *Say it loud, I'm Black and I'm proud.*
Nina Simone. *Young gifted and black.*

Videos

I am somebody—Sesame Street.
Anti-Racism song for kids/We are one (You Tube).
PBS kids talk about/Race/Racism (You Tube).
So many colors, so many shapes/Diversity song (You Tube).

Appendix B

DISPOSITIONS FOR HIGHER EDUCATION STUDENTS IN COURSES/FIELDWORK

Critically Engage with Diversity—Teacher Candidate (TC) validates, acknowledges perspectives, and includes members of social groups who have been traditionally marginalized.

a. TC interacts respectfully and empathically with people from diverse racial, cultural, linguistic, religious, ability status, class, and social backgrounds, including gender/gender identity, or sexual identity.
b. TC recognizes and validates the multiple languages and literacies, including diversity in dialect and the use of translanguaging practices such as code-meshing, of students, families, and larger school/university communities.
c. TC incorporates anti-racist, anti-bias, and culturally sustaining content and pedagogies into their practice.
d. TC designs curriculum reflective of students' lived experiences and facilitates discussions that address issues of race, gender, class, ability, and religion in a developmentally appropriate and culturally relevant manner.
e. TC able to engage with diverse ideas, consider the perspectives of others, and apply empathy to guide professional decision-making.
f. TC demonstrates skill in observing, assessing, and guiding student behavior using strength-based, culturally responsive, restorative practices.

Teach for Social Justice—Teacher Candidate (TC) works to make the classroom, school, community, and world equitable.

a. TC develops equitable relationships with students, families, and school/university colleagues/peers.
b. TC identifies inequities in the classroom, school, and/or community, and intentionally works to rectify those inequities.
c. TC assumes responsibility for the performance of all students, differentiates instruction, and designs and implements appropriate accommodations and/or modifications for learners with disabilities.
d. TC effectively interrupts and intervenes in response to observed microaggressions, verbal/physical acts of racism, classism, sexism, homophobia, religious/linguistic discrimination, and ableism in the classroom or larger school/university community.
e. TC designs and implements curriculum that incorporates critical literacy and social action.
f. TC respects and protects the confidentiality of student and family information unless disclosure serves a professional purpose, is required by law, and occurs in an appropriate setting.

Glossary

Additive: When something is added to the curriculum (like black history) but there is no room for it within the core curriculum. This is when curriculum is an afterthought and is not a central part of what children are learning.

Affinity Groups: Groups of people separated by race/culture/sex or ablism. A white affinity group would only have white members. This is utilized so that similar groups of people can share their thoughts and ideas on controversial topics, such as race, and feel supported and heard.

Ally: An ally is a white person or non-BIPOC person who actively works on themselves by critically reflecting on their role within society and who also partners in solidarity with BIPOC communities in order to fight discrimination.

Anti-bias curriculum: Curriculum/lessons that actively counter distinct stereotypes and prejudice.

Black Lives Matter: An action group founded by black women that fights against police brutality of BIPOC.

Colorism: This is about how people view the hierarchy of skin tone. The lighter the shade of a BIPOC the more accepted by white populations.

Complacency: This is when white people do not respond or actively fight against ongoing injustices but instead do nothing.

Counternarratives: These are stories/narratives from other points of view outside of normative discourses. An example of this is reading about history that is not usually covered in schools (i.e., black history).

Critical Race Theory: An ideology/concept that is academic and not taught in schools. It responds to institutional racism and is used by scholars to support research in this field.

Culturally responsive: When a teacher's activities/lessons reflect the populations in their classrooms. It values representation and understanding student's cultural backgrounds, showing respect, and honoring differences.

Equality: When a group of people strive to be considered equal to other groups within a society. Racial equality is counteracting institutional racism and strives to eliminate prejudice and stereotypes so certain groups (BIPOC) are not marginalized.

Equity: This is a monetary term that relates to which schools receive more funding (low-poverty schools) and access to materials/resources and which schools receive less funding (high poverty schools with BIPOC populations).

Funds of Knowledge: An educational theory where there is an emphasis on sharing the culture and knowledge of the school community/parents in a school setting. It involves mutual trust and respect between teachers and families.

High poverty schools: Schools in the United States that have a majority of children from a low socioeconomic status, which is usually majority BIPOC populations.

Inclusion: A concept or state of mind that a teacher utilizes in their classrooms that is inclusive of all children's needs (in learning/culture, and so on). It usually includes regular education children mixed with children with special needs.

In-service teachers: These are practicing teachers already in the field with their own classroom assignments.

Interim principal: Someone who is a temporary principal and has not necessarily gone through district protocols.

Literature circles: These are small groups of students who discuss a text critically and write or speak about their reflections/biases that are related to the readings.

Low poverty schools: Schools in the United States that have a majority of children from a higher socioeconomic status, which is usually majority white populations.

Microaggressions: When a white person intentionally or unintentionally harms a BIPOC with their words/actions.

Multicultural education: This is an ideology that teachers utilize to present multiple cultures in a classroom in a non-tourist approach. It is inclusive and honors the differences in many different cultures that are within or outside the classroom.

Post-racial society: A society where race/racism is no longer a factor at all. Many white people believe that we live in a post-racial society, after the Civil Rights movement of the 1960s. This is a myth.

Pre-service teachers: This is a teacher in training who is out in the field doing placements in order to learn how to teach.

Professional development: These are workshops provided by the district for teachers and their ongoing learning.

Racial humility: This is when someone takes the time to critically examine their own racial identity and has some understanding of their own privilege.

School readiness: A neoliberal term that emphasizes children be academically ready to do well in school. A child that is classified as non-school ready at an early age is stigmatized and can be excluded from their own learning (by pull-outs/academic intervention/special education testing, etc.). Most children identified as non-school ready are BIPOC students.

Segregated schools: This refers to de facto segregation, where a school has a majority population of one race (i.e., white, black, or Hispanic). It is not a diverse school.

SMARTGOAL: This is required by every public school teacher in the United States. In the fall of each year, the teacher writes a specific teaching goal, defines it and then goes about trying to achieve the goal by the end of the year. The administration approves the goal and then in May reviews how the teacher met this specific goal and was or was not successful. SMART stands for Specific, Measurable, Attainable, Relevant, and Time-bound.

Solidarity: A term that is about allyship between two or more groups of people. This is when people from different races/cultures work towards the same goal (racial injustice).

Suspension: When a child's behavior is deemed inappropriate and against school rules they can be suspended by the principal, which means they are removed from the classroom/work. There are in-school suspensions, usually where the child goes to another room to do work and out of school suspensions, where they have to stay home for a certain number of days.

Teachers' union: Some public districts are unionized and have staff (made up of teachers in the district) who organize and fight for teacher's rights locally and nationally.

Tone policing: This is when white people try to police or control BIPOC words and how they express themselves.

Tourist approach: When a teacher or school presents a culture from a tourist perspective that is limiting and usually stereotypical. In the end, this just perpetuates discrimination and prejudice.

Universal Design for Learning (UDL): This is a specific set of strategies to modify and accommodate to different learners in the room.

White Savior Complex: When a white person makes it their mission to help BIPOC communities, imposing their own values/ideologies.

Woke: A term used to describe a person (usually white) who has critically reflected on race and racism and is starting to understand the issues related. It is also now being co-opted by white people who are making fun of the term (i.e., woke police).

References

Adair, J. (2014) "School based agency as expanding capabilities: What it could mean for young children in the early grades," in *Harvard Educational Review*. 84 (2) pp. 217–241.

Alismail, H. (2016). "Multicultural education: Teachers' perceptions and preparation," *Journal of Education and Practice*, Vol. 7, No. 11, pp. 139–146.

Allen, Q. & White-Smith, K. (2017). "That's why I say stay in school": Black mothers' Parental involvement, cultural wealth and exclusion in their son's schooling," *Urban Education*, Vol. 53 (issue 3), pp. 1–26.

Aronson, B. (2017). "The White Savior Industrial Complex: A cultural studies analysis Of a teacher educator, savior film and future teachers," *Journal of Critical thought and Praxis,* Vol. 6, No. 3, pp. 36–54.

Asim, J. (2018). *A Child's Introduction to African American History: The Experience, People and Events that Shaped Our Country.* Black Dog and Leventhal Publishers.

Au, W. (ed.) (2014). *Rethinking Multicultural Education: Teaching for Racial and Cultural Justice.* A Rethinking Schools Publication.

Aveling, Nado (2007). "Anti-racism in schools: A question of leadership?," *Discourse: Studies in the Cultural Politics of Education*, Vol. 28, No. 1, pp. 69–85.

Bigelow, B. (2014). "Standards and tests attack Multiculturism," in *Rethinking Multicultural Education,* ed. Wayne Au. A Rethinking Schools Publication.

Bloom, S. (Sep. 2005). "Lesson of a lifetime: Her bold experiment to teach Iowa Third graders about racial prejudice divided townspeople and thrust her Onto the national stage," *Smithsonian Magazine.*

Bonilla-Silva, E. (2006). *Racism Without Racists: Colorblind Racism and the Persistence of Racial Inequality in the United States.* Rowman & Littlefield.

Case, K. & Hemmings, A. (2005). "Distancing Strategies: White women preservice Teachers and anti-racist curriculum," *Urban Education*, Vol. 40, No. 6, pp. 606–626.

Chao, T. & Jones, D. (2016). " That's not fair and why: Developing social justice mathematics activists in pre-K," *Teaching for Excellence and Equity in Mathematics*, Vol. 7, No. 1, Summer, pp. 15–21.

Cole, M. (2009). *Critical Race Theory and education: A Marxist Response.* Palgrave Macmillan.

Cowhey, M. (2004). *Black Ants and Buddhists: Thinking Critically and Teaching Differently in the Primary Grades.* Stenhouse Pub.

Davis, K., MacNaughton, G. & Smith, K. (2009). "The dynamics of whiteness: Children locating within/without," in *Race and Early Childhood Education.* MacNaughton (Ed.) Palgrave Macmillan, pp. 49–65.

Delpit, L. (2006). *Other People's Children: Cultural Conflict in the Classroom.* New Press.

Derman-Sparks, L. (Ed). (1997). "Activism and preschool children," in *Beyond Heroes and Holidays.* Washington, DC: Network of Educators on the Americas, pp. 188–192.

Derman-Sparks, L. & Phillips, C. (1997). *Teaching/Learning Anti-racism: A Developmental Approach.* Teachers College Press.

Derman-Sparks, L. & Ramsey, P. (2005). "What if all the children in my class are white? Historical and Research background," *Beyond the Journal: Young Children on the Web, NAEYC.* Vol 60 (issue 6). pp. 20–27.

DiAngelo, R. (2010). "Why can't we all just be individuals?: Countering the discourse Of individualism in anti-racist education," *UCLA Journal of Education and Information Studies*, Vol. 6, No. 1.

DiAngelo, R. (2018). *White Fragility: Why It's so Hard for White People to Talk about Racism.* Beacon Press.

Downey, D. & Pribesh, S. (2004). "When race matters: Teachers' evaluations of students' Classroom behavior," *Sociology of Education*, Vol. 77, pp. 267–282.

Eckhoff, A. (2007). "The importance of art viewing experiences in early childhood visual arts: The exploration of a master art teacher's strategies for meaningful early arts experiences," *Early Childhood Education Journal*, Vol. 35, pp. 463–472.

Epstein, T. et al. (2011). "Teaching about race in an urban history class: the effects of Culturally responsive teaching," *The Journal of Social Studies Research*, Vol. 35, pp. 2–21.

Fox, J. & Schirrmacher, R. (2015). *Art and Creative Development for Young Children.* Cengage Learning.

Gay, G. & Kirkland, K. (2003). "Developing cultural critical consciousness and self-reflection in preservice teacher education," *Theory into Practice*, Vol. 42, No. 3, pp. 181–187.

Greene, M. (1995). *Releasing the Imagination: Essays on Education, the Arts and Social Change.* Jossey-Bass.

Gregory, D. (2018). *Defining Moments in Black History: Reading Between the lines.* Amistad imprints.

Gunn, A. (2000). "Teachers' beliefs in relation to visual art education in early Childhood centres," *New Zealand Research in Early Childhood Education.* (vol 3) pp. 153–162.

References

Harris, K. (2020). "Democratic National Convention speech of Kamela Harris," (televised NBC) August 19.

Harry, B. & Klingner, J. (2006). *Why Are So Many Minority Students in Special Education? Understanding Race and Disability in Schools.* Teachers College press.

Husband, T. (2010). "He's too young to learn about that stuff: Anti-racist pedagogy and Early childhood social studies," *Social Studies Research and Practice*, Vol. 5, No. 2, pp. 61–75.

Husband, T. (2011). "I don't see color: Challenging assumptions about discussing race With young children," *Early Childhood Education Journal*, Vol. 39, pp. 365–371.

Jacobs, G. & Crowley, K. (2010). *Reaching Standards and Beyond in Kindergarten.* NAEYC and Sage Publications.

Jewell, T. (2020). *This Book Is Anti-Racist: 20 Lessons on How to Wake Up and Take Action, and Do the Work.* Frances Lincoln books.

Kendi, I. (2019). *How to Be an Anti-racist.* One world (Random House).

Khalifa, M. & Briscoe, F. (2015). "A counternarrative autoethnography exploring School districts' role in reproducing racism: willful blindness to racial inequalities," *Teachers College Record*, Vol. 117, pp. 1–34.

King, J. (2004). "Dysconscious racism: Ideology, identity and the miseducation of teachers," in *The RoutledgeFalmer Reader in Multicultural Education.* Ladson-Billings & Gillborn (Eds). Routledge, pp. 71–83.

King, L. & Brown, K. (2014). "Once a year to be black: fighting against typical black History month pedagogies," *Negro Educational Review*, Vol. 65, No. 1–4, pp. 23–43.

Kissinger, K. (2017). *Anti-Bias Education in the Early Childhood Classroom.* Routledge.

Ladson-Billings, G. (2000). "Fighting for our lives: Preparing teachers to teach African American students," *Journal of Teacher Education*, Vol. 51, No. 3, pp. 206–214.

Ladson-Billings, G. (2002). "I ain't writin' nuttin': permissions to fail and demands to succeed in urban classrooms," in *The Skin that We Speak,* ed. Lisa Delpit. New Press, pp. 109–120.

Ladson-Billings, G. (2004). "Just what is critical race theory and what's it doing in a nice field like education?," in *The RoutledgeFalmer Reader in Multicultural Education.* Ladson-Billings & Gillborn (Eds). Routledge, pp. 49–67.

Ladson-Billings, G. & Gillborn, D. (Eds.). (2004). *The RoutledgeFalmer Reader in Multicultural Education.* Routledge.

Ladson-Billings, G. (2021). "Critical Race Theory: What it is not!" in *Handbook of critical race theory in education (2nd edition).* Routledge.

Lawrence, S. & Tatum, B. (1998). "White racial identify and anti-racist education: a Catalyst for change." www.teaching for change.org, pp. 1–12.

Lazear, D. (2000). *Pathways of Learning: Teaching Students and Parents about Multiple Intelligences.* Zephyr Press.

Lee, E. & et al (Eds) (1997). *Beyond Heroes and Holidays: A Practical Guide to k-12 Anti-racist, Multicultural Education and Staff Development.* Network of Educators on the Americas.

Lee, J. (2018). "Understanding identity and practice of Asian American educators In urban schools" (dissertation). UCLA.

Lea, V. & Helfand, J. (Eds.). (2004). *Identifying Race and Transforming Whiteness in the Classroom.* Peter Lang Publishing.

Leonardo, Z. (2009). *Race, Whiteness and Education.* Routledge.

Leonardo, Z. (2013). *Race Frameworks: A Multidimensional Theory of Racism and Education.* Teachers College Press.

Leonardo, Z. (2019). "AERA division G event (Toronto, Canada)," AERA Annual International Conference.

Levy, D. (2013). *We Shall Overcome: The Story of a Song.* Disney.

Lin, M. et al. (2008). "Teaching anti-bias curriculum in teacher education programs: What and how," *Teacher Education Quarterly*, Vol. 35, No. 2, pp. 187–200.

MacNaughton, G. (2005). *Doing Foucault in Early Childhood Studies: Applying Poststructural Ideas.* Routledge.

MacNaughton, G. & Davis, K. (Eds.). (2009). *Race and Early Childhood Education: An International Approach to Identity, Politics, and Pedagogy.* Palgrave Macmillan.

Marx, S. (2004). "Exploring and challenging whiteness and white racism with white pre-service teachers," in *Identifying Race and Transforming Whiteness in the Classroom.* Lea & Helfand (Eds.). Peter Lang Publishing, pp. 132–152.

Marx, S. (2006). *Revealing the Invisible: Confronting Passive Racism in Teacher Education.* Routledge.

Mass. Department of Elementary and Secondary Education (2018). *History and Social Science Frameworks pre-k to 12.*

Maxwell, K. (2004). "Deconstructing whiteness: discovering the water," in *Identifying Race and Transforming Whiteness in the Classroom.* Lea & Helfand (Eds.). Peter Lang Publishing, pp. 153–168.

McGee, L. & Schickedanz, J. (2017). "Repeated interactive read alouds in preschool and Kindergarten." www.readingrockets.org

Membrino, A. (2019). *I look up to Misty Copeland.* Random House.

Oluo, I. (2020). *So You Want to Talk about Race.* Seal Press.

Peters, L. et al. (2019). "Conceptualization of voice: Young children as civil activists. How do They see themselves as making a difference," presented at AERA Annual Conference, New York.

Pennington, J. (2007). "Silence in the classroom/whispers in the halls: autoethnography as pedagogy in white pre-service teacher education," *Race Ethnicity and Education*, Vol. 10, No. 1, pp. 93–113.

Petit, E. (2021). "The Academic concept conservative lawmakers love to hate: How critical race theory became enemy number 1 in the battle against higher education," *The Chronicle of Higher Education,* May 12.

Phillips, S. (2016) *Brown is the New White: How the Demographic Revolution Has Created a New American Majority.* New Press.

Picower, B. (2021). *Reading, Writing, and Racism: Disrupting Whiteness in Teacher Education and in the Classroom.* Beacon Press.

Pine, G. & Hilliard III, A. (1990). "Rx for racism: Imperatives for America's schools," *Phi Delta Kappan,* April, pp. 1–10.

Public School Review.com (2020) retrieved July 2020.

Randolph, A. (2013). *The Wrong Kind of Different: Challenging the Meaning of Diversity in American Classrooms.* Teachers College press.

Rather, D. (2019). *What Unites Us: Reflections on Patriotism.* Algonquin Books.

Reynolds, P. (2019). *Say Something.* Orchard Books.

Roessel, D. & Rampersad, A. (2006). *Poetry for Young People: Langston Hughes.* Sterling Publishing.

Rosen, R. (2017). "Play as activism? Early childhood and (inter) generational politics," *Contemporary Social Science.* 12 (1–2). pp. 110–122.

Ryan, P. (2002). *When Marian Sang.* Scholastic Press.

Saad, L. (2020). *Me and White Supremacy.* Sourcebooks.

Segall, A. & Garrett, J. (2013). "White teachers talking race," *Teaching Education,* Vol. 24, No. 3, pp. 265–291.

Sharma, S. (2005). "Multicultural education: Teachers' perceptions and preparation," *Journal of College Teaching and Learning,* Vol. 2, No. 5, pp. 53–63.

Sleeter, C. (1997). "Teaching whites about racism," in *Beyond Heroes and Holidays.* Lee et al (Eds.). Network of Educators on the Americas, pp. 36–44

Sleeter, C. (2004). "How white teachers construct race," in *RoutledgeFalmer Reader In Multicultural Education.* RoutledgeFalmer, pp. 163–178.

Solomon, P. et al. (2005). "The discourse of denial: how white teacher candidates construct race, racism and white privilege," *Race, Ethnicity and Education,* Vol. 8, No. 2, pp. 147–169.

Solorzano, D. (1997). "Images and words that wound: Critical race theory, racial stereotyping, and teacher education," *Teacher Education Quarterly,* Vol. 24. No. 3, pp. 5–19.

Souto-Manning, M. & Martell, J. (2016). *Reading, Writing and Talk: Inclusive Teaching Strategies for Diverse Learners, k-2.* Teachers College Press.

St. Denis, V. & Schick, C. (2003). "What makes anti-racist pedagogy in teacher education Difficult? Three popular ideological assumptions," *The Alberta Journal of Educational Research.* Vol. XLIX, No. 1, pp. 55–69.

Tager, M. (2017). *Challenging the School Readiness Agenda in Early Childhood Education.* Routledge.

Tager, M. (2019). *Technology Segregation: Disrupting Racist Frameworks in Early Childhood Education.* Lexington Books.

Tatum, B. (2017). *Can We Talk About Race? And Other Conversations in an Era of School Resegregation.* Beacon Press.

U.S. Department of Education (2013–14). Office of Civil Rights. www.2ed.gov.

Van De Mieroop, K. (2016). "On the advantage and disadvantage of black history month For life: The creation of the post racial era," in *History and Theory 55–1.* pp. 3–24, Wesleyan University.

West, C. (1993). *Race Matters.* Beacon Press.

West, C. (2020). "Deep Education" speech at Westfield State University, Massachusetts (March).

Wilkerson, I. (2020). *Caste: The Origins of Our Discontents.* Random House.

Woodson, J. (2001). *The Other Side.* GP Putnam and Sons.

Index

affinity Groups, 167, 175, 181–82
agency, 11, 22, 29–31, 79–81, 119, 124, 127–29, 132
Alice, Ms., 15–16, 22–24, 27, 50–51, 55–57, 83, 85, 88–91, 95, 100–101, 147–49, 159–60
Anderson, Marion, 80, 89
Angelou, Maya, 95

Baker Street School, 5, 26, 121, 150
biases, 3, 8, 11, 20, 29, 81–82, 105, 111–14, 125–27, 132–33, 138–45, 165, 168, 174–75
Black Lives Matter, 11, 32, 37–38, 89, 153, 164
Bridges, Ruby, 7, 77–78, 88–89
Broadbent, Ms., 1–3, 15–17, 20–21, 35–36, 48–49, 51–52, 61–62, 65–66, 74–75, 85–86, 88, 102–3, 105, 108, 126, 156–57, 166, 169–70

Civil Rights Movement, 3, 24, 33, 38, 57, 69, 74, 79–80, 86, 89, 91–92, 94, 115, 121–22, 126, 129, 147, 154
colorblind discourse, 2–3, 8–9, 24, 34, 39, 47, 79–80, 136, 142, 167
colorism, 60, 62–65, 175
Coltrane School, 1, 5, 20, 65, 85, 119, 149, 156–57

committee work, 168–70, 173–75
community building, 14, 18, 20, 25–26, 54
COVID-19. *See* pandemic
Critical Race Theory, 6–7, 35, 86, 153, 171
culturally responsive, 70, 73, 79–80, 155

dance/movement, 11, 33, 60, 70–71, 74
developmentally appropriate practices, 4, 20, 50, 87, 120, 126–27, 156, 169
dramatic arts, 55, 66, 71–72, 74, 113–14, 143

empathy, 14, 18–21, 23, 37, 128, 138, 140–43

fairness, 3, 25, 45, 56, 117–21, 124–25, 128, 132, 152
Fern, Ms., 15, 17, 22–23, 25, 28, 35, 37, 43–46, 63–65, 90, 92, 97–98, 100–101, 103, 117, 119, 122–23, 148–52, 156–59, 164–66, 168–69
Funds of Knowledge, 160

Gandhi, Mahatma, 88–91

higher education classrooms, 2, 11, 28–30, 38–41, 54–57, 72–75, 80–81,

93–95, 105, 111–14, 117, 125–29, 138–45, 159–61, 167–76
Houston, Ms., 15–16, 19–21, 24–25, 49–51, 59–60, 67–69, 71–72, 77–78, 87, 102, 119–20, 141, 149, 153–56
Hughes, Langston, 95, 107–8

identity. *See* racial, identity
indigenous populations, 100–101, 149
individualism, 44, 46–47
interruption, 165–66
intersectionality, 14–15, 28

Jim Crow Laws, 53, 69, 80, 92, 94, 115

King, Martin Luther (Jr.), 31, 79, 87–88

Lewis, John, 87, 89
lifelong learning, 10, 14, 26–27, 29, 123, 167, 175
Longwood Elementary, 5–6, 21, 78, 119, 150

Maltes, Ms., 13–15, 18, 26, 36, 67, 99, 104, 121, 150
meritocracy, 44, 47, 142
microaggressions, 52–54, 57
music, 60, 66, 68–70

Packard Elementary, 5–6, 55, 147
pandemic, 6, 18, 45–46, 49, 103, 157, 159, 163, 165, 176
parental support, 148–51, 161
Parks, Rosa, 31–33, 69, 79, 87–88, 94
play, 71–72, 113, 117, 124–25, 140, 150, 155
poverty, 49, 51, 134
professional development, 37, 86, 157–58, 163, 168–69

racial: humility, 132, 138, 142; identity, 2–3, 11, 17, 25–26, 28, 63, 66, 68, 72, 74, 99, 101, 104, 112, 131–43, 150, 158–59, 168, 175
racism, 2–4, 7–11, 14, 17–18, 22–29, 34–36, 40–41, 44, 47–48, 52, 55–57, 60, 69, 71, 78–83, 86, 89–90, 94–95, 100, 103, 105, 114, 116–22, 126–28, 133, 138, 140, 142, 150–51, 153, 158, 164–71, 175–76
reconstruction, 33, 53, 80, 92, 94
role play, 19, 55, 74, 132–33, 142–44, 154, 159

segregation, 33, 54–55, 65, 77–78, 92, 94–95, 174
skin tone, 60–62, 64–68, 72–75, 102, 105, 107–13, 136–37
slavery, 24, 34, 53, 69, 79–80, 85–86, 92, 94–95, 112, 114, 151, 153
SMARTGOAL, 158–59
Smithfield Elementary, 3, 5, 52, 91
solidarity, 79, 117, 164, 171
standards, 20, 62, 79, 81–87, 95, 122, 176

tone policing, 166
tourist approach, 33, 61, 86, 169
Truth, Sojourner, 24, 33, 80, 89
Tubman, Harriet, 32, 89, 94, 111

underground railroad, 94
unions, 50, 157–58, 169
Universal Design for Learning, 127

Verano, Ms., 3, 10, 15, 17, 27, 36, 52–54, 66–67, 81–83, 91, 105–10, 115–17, 120–22, 126, 135–37, 150–51, 153, 157–58

West, Cornell, 95, 117, 138, 145, 165, 174
white: discomfort, 4, 8, 133, 135, 137–38, 153; privilege, 9, 40, 43–44, 49–50, 87, 112, 131–38, 142–44, 151, 153, 166, 171, 174; saviorism, 132–34, 171; supremacy, 8, 11, 23, 44–47, 53, 63, 65, 79–80, 122, 134–38, 151, 175
Woodson, Carter, 32, 80
Woodson, Jacquelyn, 100–101

About the Author

Dr. Miriam Tager is currently associate professor of early childhood education at Westfield State University in Massachusetts. Her previous books include *Challenging the School Readiness Agenda in Early Childhood Education* (2017) and *Technology Segregation: Disrupting the Racist Frameworks in Early Childhood Education* (2019). She is one of the rotating co-chairs of the Anti-Racist Education Committee in her department and facilitates faculty workshops for her colleagues. Her research interests include Anti-Racist pedagogy, critical pedagogy, and critical early childhood education policy. She currently lives in Northampton with her wife of twenty-three years (Robin) and two daughters, Ella (16) and Lily (9), and a dog named Leo.

www.ingramcontent.com/pod-product-compliance
Lightning Source LLC
Chambersburg PA
CBHW061714300426
44115CB00014B/2688